Trauma and Memory

Editors:
Herta Flor
Michèle Wessa

Zeitschrift für Psychologie
Journal of Psychology

Vol. 218, No. 2, 2010

HOGREFE

Library of Congress Cataloging in Publication

is available via the Library of Congress Marc Database under the
LC Control Number 2010921355

Library and Archives Canada Cataloguing in Publication

Trauma and memory / editors: Herta Flor, Michèle Wessa.

Published as part of the journal Zeitschrift für Psychologie = Journal of Psychology, vol. 218, no. 2, 2010.

Includes bibliographical references.
ISBN 978-0-88937-387-7

1. Psychic trauma. 2. Post-traumatic stress disorder. 3. Memory.
I. Flor, Herta II. Wessa, Michèle III. Title: Zeitschrift für Psychologie.

RC552.T7T734 2010 616.85'21 C2010-900725-5

PUBLISHING OFFICES
USA: Hogrefe Publishing, 875 Massachusetts Avenue, 7th Floor, Cambridge, MA 02139
Phone (866) 823-4726, Fax (617) 354-6875; E-mail customerservice@hogrefe-publishing.com
EUROPE: Hogrefe Publishing, Rohnsweg 25, 37085 Göttingen, Germany
Phone +49 551 49609-0, Fax +49 551 49609-88, E-mail publishing@hogrefe.com

SALES & DISTRIBUTION
USA: Hogrefe Publishing, Customer Services Department, 30 Amberwood Parkway, Ashland, OH 44805, Phone (800) 228-3749, Fax (419) 281-6883, E-mail customerservice@hogrefe.com
EUROPE: Hogrefe Publishing, Rohnsweg 25, 37085 Göttingen, Germany
Phone +49 551 49609-0, Fax +49 551 49609-88, E-mail publishing@hogrefe.com

OTHER OFFICES
CANADA: Hogrefe Publishing, 660 Eglinton Ave. East, Suite 119-514, Toronto, Ontario M4G 2K2
SWITZERLAND: Hogrefe Publishing, Länggass-Strasse 76, CH-3000 Bern 9

Hogrefe Publishing
Incorporated and registered in the Commonwealth of Massachusetts, USA, and in Göttingen, Lower Saxony, Germany

ISBN 978-0-88937-387-7

Contents

Memory and Posttraumatic Stress Disorder

A Matter of Context?

Herta Flor and Michèle Wessa

Department of Cognitive and Clinical Neuroscience, Central Institute of Mental Health, University of Heidelberg, Mannheim, Germany

In this issue of the *Zeitschrift für Psychologie / Journal of Psychology* we have assembled a number of articles and comments that deal with the relationship of trauma and memory, with an emphasis on the role of memory mechanisms in posttraumatic stress disorder (PTSD). There is uniformity in the assumption that memory is severely altered by traumatic events, but memory deficits may also contribute to the development of stress-related disorders. Although there is agreement that in PTSD memory mechanisms are at the core of the disorder, there is disagreement on the nature of the pathology and to what extent additional factors such as appraisal of the deficit are of importance. As Ehlers (2010) notes, there is clear evidence of a preponderance of emotional memories that are often sensory, fast, tied to very aversive moments of the traumatic experience, experienced as immediate rather than past, and related to non-declarative learning processes such as Pavlovian conditioning and priming. Whereas these memories seem to predominate, generalize (see Lissek & Grillon, 2010), and fail to extinguish (Wessa & Flor, 2007), episodic memories of the trauma and life in general seem to be affected, be it by fragmentation (Brewin, 2007), lack of connectedness (Michael, Ehlers, Halligan, & Clark, 2005), or overgeneralization (Schönfeld, Ehlers, Böllinghaus, & Rief, 2007). Early theories about memory mechanisms in PTSD suggested that the documented reduction of hippocampal volume in PTSD might lead to a dissociation of declarative and non-declarative memories (Elzinga & Bremner, 2002). However, these alterations are not as straightforward as it might seem since it could be shown that recall of trauma-related materials is similar in traumatized persons with and without PTSD (Wessa, Jatzko, & Flor, 2006). Retrieval-induced forgetting is also not significantly different in PTSD versus non-PTSD subjects as shown by Koessler and colleagues (2010). Diener, Flor, and Wessa (2010) demonstrate a specific deficit in encoding but not retrieval of episodic memory that is associated with hyperarousal symptoms. This suggests that a very thorough analysis of memory mechanisms is needed and that categories such as declarative/non-declarative or episodic versus semantic need to be further differentiated and specific aspects of these memory processes – such as elaboration, connectedness, or trauma-relevance – need to be considered. For example, the reduced hippocampal volumes could also lead to reduced context conditioning, which is also a form of emotional associative learning, whereas cue conditioning, which is more amygdala-dependent, seems to be enhanced. We (Lang et al., 2009) and others (Alvarez, Biggs, Chen, Pine, & Grillon, 2008; Marschner, Kalisch, Vervliet, Vansteenwegen, & Büchel, 2008) have shown that the hippocampus is involved in context conditioning in human beings and we have preliminary data that indicate impaired context conditioning in persons with small hippocampal volumes (Pohlack, Liebscher, Ridder, Lipinski, & Flor, 2009). A detailed examination of contextual memory in PTSD seems therefore warranted.

Context is also important for extinction learning where the organism has to learn to associate the conditioned stimuli with a certain context, no longer with a danger. Bouton and colleagues (2006) and others have emphasized the important role of context for extinction. Disordered context conditioning might therefore not only contribute to the feeling of "nowness" that characterizes the intrusions of PTSD patients and to the inability to feel safe (since safe and dangerous contexts cannot be properly differentiated) but may also impair the extinction of the cue-conditioned fear response since the extinction context has not been associated to the cues. This reasoning is in line with the proposal by Schauer and Elbert (2010), who argue that it is important to consider the peritraumatic defense processes that are activated and that subgroups of patients can be identified that are at different positions in the defense cascade. They specifically emphasize that memory processes are substantially different if persons are putting on a peritraumatic sympathetic activation versus those who went down the entire defense cascade where a parasympathetic dominance and dissociation prevail. This depends on the type of trauma and possibilities of the organism for optimal response. Extinction learning is especially hampered by dissociative

DOI: 10.1027/0044-3409/a000012

responses (Ebner-Priemer et al., 2009) and must be adapted in these patients. In line with this, the study by Mauchnik, Ebner-Priemer, Bohus, and Schmahl (2010) showed differential conditioning in patients with borderline personality disorder with and without PTSD. This points to the necessity to carefully assess comorbidity with other disorders (depression is, e.g., also important) but also to delineate and consider modulating factors such as dissociation (Ebner-Priemer et al., 2009). The need to enhance extinction learning is also emphasized by Davis (2010), who suggests that pharmacological enhancers such as d-cycloserine, a partial NMDA receptor agonist, might improve extinction also in PTSD patients, perhaps by promoting contextual learning (see also Bouton, Vurbic, & Woods, 2008). The elevated false alarm rate reported in Ugandan PTSD patients in the retrieval-induced forgetting procedure by Koessler et al. (2010) also suggests that the contextual binding needed to differentiate traumatic from nontraumatic items may be disturbed and this would also contribute to the generalization reported by Lissek and colleagues (2008) and Lissek and Grillon (2010). In addition, Frewen and Lanius (2010) observed that emotional imagery triggered more trauma-related episodic memory in PTSD patients and this also elicited stronger responses to the script-driven imagery scenes and was associated with a reduced ventromedial prefrontal response suggesting a reduction in inhibitory power related to trauma-related learning. Interestingly, the vividness of mental imagery did not explain differences between PTSD and non-PTSD patients in a study by Jelinek and colleagues (2010). Mental imagery ability was, however, predictive of recovery from PTSD, with those who recovered showing less vivid mental imagery. How this ability is related to the retrieval of specific trauma memories has not yet been investigated, nor has imagery ability for traumatic versus nontraumatic materials been assessed. Moreover, the interaction of cue and context conditioning and episodic traumatic and nontraumatic memory processes must be further delineated.

The study by Dörfel, Werner, Schaefer, and Karl (2010) found a close association between increased PTSD symptoms and more brain activation in areas relevant for visual mental imagery (e.g., precuneus and occipital cortex) and decreases in areas involved in the orientation toward the environment or keeping the balance between internal and external process monitoring (e.g., supramarginal gyrus). The pattern of brain activations and associations with memory and neuropsychological performance also points to the role of visuo-spatial impairment and insufficient context integration in PTSD that might hamper extinction. An even more dramatic change in memory function is present in the patients described by Staniloiu and Markowitsch (2010) who suffer from dissociative amnesia where a complete shutdown of autobiographic-episodic memory is present as a consequence of stress. The authors report overall reduction in brain metabolism, selective small fiber degeneration as well as specific alterations primarily in right fronto-temporal cortices.

The contributions of this issue show that the area of trauma and memory is in the process of extensive theory building and differentiated empirical research. The use of multiple measures of learning and memory on the subjective, behavioral, and physiological level, the analysis of the time frame of learning and memory, and the consideration of evolutionary theories will greatly enhance our understanding of the role of memory in stress-related disorders such as PTSD.

Acknowledgments

Preparation of this article and the research reported here was greatly facilitated by the Collaborative Research Center 636 "Learning, Memory and Brain Plasticity: Implications for psychopathology" funded by the Deutsche Forschungsgemeinschaft.

References

Alvarez, R. P., Biggs, A., Chen, G., Pine, D. S., & Grillon, C. (2008). Contextual fear conditioning in humans: Cortical-hippocampal and amygdala contributions. *Journal of Neuroscience, 28*, 6211–6219.

Bouton, M. E., Vurbic, D., & Woods, A. M. (2008). D-cycloserine facilitates context-specific fear extinction learning. *Neurobiology of Learning and Memory, 90*, 504–510.

Bouton, M. E., Westbrook, R. F., Corcoran, K. A., & Maren, S. (2006). Contextual and temporal modulation of extinction: Behavioral and biological mechanisms. *Biological Psychiatry, 60*, 352–360.

Brewin, C. R. (2007). Autobiographical memory for trauma: Update on four controversies. *Memory, 15*, 227–248.

Davis, M. (2010). Facilitation of fear extinction and psychotherapy by D-cycloserine. *Zeitschrift für Psychologie / Journal of Psychology, 218*, 149–150.

Diener, S. J., Flor, H., & Wessa, M. (2010). Learning and consolidation of verbal declarative memory in patients with posttraumatic stress disorder. *Zeitschrift für Psychologie / Journal of Psychology, 218*, 135–140.

Dörfel, D., Werner, A., Schaefer, M., & Karl, A. (2010). Pilot neuroimaging study in civilian trauma survivors: Episodic recognition memory, hippocampal volume, and posttraumatic stress disorder symptom severity. *Zeitschrift für Psychologie / Journal of Psychology, 218*, 128–134.

Ebner-Priemer, U. W., Mauchnik, J., Kleindienst, N., Schmahl, C., Peper, M., Rosenthal, M. Z., ... Bohus, M. (2009). Emotional learning during dissociative states in borderline personality disorder. *Journal of Psychiatry and Neuroscience, 34*, 214–222.

Ehlers, A. (2010). Understanding and treating trauma memories in posttraumatic stress disorder. *Zeitschrift für Psychologie / Journal of Psychology, 218*, 141–145.

Elzinga, B. M., & Bremner, J. D. (2002). Are the neural substrates of memory the final common pathway in posttraumatic stress disorder (PTSD)? *Journal of Affective Disorders, 70*, 1–17.

Frewen, P. A., & Lanius, R. A. (2010). Non-idiographic emotional script-driven imagery in posttraumatic stress disorder: Impact of priming of episodic recall and self-referential processing. *Zeitschrift für Psychologie / Journal of Psychology, 218*, 89–95.

Jelinek, L., Randjbar, S., Kellner, M., Untiedt, A., Volkert, J., Muhtz, C., & Moritz, S. (2010). Intrusive memories and modality-specific mental imagery in posttraumatic stress disorder (PTSD). *Zeitschrift für Psychologie / Journal of Psychology, 218*, 64–70.

Koessler, S., Wöhrmann, C., Zwissler, B., Pfeiffer, A., Ertl, V., & Kissler, J. (2010). Does remembering cause forgetting in chronically stressed people? A study of Ugandan civil war refugees with and without PTSD. *Zeitschrift für Psychologie / Journal of Psychology, 218*, 71–79.

Lang, S., Kroll, A., Lipinski, S. J., Wessa, M., Ridder, S., Christmann, C., . . . Flor, H. (2009). Context conditioning and extinction in humans: Differential contribution of the hippocampus, amygdala and prefrontal cortex. *European Journal of Neuroscience, 29*, 823–832.

Lissek, S., Biggs, A. L., Rabin, S. J., Cornwell, B. R., Alvarez, R. P., Pine, D. S., & Grillon, C. (2008). Generalization of conditioned fear-potentiated startle in humans: Experimental validation and clinical relevance. *Behaviour Research and Therapy, 46*, 678–687.

Lissek, S., & Grillon, C. (2010). Overgeneralization of conditioned fear in the anxiety disorders: Putative memorial mechanisms. *Zeitschrift für Psychologie / Journal of Psychology, 218*, 146–148.

Marschner, A., Kalisch, R., Vervliet, B., Vansteenwegen, D., & Büchel, C. (2008). Dissociable roles for the hippocampus and the amygdala in human cued versus context fear conditioning. *Journal of Neuroscience, 28*, 9030–9036.

Mauchnik, J., Ebner-Priemer, U. W., Bohus, M., & Schmahl, C. (2010). Classical conditioning in borderline personality disorder with and without posttraumatic stress disorder. *Zeitschrift für Psychologie / Journal of Psychology, 218*, 80–88.

Michael, T., Ehlers, A., Halligan, S. L., & Clark, D. M. (2005). Unwanted memories of assault: What intrusion characteristics are associated with PTSD? *Behavior Research and Therapy, 43*, 613–628.

Pohlack, S., Liebscher, C., Ridder, S., Lipinski, S., & Flor, H. (2009). The role of hippocampus and context conditioning in posttraumatic stress disorder: A cross-sectional study in traumatized and non-traumatized paramedics. *Psychophysiology, 46*(S1), 126.

Schauer, M., & Elbert, T. (2010). Dissociation following traumatic stress: Etiology and treatment. *Zeitschrift für Psychologie / Journal of Psychology, 218*, 109–127.

Schönfeld, S., Ehlers, A., Böllinghaus, I., & Rief, W. (2007). Overgeneral memory and suppression of trauma memories in post-traumatic stress disorder. *Memory, 15*, 339–352.

Staniloiu, A., & Markowitsch, H. J. (2010). Searching for the anatomy of dissociative amnesia. *Zeitschrift für Psychologie / Journal of Psychology, 218*, 96–108.

Wessa, M., & Flor, H. (2007). Failure of extinction of fear responses in posttraumatic stress disorder: Evidence from second-order conditioning. *American Journal of Psychiatry, 164*, 1684–1692.

Wessa, M., Jatzko, A., & Flor, H. (2006). Retrieval and emotional processing of traumatic memories in posttraumatic stress disorder: Peripheral and central correlates. *Neuropsychologia, 44*, 1683–1696.

Herta Flor

Institut für Neuropsychologie und Klinische Psychologie
Ruprecht-Karls-Universität Heidelberg
Zentralinstitut für Seelische Gesundheit
J5
68159 Mannheim
Germany
Tel. +49 621 1703 6302
Fax +49 621 1703 6305
E-mail herta.flor@zi-mannheim.de

Original Article

Intrusive Memories and Modality-Specific Mental Imagery in Posttraumatic Stress Disorder

Lena Jelinek,[1] Sarah Randjbar,[1] Michael Kellner,[1] Angnes Untiedt,[1] Jana Volkert,[2] Christoph Muhtz,[1] and Steffen Moritz[1]

[1]Department of Psychiatry and Psychotherapy, University Medical Center Hamburg-Eppendorf, Hamburg, Germany, [2]Department of Medical Psychology, University Medical Center Hamburg-Eppendorf, Hamburg, Germany

Abstract. Posttraumatic stress disorder (PTSD) is characterized by vivid intrusive memories of the trauma. Among these, visual sensations of the trauma are most commonly reported. However, intrusions may involve other senses as well (e.g., acoustic, olfactory, or bodily sensations). It has been proposed that enhanced mental imagery may predispose individuals with traumatic experiences to intrusions and ultimately to PTSD. A total of 58 victims of interpersonal violence with current (n = 20), past (n = 19), and no lifetime PTSD (n = 19) as well as non-traumatized controls (n = 23) were assessed with the Vividness of Visual Imagery Questionnaire (VVIQ) and a modality-specific imagery questionnaire. Moreover, the sensory quality of the traumatic intrusions was assessed in traumatized participants. Participants with recovered PTSD displayed less overall mental imagery than the other three groups who were indistinguishable. No relation was found between the modality-specific mental imagery and the sensory quality of the intrusions. The impact of mental imagery on intrusive memories in PTSD is complex. Less mental imagery appears beneficial in the recovery process, but does not prevent the development of intrusive symptoms in the first place. Further investigation of perceptual and memory vividness as well imagery control (i.e., to sustain, modify, or terminate an image) also including trauma-related material may be important for trauma-specific interventions.

Keywords: PTSD, memory, intrusions, imagery

Posttraumatic stress disorder (PTSD) is characterized by highly distressing intrusive memories of the trauma (American Psychiatric Association [APA], 1994). As the term "reexperiencing" suggests, these memories are often extremely vivid with lifelike perceptual features (cf. Ehlers, Hackmann, & Michael, 2004). Similar to real-life experiences, they may involve multiple senses, such as visual, acoustic, olfactory, or bodily sensations; yet, visual sensations are most commonly reported (Ehlers et al., 2002; Hackmann, Ehlers, Speckens, & Clark, 2004).

Models of PTSD etiology are challenged to explain the pathogenesis and nature of these intrusive memories. One mechanism that has been suggested to predispose individuals to more vivid memories of the trauma (and ultimately to PTSD) is the general ability to lifelike mental imagery (see Bryant & Harvey, 1996; Kosslyn, 2005). Mental imagery has been defined as a "quasi-perceptual experience" similar to a perceptual experience, but occurring without the corresponding external stimuli (Thomas, 1999). It is not restricted to visual images but may occur in any sensory system (Kosslyn, 2005) and engages similar neural circuits as the primary sensory channels (Borst & Kosslyn, 2008; Ganis, Thompson, & Kosslyn, 2004). Although the ability for mental imagery may vary for each sensory quality in individuals, modalities are pooled and reported as one generalized score in most studies. Accordingly, studies investigating mental imagery in PTSD have mainly reported results for the generalized ability by using the total score of the Questionnaire of Mental Imagery (QMI, Sheehan, 1967). However, studies investigating mental imagery in PTSD are rare. Stutman and Bliss (1985) reported superior overall mental imagery in Vietnam veterans with high versus low PTSD symptoms. This general finding of enhanced mental imagery was not supported by two later studies also using the QMI (Karatzias, Power, Brown, & McGoldrick, 2009) or a modified version of the instrument (Laor et al., 1999). Moreover, in the study by Laor and colleagues (1999) a negative relation was found between imagery vividness and physiological response to trauma-related stimuli in a group with low PTSD symptoms, indicating that superior imagery vividness might even serve as a protective function in low levels of PTSD symptomatology.

To the best of our knowledge, the only study focusing on a specific sensory quality was conducted by Bryant and Harvey (1996) investigating visual sensations by means of the Vividness of Visual Imagery Questionnaire (VVIQ,

DOI: 10.1027/0044-3409/a000013

Marks, 1989). They found that visual imagery was in fact best in survivors of motor vehicle accidents with low anxiety in comparison to those who developed PTSD or specific phobia subsequent to the accident. Still, within the PTSD group higher levels of flashbacks were associated with overall higher visual imagery.

To summarize, mental imagery has mainly been investigated as a generalized ability (Karatzias et al., 2009; Laor et al., 1999; Stutman & Bliss, 1985) although traumatic as well as non-arousing imagery may include different senses. The aim of the current study was to fill this gap and to investigate modality-specific mental imagery in PTSD and its relation to the sensory quality of intrusions. We hypothesized that victims of interpersonal violence with PTSD would display the most lifelike mental imagery. Furthermore, we hypothesized a relation between the ability to modality-specific imagery and the sensory quality of intrusions, for example, that someone with a good olfactory mental imagery is more likely to experience olfactory intrusions.

Methods

Sample

Fifty-eight victims of interpersonal violence were recruited by means of advertisement or contacts through the Department for Psychiatry and Psychotherapy of the University Medical Center Hamburg (Germany). Participants were screened via telephone interviews to ensure that all participants were fluent in German, between 18 and 70 years old, and had no neurological disorder or lifetime psychotic symptoms. In addition a healthy control group (n = 23) with no lifetime traumatic event or psychiatric disorder was recruited. The study was approved by the Ethics Committee of the Medical Board Hamburg. Prior to participation, participants were informed about the study rationale, the approximate duration of assessment, and the different procedures involved in verbal and written form. All participants provided full informed consent.

Measures

Demographic Characteristics and Psychopathology

First, a short standardized demographic interview (e.g., age) including trauma-related questions (e.g., date of trauma) was conducted. PTSD diagnosis relied on the PTSD section of the Structured Clinical Interview for DSM-IV (SCID; First, Spitzer, Gibbon, & Williams, 1996). Twenty victims of interpersonal violence fulfilled criteria for current PTSD (PTSD group), 19 fulfilled the criteria for PTSD in the past and were recovered at the time of the assessment (recovered group), and 19 never fulfilled PTSD criteria (non-PTSD group). Comorbid diagnoses in patients and the absence of psychiatric diagnoses in healthy controls, respectively, were determined using the Mini International Neuropsychiatric Interview (MINI; Sheehan et al., 1998). The severity of present PTSD symptoms was assessed using the Posttraumatic Stress Diagnostic Scale (PDS; Foa, Cashman, Jaycox, & Perry, 1997). Current levels of depression were assessed using the Hamilton Depression Rating Scale (HDRS; Hamilton, 1960). Levels of general (trait) and current anxiety (state) were measured using the State-Trait Anxiety Inventory (STAI; Laux, Glanzmann, Schaffner, & Spielberger, 1981).

Intrusions Interview

To specify type and severity of intrusions a modified version of the Intrusions Interview (Hackmann et al., 2004; Speckens, Ehlers, Hackmann, & Clark, 2006) was conducted with traumatized participants. In this interview, participants are asked whether they reexperienced or have ever reexperienced the trauma recently in the following ways: visually, olfactorily, acoustically, emotionally, in form of bodily sensations, actions, and/or thoughts. Participants, who recently suffered from intrusions, were also asked about the frequency, vividness, and distress of intrusions as well as the extent to which intrusions seemed to be happening here and now in the past 7 days. Each item is rated on a scale from 1 (not at all) to 100 (very much). In the study by Speckens and colleagues (2006) the retest-reliability for the Intrusion Questionnaire ranged between $r = .61$ and $r = .72$ for the four rating scales.

Imagination

Vividness of Visual Imagery Questionnaire

To assess the vividness of visual imagery the Vividness of Visual Imagery Questionnaire (VVIQ, Marks, 1989) was used. The questionnaire contains 32 items consisting of four real-life scenes or objects (e.g., Scenario 1: "Think of some relative or friend whom you frequently see (but who is not with you at present) and consider carefully the picture that comes before your mind's eye"; Item 1: "The exact contour of face, head, shoulders, and body."). The scenarios were read to the participant by the interviewer. Participants were instructed to imagine the scenario as vivid and clear as possible. Subsequently they were asked to rate the vividness of the imagery on a 5-point Likert scale (1 = "No image at all, you only "know" that you are thinking of an object"; 5 = "Perfectly clear and as vivid as normal vision."). The VVIQ consists of two parts. In the first part participants are instructed to keep their eyes open and in the second part they should close their eyes during imagination. As summarized by Campos and Perez-Fabello (2009), the VVIQ has shown good reliability and validity in prior studies.

Modality-Specific Imagery Questionnaire

For the present study a new self-rating scale, based on the Creative Imagination Scale (CIS; Barber & Wilson, 1978), was developed by the authors, specifically tailored to the purpose of the present study: the Modality-Specific Imagery Questionnaire (MIQ). The MIQ contains seven items, each assessing a different sensory quality of mental imagery: visual, acoustic, olfactory, emotional, and bodily sensations (warmth, coldness, and heaviness). The participants were instructed to imagine situations/objects as vividly and clearly as possible (e.g., bodily sensations of coldness: "Please imagine, you are drinking a cold glass of mountain water on a hot summer day.") and to subsequently rate clarity and vividness of the imagination compared to real-life perception on a 5-point scale.

Statistical Analyses

For the majority of the statistical analysis the data of 81 participants were used. For some of the calculations the number of participants was reduced, due to missing data of the STAI. This is indicated in the corresponding tables. For data analysis SPSS version 15.0 for Windows was used. An alpha level of .05 (two-tailed) was used for all statistical tests. As modality-specific mental imagery was investigated for the first time univariate comparisons were planned for exploratory purposes to follow up general models independent of significance.

Results

As can be seen in Table 1, the groups did not differ with regard to age, gender, or verbal intelligence. Eleven traumatized participants with PTSD currently received psychotropic medication (three were medicated with antidepressant agents, one with a neuroleptic agent, four with soporifics, two with both a combination of a neuroleptic and an antidepressant or an antidepressant and a soporific, and one with a combination of a neuroleptic, an antidepressant, and a soporific). Additionally, one participant of the recovered group was medicated with an antidepressant agent. As expected, the three traumatized groups differed with regard to PDS total and subscores, depression as well as frequency, vividness, distress, and the here and nowness of intrusions (also see Table 2). Groups also differed with regard to state and trait anxiety as measured by the STAI. The reported qualities of reexperiencing the traumatic event are displayed in Table 3. The most commonly reported intrusions were visual, emotional, or bodily sensations.

Vividness of Visual Imagery Questionnaire

As displayed in Table 2, groups differed with regard to visual imagery in the VVIQ. Bonferroni-corrected post hoc tests showed that participants with recovered PTSD had poorer overall mental imagery than traumatized participants without PTSD and non-traumatized controls. The other groups did not differ with regard to imagery vividness.

Modality-Specific Imagery Questionnaire

A 4 × 7 mixed ANOVA with Group (PTSD, recovered, non-PTSD, and non-Trauma) as between-subject factor and Modality (visual, acoustic, olfactory, emotional, warmth, coldness, and heaviness) as within-subject factor and level of Mental Imagery as dependent variable was calculated (see Figure 1). Groups differed with regard to Mental Imagery, $F(3, 77) = 0.39, p < .05$, and Mental Imagery differed for the various modalities, $F(6, 462) = 14.63, p < .001$. The Group × Modality interaction, however, was nonsignificant, $F < 0.9$, $p > .6$. Bonferroni-corrected post hoc test revealed that the recovered PTSD group displayed lower imagery vividness than the non-PTSD group. As modality-specific mental imagery was investigated for the first time, we performed univariate comparisons separate for each modality for exploratory purposes. Analyses showed that groups did not differ in imagery vividness of visual, emotional, and bodily sensations of warmth and heaviness ($ps > .1$). However, group differences were found with regard to mental imagery of olfactory, $F(3, 77) = 3.98, p < .01$, and acoustic experiences,

Table 1. Demographic characteristics of the sample

Variable	PTSD (*P*) (*n* = 20)	Recovered PTSD (*R*) (*n* = 19)	Non-PTSD (n*P*) (*n* = 19)	Non-Trauma (n*T*) (*n* = 23)	Statistics
Age	36.70 (10.68)	32.00 (8.83)	29.11 (6.11)	34.35 (11.24)	$F(3, 77) = 2.27$
Gender (f/m)	16/4	13/6	13/6	15/8	$\chi^2(3) = 1.25$
Verbal intelligence	27.35 (4.60)	29.11 (3.45)	29.21 (4.30)	29.22 (3.79)	$F(3, 77) = 1.03$
Psychopathology					
PDS (total score)	31.45 (8.61)	9.00 (7.32)	4.42 (4.77)	–	$F(2, 55) = 81.32$**
PDS intrusions	9.20 (4.03)	1.89 (2.23)	1.21 (1.65)	–	$F(2, 55) = 47.30$**
PDS avoidance	12.40 (3.32)	4.00 (3.82)	1.26 (1.97)	–	$F(2, 55) = 67.24$**
PDS arousal	9.85 (3.62)	3.11 (2.54)	1.95 (1.87)	–	$F(2, 55) = 46.05$**
HDRS	15.95 (7.40)	6.47 (4.34)	2.42 (2.59)	–	$F(2, 55) = 34.64$**
STAI (state)	43.46 (14.38)[a]	40.20 (13.13)[b]	37.73 (7.76)[b]	31.22 (6.48)	$F(3, 60) = 4.44$* $P > nT$
STAI (trait)	50.36 (13.03)[a]	41.00 (10.79)[b]	34.47 (6.44)[b]	33.17 (8.55)	$F(3, 60) = 9.19$* $P > nP, nT$

Note. [a]$n = 11$, [b]$n = 15$; *$p < .01$. **$p < .001$.

Table 2. Means and standard deviations with regard to intrusions and mental imagery

Variable	PTSD (*P*) (*n* = 20)	Recovered PTSD (*R*) (*n* = 19)	Non-PTSD (n*P*) (*n* = 19)	Non-Trauma (n*T*) (*n* = 23)	Statistics
Intrusion interview					
Intrusion frequency	51.00 (29.76)	3.95 (13.80)	5.26 (14.67)	–	$F(2, 55) = 31.16^{**}$
Intrusion vividness	62.70 (33.05)	8.95 (21.83)	8.42 (20.62)	–	$F(2, 55) = 28.43^{**}$
Intrusion distress	71.95 (34.39)	9.47 (22.72)	6.32 (16.06)	–	$F(2, 55) = 40.69^{**}$
Intrusion here and nowness quality	48.00 (41.37)	2.63 (7.34)	0.26 (1.15)	–	$F(2, 55) = 23.35^{**}$
Mental imagery					
VVIQ	122.80 (20.34)	105.68 (25.35)	124.05 (16.36)	123.26 (19.74)	$F(3, 77) = 3.56^{*}$ $R <$ nP, nT
MIQ (total score)	25.30 (5.44)	22.16 (5.56)	27.11 (3.54)	25.13 (4.12)	$F(3, 77) = 3.58^{*}$ $R <$ nP

Note. $^{*}p < .05$. $^{**}p < .001$.

Table 3. Quality of intrusions experienced within the last 7 days (ever experienced). Traumatized participants only

	PTSD (*P*) (*n* = 20)	Recovered PTSD (*R*) (*n* = 19)	Non-PTSD (n*P*) (*n* = 19)	Average
Visual	55% (90%)	11% (84%)	21% (58%)	29% (78%)
Olfactory	10% (25%)	0% (0%)	5% (16%)	5% (14%)
Acoustic	25% (50%)	11% (32%)	0% (26%)	12% (36%)
Emotional	75% (85%)	21% (84%)	16% (53%)	38% (74%)
Bodily sensations	65% (90%)	5% (53%)	0% (32%)	24% (59%)
Actions	30% (45%)	0% (37%)	5% (5%)	12% (29%)
Thoughts	40% (55%)	0% (37%)	11% (26%)	17% (40%)

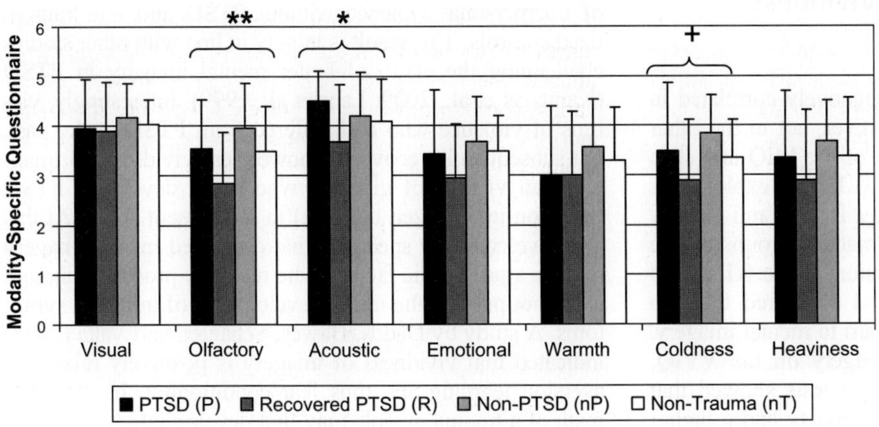

Figure 1. Means and standard deviations of mental imagery as measured by the MIQ. *Note.* $^{+}p < .1$. $^{*}p < .05$. $^{**}p < .01$.

$F(3, 77) = 2.85, p < .05$, and at trend level for the experience of coldness, $F(3, 77) = 2.62, p = .06$, indicating that mental imagery is less vivid in victims of violence who recovered from PTSD (see Figure 2).

Relation Between Intrusions and Imagery Vividness

Mental imagery as measured by the VVIQ and the MIQ did not correlate with the extent of intrusions as measured by the intrusion subscale of the PDS (neither in the total sample, $rs < .13$, $ps > .3$, nor in each of the subsamples). Similarly, no relation was found between mental imagery and frequency, vividness and distress of the intrusions as measured by the intrusions interview ($rs < .17$, $ps > .1$). However, a significant positive relation was observed between the here and nowness of intrusions and the total score of the VVIQ, $r = .28, p < .05$. Still, no correlation was found between the total score of the MIQ and the here and nowness of intrusions ($p > .5$).

To investigate the relationship between modality-specific imagery and the modality of intrusions, traumatized

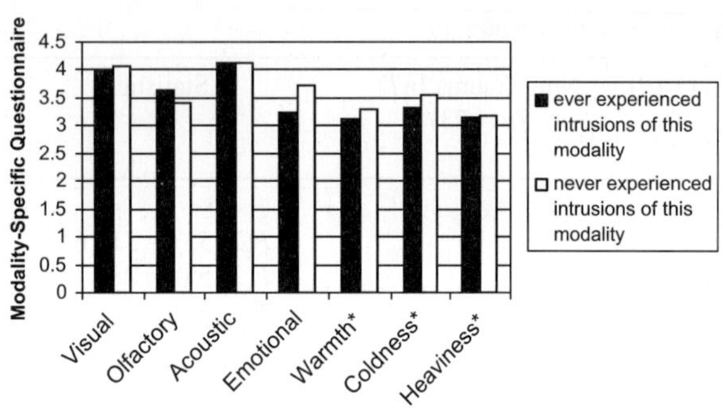

Figure 2. Traumatized participants who ever or never reexperienced the trauma in form of the specific modality according to the Intrusions Interview and performance on the corresponding subscale of the MIQ.
Note. * = group allocation according to reexperiencing in form of bodily sensations.

participants were divided into participants who have ever versus who never experienced intrusions of a specific sensory quality (according to the intrusions interview: visual, olfactory, acoustic, emotional, and bodily sensations). The corresponding groups were then compared on mental imagery of the relevant modality of the MIQ (see Figure 2). However, no relation was found between the modality-specific mental imagery and the sensory quality of intrusions (all $t < |1.51|$, all $p > .1$).

Relation Between Imagery Vividness and Anxiety

Anxiety and mental imagery were negatively correlated in the PTSD sample (see Table 4), however, not in the other subgroups (except for the total score of the MIQ and state anxiety in the non-Trauma group). To further explore this result and to follow up the results by Bryant and Harvey (1996), we subdivided the three traumatized groups by the median score (=37) on the state version of the STAI into those with high and low anxiety and compared them to non-traumatized participants with regard to mental imagery. Groups differed in visual mental imagery on the VVIQ, $F(6, 57) = 2.67$, $p < .05$. Uncorrected *t* tests showed that participants with PTSD and low state anxiety had a higher imagery score than all other groups. Groups differed also with regard to visual mental imagery on the MIQ, $F(6, 57) = 2.78$, $p < .05$. *T*-tests indicated that participants with PTSD and low anxiety had a higher imagery than participants who recovered from PTSD and non-traumatized participants. However, in both analyses the sample size of this subsample was small ($n = 5$) and when controlled for multiple testing most of these differences disappeared.

Relation Between Imagery Vividness and Age and Medication

As reduced imagery vividness has previously been related to age (Dror & Kosslyn, 1994) and as the age range of our sample was rather large, we additionally correlated age and imagery vividness. However, no relation was found between age and mental imagery (all $r < |.13|$, all $p > .3$). To investigate the influence of medication on imagery vividness, medicated and unmedicated PTSD patients were compared with regard to imagery vividness, revealing no group differences (all $t < |0.76|$, all $p > .4$).

Discussion

The aim of the present study was to investigate modality-specific mental imagery in PTSD and particularly its relationship with the sensory quality of the intrusions. In line with previous theoretical assumptions (cf. Bryant & Harvey, 1996; Kosslyn, 2005) we hypothesized that mental imagery would be superior in victims of interpersonal violence with PTSD. Unexpectedly, victims of interpersonal violence with PTSD showed a similar ability to mental imagery as victims of interpersonal violence without PTSD and non-traumatized controls. This result is largely in line with other studies challenging the claim of better mental imagery in PTSD (Karatzias et al., 2009; Laor et al., 1999). Interestingly, victims of violence who had suffered from PTSD in the past, but subsequently recovered showed less vivid mental imagery than victims of violence who never developed PTSD (and non-traumatized controls) in the present study. At this point we can only speculate that decreased mental imagery may be a prognostic factor in the recovery process, although it did not prevent the initial development of intrusive symptoms. A study by Dadds, Hawes, Schaefer, and Vaka (2004) indicated that vividness of imagery is positively related to aversion learning and thus fear conditioning. In the aftermath of a trauma, people may first develop intrusions, however, those who tend to experience less vivid traumatic imagery (due to less vivid general mental imagery) may be less likely to be fear conditioned, potentially leading to a recovery from reexperiencing symptoms. However, we do not know at what point in time recovery occurred in

Table 4. Pearson correlation between mental imagery and anxiety as measured by the STAI

	PTSD (*P*) (*n* = 11)		Recovered PTSD (*R*) (*n* = 15)		Non-PTSD (*nP*) (*n* = 15)		Non-Trauma (*nT*) (*n* = 23)	
	STAI trait	STAI state	STAI trait	STAI state	STAI trait	STAI state	STAI trait	STAI state
VVIQ	−.90***	−.79**	−.04	−.08	−.07	.02	.03	−.10
MIQ	−.78*	−.73*	.23	.12	−.23	.38	−.32	−.55**

Note. *$p < .05$. **$p < .01$. ***$p < .001$.

our current sample or whether participants recovered with the help of a therapist or on their own account. These questions should be addressed in subsequent research.

Exploratory analyses performed in a subsample indicated that the expected pattern of more lifelike mental imagery in PTSD was only present in those with low anxiety. Moreover, a negative relation between anxiety and mental imagery was found within the PTSD group. This result is largely in line with findings of Bryant and Harvey (1996) reporting that the ability to experience mental imagery diminishes as levels of anxiety increase. It seems that anxiety obstructs cognitive processes required for individuals with PTSD to experience mental imagery.

Apart from anxiety, we investigated the influence of other factors on mental imagery, such as age and medication, to secure our results against their potential influence. In the present sample neither age nor status of medication was related to mental imagery. However, medication ranged from neuroleptics over antidepressants to soporifics highly restricting differential conclusions on specific substances.

The second aim of the study was to investigate the relation between modality-specific mental imagery and the sensory quality of intrusions. We postulated that better mental imagery for a specific modality would lead to a higher likelihood to develop intrusions in that particular modality. The expected relation, however, was not found: Traumatized subjects who ever reexperienced their trauma in a specific quality (e.g., olfactory intrusion) did not display better mental imagery in that modality (e.g., mental imagery of olfactory sensations). To our knowledge, this study was the first to investigate this relation, using an imagery task specifically designed for this purpose (MIQ) as well as a widely used task for visual mental imagery (VVIQ; Marks, 1989). However, our trauma sample consisted of victims of interpersonal violence, who may differ from other trauma samples.

We would also like to address several shortcomings of the present study. First, while the sample size can be considered sufficient for the overall analysis, when additionally comparing high and low anxious subgroups, our sample size was significantly reduced. Thus, results can only be considered preliminary. Second, the MIQ is a new questionnaire that was specifically constructed for the purpose of the study. While it is based on the established CIS (Barber & Wilson, 1978), the psychometric properties of the MIQ have not yet been investigated and may thus have compromised our results. Third, the follow-up of the nonsignificant interaction between modality and group for the MIQ with univariate comparisons (separate for each modality) can be questioned. As the present study was the first to investigate modality-specific imagery in PTSD the performed univariate comparisons were conducted for exploratory purposes. A fourth limitation of the study is the cross-sectional design. We cannot rule out the possibility that mental imagery was enhanced before the traumatic event in participants who later developed PTSD and that the willingness to engage in imagery changed as a consequence of the disorder. To answer this question, prospective studies are needed.

When replicated, our findings may have important implications for therapeutic interventions. First, when using (nontraumatic) guided imagery, for example, for relaxation, highly anxious traumatized patients may have difficulties engaging in imagery. Second, when using trauma-specific interventions such as imaginal exposure, reduced mental imagery may influence the outcome (however, see Rauch, Foa, Furr, & Filip, 2004). Moreover, the measures we employed do not differentiate between vividness and control of imagery, that is, to sustain, modify, or terminate an image. This may also be important for trauma-specific interventions using imagery, such as imagery rescripting (Smucker, 2005). However, mental imagery for non-traumatic stimuli may not be highly associated with the ability for trauma-related (highly arousing) imagery in traumatized individuals and the described mechanisms of cognitive control may function differently when high-arousing material is used. As startle hyperreactivity is also suggested to serve as a key factor in the development of PTSD (e.g., Pole et al., 2009), processes of mental imagery may especially differ under conditions of high arousal in PTSD. Future studies implementing traumatic as well as non-traumatic material would benefit from including objective measures of imagery control, such as a mental rotation task, and executive functioning to explore the relevance and influence of imagery control thoroughly.

Acknowledgments

We would like to thank Annie Bessette, Dr. Karl-Heinz Biesold, and Dipl-Psych. Klaus Barre for their help with the recruitment of participants.

References

American Psychiatric Association (APA). (1994). *Diagnostic and statistical manual of mental disorders* (4th ed.). Washington, DC: Author.

Barber, T. X., & Wilson, S. C. (1978). The Barber Suggestibility Scale and the Creative Imagination Scale: Experimental and clinical applications. *American Journal of Clinical Hypnosis, 21*, 84–108.

Borst, G., & Kosslyn, S. M. (2008). Visual mental imagery and visual perception: Structural equivalence revealed by scanning processes. *Memory & Cognition, 36*, 849–862.

Bryant, R. A., & Harvey, A. G. (1996). Visual imagery in posttraumatic stress disorder. *Journal of Traumatic Stress, 9*, 613–619.

Campos, A., & Perez-Fabello, M. J. (2009). Psychometric quality of a revised version Vividness of Visual Imagery Questionnaire. *Perceptual and Motor Skills, 108*, 798–802.

Dadds, M. R., Hawes, D., Schaefer, B., & Vaka, K. (2004). Individual differences in imagery and reports of aversions. *Memory, 12*, 462–466.

Dror, I. E., & Kosslyn, S. M. (1994). Mental imagery and aging. *Psychology and Aging, 9*, 90–102.

Ehlers, A., Hackmann, A., & Michael, T. (2004). Intrusive reexperiencing in post-traumatic stress disorder: Phenomenology, theory, and therapy. *Memory, 12*, 403–415.

Ehlers, A., Hackmann, A., Steil, R., Clohessy, S., Wenninger, K., & Winter, H. (2002). The nature of intrusive memories after trauma: The warning signal hypothesis. *Behavior Research and Therapy, 40*, 995–1002.

First, M. B., Spitzer, R. L., Gibbon, M., & Williams, J. B. W. (1996). *Structured clinical interview for DSM-IV axis I disorders*. Washington, DC: American Psychiatric Press.

Foa, E. B., Cashman, L., Jaycox, L., & Perry, K. (1997). The validation of a self-report measure of posttraumatic stress disorder: The Posttraumatic Diagnostic Scale. *Psychological Assessment, 9*, 445–451.

Ganis, G., Thompson, W. L., & Kosslyn, S. M. (2004). Brain areas underlying visual mental imagery and visual perception: An fMRI study. *Cognitive Brain Research, 20*, 226–241.

Hackmann, A., Ehlers, A., Speckens, A., & Clark, D. M. (2004). Characteristics and content of intrusive memories in PTSD and their changes with treatment. *Journal of Traumatic Stress, 17*, 231–240.

Hamilton, M. (1960). A rating scale for depression. *Journal of Neurology, Neurosurgery and Psychiatry, 23*, 56–62.

Karatzias, T., Power, K., Brown, K., & McGoldrick, T. (2009). Vividness of mental imagery in posttraumatic stress disorder (PTSD): The role of depression. *Journal of Behavior Therapy and Experimental Psychiatry, 40*, 352–358.

Kosslyn, S. M. (2005). Reflective thinking and mental imagery: A perspective on the development of posttraumatic stress disorder. *Development and Psychopathology, 17*, 851–863.

Laor, N., Wolmer, L., Wiener, Z., Sharon, O., Weizman, R., Toren, P., & Ron, S. (1999). Image vividness as a psychophysiological regulator in posttraumatic stress disorder. *Journal of Clinical and Experimental Neuropsychology, 21*, 39–48.

Laux, L., Glanzmann, P., Schaffner, P., & Spielberger, C. D. (1981). *Das State-Trait-Angstinventar (STAI)* [The State-Trait Anxiety Inventory]. Weinheim, Germany: Beltz Test.

Marks, D. F. (1989). Construct validity of the Vividness of Visual Imagery Questionnaire. *Perceptual and Motor Skills, 69*, 459–465.

Pole, N., Neylan, T. C., Otte, C., Henn-Hasse, C., Metzler, T. J., & Marmar, C. R. (2009). Prospective prediction of posttraumatic stress disorder symptoms using fear potentiated auditory startle responses. *Biological Psychiatry, 65*, 235–240.

Rauch, S. A., Foa, E. B., Furr, J. M., & Filip, J. C. (2004). Imagery vividness and perceived anxious arousal in prolonged exposure treatment for PTSD. *Journal of Traumatic Stress, 17*, 461–465.

Sheehan, D. V., Lecrubier, Y., Sheehan, K. H., Amorim, P., Janavs, J., Weiller, E., ... Dunbar, G. C. (1998). The MINI International Neuropsychiatric Interview (MINI): The development and validation of a structured diagnostic psychiatric interview. *Journal of Clinical Psychiatry, 59*(suppl. 20), 22–23.

Sheehan, P. W. (1967). A shortened form of Betts' questionnaire upon mental imagery. *Journal of Clinical Psychology, 23*, 386–389.

Smucker, M. R. (2005). Imagery rescripting and reprocessing therapy. In A. Freeman, S. H. Felgoise, C. M. Nezu, A. M. Nezu, & M. A. Reinecke (Eds.), *Encyclopedia of cognitive behavior therapy* (pp. 226–229). New York, NY: Springer.

Speckens, A. E., Ehlers, A., Hackmann, A., & Clark, D. M. (2006). Changes in intrusive memories associated with imaginal reliving in posttraumatic stress disorder. *Journal of Anxiety Disorders, 20*, 328–341.

Stutman, R. K., & Bliss, E. L. (1985). Posttraumatic stress disorder, hypnotizability, and imagery. *American Journal of Psychiatry, 142*, 741–743.

Thomas, N. J. T. (1999). Are theories of imagery theories of imagination? An active perception approach to conscious mental content. *Cognitive Science, 23*, 207–245.

Lena Jelinek

Department of Psychiatry and Psychotherapy
University Medical Center Hamburg-Eppendorf
Martinistr. 52
20246 Hamburg
Tel. +49 40 7410 57539
Fax +49 40 7410 57566
E-mail l.jelinek@uke.uni-hamburg.de

Original Article

Does Remembering Cause Forgetting in Chronically Stressed People?

A Study of Ugandan Civil War Refugees With and Without PTSD

Susanne Koessler,[1] Christian Wöhrmann,[1] Bastian Zwissler,[1] Anett Pfeiffer,[1,2] Verena Ertl,[1,2] and Johanna Kissler[1]

[1]Department of Psychology, University of Konstanz, Germany, [2]VIVO – Victim's Voice, Nongovernmental Organization, Konstanz, Germany

Abstract. People suffering from Posttraumatic Stress Disorder (PTSD) often have reduced episodic memory performance as well as intrusions and flashbacks of traumatic events. Hippocampal and prefrontal dysfunctions are assumed to be responsible. Using a modified retrieval-induced forgetting paradigm, we investigated episodic memory performance in a group of German participants and in civil war victims with and without PTSD in Northern Uganda. Retrieval-induced forgetting is an adaptive mechanism in memory and refers to the fact that retrieval of target elements impairs subsequent recall of related material. Retrieval-induced forgetting depends on medio-temporal and prefrontal functions and acute stress eliminates the effect. Here, using a pictorial retrieval-induced forgetting paradigm, retrieval-induced forgetting was found in a German group, but not in Ugandan refugees, neither in those with nor without PTSD. As both groups were exposed to multiple, often severely traumatic events, stress exposure in both Ugandan groups may account for this finding. Specific to Ugandan refugees with PTSD, an elevated false alarm rate during recognition testing was found, although even refugees without PTSD had higher false alarm rates than the German group. In the civil war victims, stress-induced memory dysfunction may impair hippocampus-mediated contextual binding, eliminating retrieval-induced forgetting and reducing the ability to differentiate between old and new pictures. Traumatic stress may additionally disrupt prefrontal inhibition mechanisms, leading to an inability to suppress false alarms.

Keywords: PTSD, stress, memory inhibition, episodic memory, retrieval-induced forgetting

Each time we remember an item or event, memory for this item or event is strengthened (Carrier & Pashler, 1992; Hogan & Kintsch, 1971; Roediger & Karpicke, 2006) and the likelihood of its successful future recollection increases. This mechanism is very powerful, has long been known to psychology (Gates, 1917), and is intuitively plausible to the layperson. Less intuitive, however, is the fact that by remembering certain aspects of an episode, other parts of that episode are automatically suppressed, a phenomenon known as retrieval-induced forgetting (e.g., Anderson, Bjork, & Bjork, 1994).

Retrieval-induced forgetting effects have been demonstrated in both free recall (e.g., Amir, Badour, & Freese, 2009; Anderson et al., 1994) and recognition (e.g., Hicks & Starns, 2004; Spitzer, Hanslmayr, Opitz, Mecklinger, & Bäuml, 2009), in classical laboratory experiments with newly learned material (e.g., Ciranni & Shimamura, 1999) as well as with individual emotional autobiographical memories (Barnier, Hung, & Conway, 2004) and even in social situations (Cuc, Koppel, & Hirst, 2007). Social sharing of even very salient memories, such as memories of the 9/11 attacks, has been demonstrated to reduce the availability of related, initially similarly salient memories. This and related findings lend momentum to the hypothesis that retrieval-induced forgetting may play a key role in the construction of collective memories (Coman, Manier, & Hirst, 2009).

Across the life-span retrieval-induced forgetting effects have been found in first and fourth graders (Zellner & Bäuml, 2005), young adults (Anderson, Bjork, & Bjork, 2000), and also in elderly people (Aslan, Bäuml, & Pastotter, 2007; Gomez-Ariza, Pelegrina, Lechuga, Suarez, & Bajo, 2009). On a neural level, medio-temporal structures appear critical for retrieval-induced forgetting as the effect is abolished in people with medio-temporal lobe lesions (Conway & Fthenaki, 2003). Moreover, recent neuroimaging studies point to an involvement of prefrontal brain structures (Kuhl, Dudukovic, Kahn, & Wagner, 2007; Wimber, Rutschmann, Greenlee, & Bäuml, 2009). Overall, a growing body of literature shows that retrieval-induced forgetting is a very basic mechanism of human memory control that secures access to selected material and suppresses nonselected competing information.

Although a widely reported mechanism, in some populations retrieval-induced forgetting may not arise. Phenomenologically, patients with Posttraumatic Stress Disorder (PTSD) who suffer from recurrent disturbing memories of

DOI: 10.1027/0044-3409/a000014

traumatic events can be suspected to have deficient retrieval-induced forgetting. In these patients, recall of certain, often peripheral, details of an episode instead of suppressing related information, appears to trigger recall of additional elements that the patients experience in the form of flashbacks or intrusive thoughts. Experimentally, recent research has shown that acutely experienced stress disrupts retrieval-induced forgetting in students, the reduction in the retrieval-induced forgetting effect being inversely related to participants' cortisol levels (Koessler, Engler, Riether, & Kissler, 2009).

Dysregulation of the glucocorticoid (e.g., cortisol) and adrenaline releasing hypothalamic-pituitary-adrenergic (HPA) axis is assumed to play a key role in the development and maintenance of PTSD (e.g., see further Yehuda, 2002). Extreme levels of cortisol release during a traumatic event can be neurotoxic to the hippocampus (McEwen, 1999). Reduced hippocampal volumes are assumed to be related to impaired episodic memory, primarily regarding the ability to bind individual details to context cues which is the very ability that retrieval-induced forgetting depends on (Bäuml, 2006). Reduced hippocampal volumes and hippocampal dysfunction have been reported in PTSD, although it is unclear whether these are a consequence of chronic stress or PTSD or a risk factor for its development or perhaps both (cf. Bremner, 2001; Gilbertson et al., 2002; Sapolsky, 2002).

Although perhaps less well investigated than the hippocampus, the prefrontal cortex is also a target site for the effects of stress hormones as it is likewise densely populated with glucocorticoid receptors and indeed several studies indicate prefrontal cortex dysfunctions in PTSD (Koenen et al., 2001; Vasterling, Brailey, Constans, & Sutker, 1998). Prefrontal cortex is assumed to be involved in behavior control functions such as response inhibition and in memory it plays an important role in retrieval monitoring (Henson, Shallice, & Dolan, 1999) which may explain its activation during retrieval-induced forgetting (see above). PTSD patients' higher levels of intrusions during free recall as well as more false alarms in recognition memory tasks have also been related to prefrontal dysfunction (Vasterling et al., 1998).

Retrieval-induced forgetting may be altered in people who have experienced severe traumatic stress for a number of reasons, but only one very recent study has addressed the issue empirically: Amir and colleagues (2009) investigated retrieval-induced forgetting in trauma-exposed North American undergraduates. Three hundred fifty college students were screened for traumatic events and PTSD symptoms. Seventeen of these fulfilled PTSD criteria as reflected by a Posttraumatic Diagnostic Scale (PDS; Foa, Cashman, Jaycox, & Perry, 1997) score of at least 11, and 15 reported at least one traumatic event, but did not fulfill criteria for a diagnosis. Sixteen students reporting neither traumatic events nor PTSD-related symptoms served as the control group. The three groups participated in a typical verbal retrieval-induced forgetting experiment. They learned words belonging to different categories (e.g., Fruit – Banana, Drink – Beer, etc.) and retrieval-practiced some of the words from some of the categories via category plus word stem cued recall (e.g., Fruit – Ba_____). During final recall they were quizzed about all initially learned words by way of a category-name-cued recall (e.g., Drink – _____; Fruit – ____; etc.). Results showed standard retrieval-induced forgetting in the non-traumatized control group with a recall enhancement for the practiced material and recall suppression for the non-practiced items from the practiced categories in comparison to items from never-practiced categories. By contrast, neither of the trauma-exposed groups showed retrieval-induced forgetting. Specifically the PTSD group also showed a smaller benefit from retrieval practice than the other two groups. Thus, this study indicates that American undergraduates with traumatic life events and/or qualifying for a diagnosis of PTSD have altered retrieval-induced forgetting.

Fortunately, most industrialized societies are relatively safe and the likelihood of experiencing traumatic events is comparatively low. However, the more different traumatic events an individual experiences, the more likely is the development of PTSD (Neuner et al., 2004). Consequently, in war-torn societies that suffer from violent conflict, PTSD prevalence is high (Karunakara et al., 2004), posing considerable threats for collective social and cognitive functioning, and perhaps even jeopardizing the formation of consistent and positive collective memories (Coman, Brown, Koppel, & Hirst, 2009). Therefore, the experimental study of relevant cognitive phenomena in non-Western societies and these cognitive phenomena's alteration by traumatic stress are needed to scientifically assess the cognitive and ultimately social consequences of violence and trauma.

The present study examined retrieval-induced forgetting in trauma victims with and without PTSD in a crisis region in East Africa (Northern Uganda) affected by ethnic conflict, civil war, and terror. Most of the Ugandan participants had been abducted as children by a guerrilla group called the "Lord's Resistance Army." Typical traumatic events included the abduction itself, rape, beatings and maltreatment, being threatened at gunpoint, witnessing torture, mutilations, killings and abductions of others, or being forced to commit crimes and acts of violence. Since this population differs on many educational, cultural, and social factors from populations normally studied in industrialized countries, a language-free recognition memory-based pictorial retrieval-induced forgetting paradigm was created. Photographs belonging to different categories (e.g., flowers and faces) were presented for learning. Then, participants were presented with partly occluded versions of some of the pictures for retrieval practice with the instruction to recall what the original picture looked like. A final old-new recognition memory test on all initially presented pictures and an equal number of thematically similar distractors followed (see Figure 1). The design was first tested in a group of German students and then used with the Ugandan internally displaced persons (IDPs). At the time this study was planned and conducted, we expected a significant retrieval-induced forgetting effect in the German group and in IDPs without PTSD, but not in the Ugandan IDPs with a PTSD diagnosis. Based on Amir et al.'s (2009) recent results, however, an absence of retrieval-induced forgetting in both Ugandan groups is conceivable due to both groups' exposure to severe stress. Finally, we anticipate poorer discrimination performance in PTSD, reflected in a higher false alarm rate.

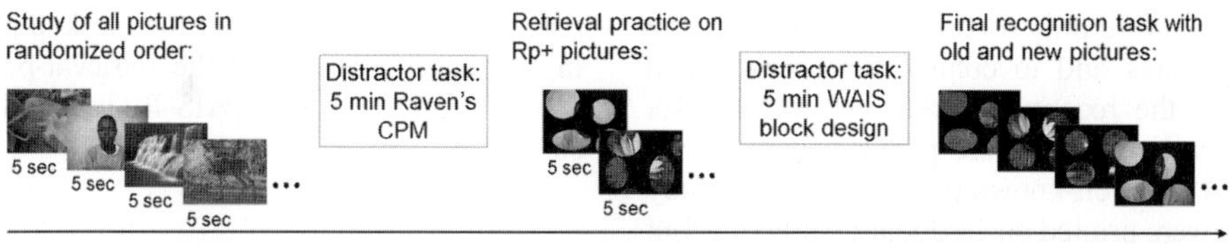

Figure 1. Experimental procedure. The experiment consisted of three phases which were separated by two distractor tasks. First (left) a series of pictures belonging to different categories was learned. After 5 min of Raven's Coloured Progressive Matrices, a cued retrieval-practice phase followed (middle). Participants had to recall the entire picture with the help of partly occluded exemplars. After another 5 min of distractor task, a final recognition test, were all initially presented pictures were re-presented together with similar new pictures, followed. For final recognition pictures were again partly occluded.

Methods

German Participants

Thirty-one healthy German students (26 females) from the University of Konstanz with a mean age of 23.32 (*SD* = 2.53) were tested to validate the present pictorial retrieval-induced forgetting design. All participants were free of medication and had been screened with the German Version of the Beck Depression Inventory (BDI; Hautzinger, Bailer, Worall, & Keller, 1994) and the State Trait Anxiety Inventory (STAI; Laux, Glanzmann, Schaffner, & Spielberger, 1981). Mean BDI score was 3.87 (*SD* = 4.06), mean STAI-S score was 32.77 (*SD* = 7.42), and mean STAI-T score was 36.53 (*SD* = 8.67). All obtained scores were within the normal range (cf. Hautzinger et al., 1994; Laux et al., 1981) and were similar to scores of other student samples from our laboratory. None of the German participants had traumatic events comparable to the Ugandan samples and all participants were free of PTSD or partial PTSD diagnosis (cf. Twamley, Hami, & Stein, 2004). Participants provided written informed consent and received a small financial compensation (5€ ~ US$7.20) for their participation.

Ugandan Participants

Forty-seven Ugandan participants (36 females) with a mean age of 20.79 (*SD* = 4.15) participated in this study. They were all inhabitants of two IDP camps (Awer and Parabongo) near the city of Gulu in Northern Uganda. The participants had all been clinically diagnosed in a large ongoing study on mental health and organized violence. For PTSD diagnosis, the PDS (Foa et al., 1997) was used. The PDS is normally applied as a self-report instrument, but due to local circumstances was administered with the assistance of trained interviewers. The PDS has good psychometric properties with a Cronbach's Alpha of .92, a test-retest reliability of .83, and a kappa of .74 between the PDS and the SCID. The analysis of the convergent validity reveals a kappa of .65 between PDS and SCID (Foa et al., 1997; Odenwald et al., 2007). The PTSD group (*N* = 24) had a mean score of 19.63 (*SD* = 4.99, range 15–33) on the PDS (with 15 being the cutoff for a PTSD diagnosis; cf. Odenwald et al., 2007) and fulfilled all PTSD criteria according to DSM-IV, whereas all of the Non-PTSD group members (*N* = 23) had a mean PDS score of zero. Both groups exhibited a high number of traumatic events. People in the non-PTSD group had on average 10.91 (*SD* = 7.22) traumatic experiences and people in the PTSD group had on average 20.92 (*SD* = 10.45) traumatic events. This difference was significant ($F(1, 45) = 14.45$, $p < .001$). All participants had similar education levels with 2 years of formal schooling at some point in their lives. They spoke the Ugandan dialect of Luo. During the experiment, which took place in the participants' huts, a trained local interpreter translated the experimenter's standardized instructions and the subjects' answers. Participants provided informed consent and received a payment of 3,000 Ugandan Shillings (USh 3,000 ~ US$1.80).

Experimental Procedure

All participants were tested in single sessions with one session taking ~ 45 min. Investigators introduced themselves and gave some general information about the study to the students or explained to the Ugandan participants the reason of the visit in general terms. Possible questions were answered before the start of the experiment. The experiment consisted of a study phase, a retrieval-practice phase, and a final test phase. Pictorial material was used in all three phases. Between study and retrieval-practice phase, a 5-min probe of Raven's Coloured Progressive Matrices (CPM; Bulheller & Häcker, 2006) was incorporated as a distractor task. As a second distractor task, a 5-min run with the Wechsler Adult Intelligence Scale-Revised (WAIS-R; Tewes, 1991) performance subscale of block design followed the retrieval practice and preceded the final test phase. The sequence of the experimental events is depicted in Figure 1.

Material

Colored pictures from four different semantic categories (antelopes, faces, flowers, and waterfalls) were used as stimulus material. Each category comprised six exemplars resulting in 24 relevant pictures for the study phase. Additionally, filler pictures stemmed from two further categories (birds and elephants). These were only used to counterbalance the sequence of the pictures and to control for primacy and recency effects. For the recognition task in the final test phase 24 (six per category) new lure pictures were shown in addition to the 24 old, well-known pictures from the study phase. All pictures were printed on cardboard cards of about 9 × 13 cm size that were presented by the experimenter during the study. One sample picture from each of the relevant categories can be seen in Figure 1.

Study Phase

In order to counterbalance the sequence of the pictures across participants, two differently randomized study lists had been generated. Each list consisted of 24 block-randomized pictures. Each block consisted of four items and contained one exemplar from each category. No two pictures from the same category were presented in sequence. The list started and ended with a picture from one of the filler categories, resulting in 28 study pictures overall. The experimenter showed the items from one of these lists to the participant. Each picture was shown for 5 s and the participants were asked to look carefully at the picture and to memorize it for later. All pictures were presented a second time in the same order.

Retrieval Practice Phase

The participants retrieval-practiced half of the six exemplars from two of the four relevant categories. This resulted in six relevant retrieval-practiced (Rp+) pictures, the remaining unpracticed pictures from the practiced categories (Rp−), and the control pictures from the completely never-practiced categories (Nrp). By using four different retrieval-practice lists, the assignment of categories and items to retrieval practice or no retrieval practice was counterbalanced across subjects and groups. At the beginning and at the end of each list, filler category pictures were presented to avoid successive presentation of items of the same category and to control for primacy and recency effects. The typical word stem completion task in verbal retrieval-induced forgetting (e.g., Anderson et al., 1994) was replaced by the presentation of partly occluded pictures in our pictorial retrieval-induced forgetting design. All "to-be-retrieval-practiced" pictures were partly occluded using a black rectangle with the size of the picture and four or five transparent ellipses, through which parts of the picture could be seen. Six different such masks were generated and randomly assigned to each of the items. Examples of two masked pictures are shown in Figure 1.

The participants were asked to use the masked pictures as cues to recall and imagine the whole picture from the study phase. Previous work has shown that a retrieval-attempt in the retrieval-practice phase is sufficient to cause the retrieval-induced forgetting effect. Retrieval success itself is not necessary (Storm, Bjork, Bjork, & Nestojko, 2006). Each item was shown for 5 s and the experimenter repeated the presentation of the masked pictures once again in the same order. After the retrieval-practice phase there was a 5-min run of the WAIS-R (Tewes, 1991) block design subtest.

Final Test Phase

During the final test, all 24 initially learned old pictures and 24 new lure pictures, six lure pictures per category, were successively shown in a randomized order. All presented items were partly occluded with the masks from the retrieval-practice phase. Masks and pictures were randomly paired, but for Rp+ pictures, the masks on the final test differed from the ones used during retrieval practice. Retrieval-induced forgetting on this final test is measured as the difference in recognition performance between Nrp minus Rp− items. The retrieval-practice effect is reflected in the difference between Rp+ minus Nrp items.

For the final test, four differently randomized lists of old and new pictures were created. Lists were counterbalanced across the participants and samples. The presentation always started with two masked filler items. Old and new pictures were presented randomly under the constraints that (1) the same number of old and new items was shown in the first 24 and last 24 test trials; (2) no two old items from a given category were ever tested before at least one lure item from the same category was tested, and vice versa; (3) no items requiring the same correct response (target or lure) appeared more than four times in a row; and (4) pictures of the same category were not presented successively. After presentation of each picture, participants were asked to judge the item as old or new. In Uganda, the interpreter translated the participant's answer and the experimenter took the responses down on a prepared data sheet. After the final test phase, all participants were informed about the aim of the study. After answering any remaining questions about the study, the participants received their financial compensation.

Distractor Tasks

Two distractor tasks were used in the study. The first distractor task intervened between study and retrieval practice and the second one followed the retrieval-practice phase.

After the study phase the participants solved matrices from the CPM for 5 min. In each test item, the participants were asked to identify the missing segment (among six presented alternatives) that was required to complete a larger pattern. The experimenter took down the number of performed and solved items.

Five minutes of the WAIS-R block design intervened between retrieval-practice and final test phase. The test required the participants to put sets of cubes together to match different 2D patterns on printed cards. The first test item was used for demonstration to explain the task. As in the first distractor task, the experimenter wrote down the number of performed and correctly solved test items.

Data Analysis

For data analysis, proportions of recognized items were calculated. Due to inhomogeneity of variance, all proportions were arcsine transformed as suggested by Winer (1971) to stabilize the variances and to normalize the data before repeated-measures analyses of variance (ANOVAs) were calculated. For a better display in graphics the arcsine values were retranslated to proportions using the sine transform (cf. Zar, 1984). Because particularly in populations with excessive false alarm rates, false alarms may affect and possibly obscure memory effects, all effects of interest were analyzed both for hit and recognition rates as indexed by hit rates minus false alarm rates using ANOVAs. Significant effects were followed up with two-tailed *t* tests.

Results

German Participants

Retrieval Practice Effect

Perhaps due to their overall very high performance, the German participants did not exhibit a significant retrieval practice effect. Recognition memory on Rp+ items was not higher than on Nrp items, either for hit rates ($F(1, 30) < 1$) or for recognition rates ($F(1, 30) < 1$) as indexed by hit rates minus false alarm rates. Figure 2 depicts Rp+, Nrp as well as Rp− recognition rates, the latter being critical for retrieval-induced forgetting as detailed in the following paragraph.

Retrieval-Induced Forgetting Effect

A retrieval-induced forgetting effect was found in the German sample. Hit rate for Nrp items was significantly higher than for Rp− items ($F(1, 30) = 6.36$; $p < .05$) and although somewhat attenuated, the effect was still visible in the false-alarm-corrected recognition rates ($F(1, 30) = 3.86$; $p = .059$), indicating that the manipulation also induced a small response bias which contributed to the retrieval-induced forgetting effect. See Figure 2 for false-alarm-corrected Nrp and Rp− recognition rates.

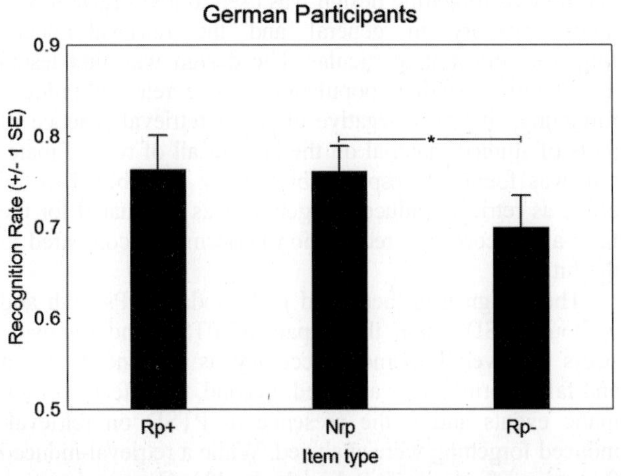

Figure 2. Recognition rates for retrieval-practiced (Rp+) items, non-retrieval-practiced items for never-practiced categories (Nrp), and unpracticed items from practiced categories (Rp−) in the German group.

Ugandan Participants

Hit Rate

Hit rates did not differ between Ugandans with and without PTSD ($F(1, 45) < 1$). However, hit rates in both Ugandan groups were lower than in the German group (all three groups: $F(2, 75) = 13.66$; $p < .0001$, Ugandan Non-PTSD vs. German: $t(52) = -5.62$, $p < .001$; Ugandan PTSD vs. German: $t(53) = -3.72$; $p < .001$).

False Alarm

False alarm rates for the three groups of participants are shown in Figure 3. As expected, false alarm rate was significantly higher in the PTSD than the Non-PTSD group ($F(1, 45) = 5.07$; $p < .05$). Additionally, both Ugandan groups had significantly higher false alarm rates than the German sample ($F(2, 75) = 73.91$; $p < .0001$; Ugandan Non-PTSD vs. German: $t(52) = 8.61$; $p < .001$; Ugandan PTSD vs. German: $t(53) = 12.96$; $p < .0001$).

Retrieval Practice Effect

Using hit rates, a Group (Non-PTSD, PTSD) × Item type (Rp+, Nrp) ANOVA revealed that Rp+ pictures were better recognized than Nrp pictures ($F(1, 75) = 6.49$; $p = .01$) indicating a retrieval practice effect. No significant main effect for the factor group ($F(1, 45) = 1.00$; $p > .30$) and

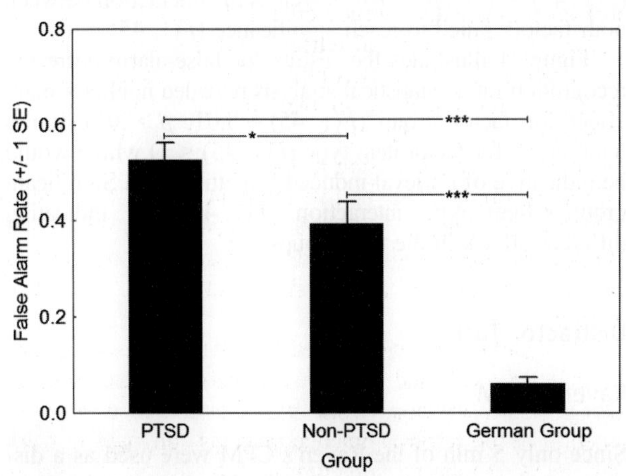

Figure 3. False alarm rates in the Ugandan PTSD group, the Ugandan Non-PTSD group, and the German group.

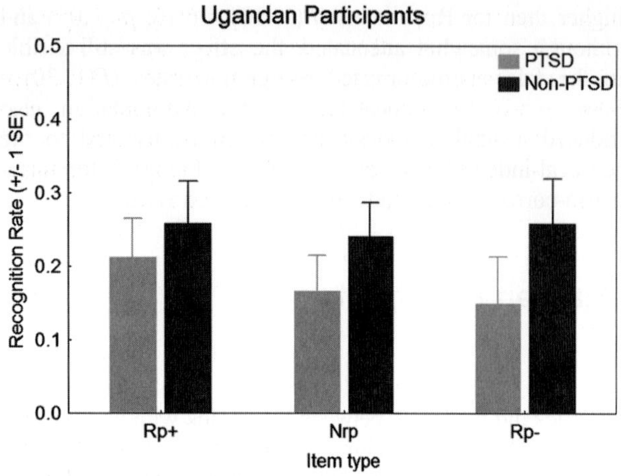

Figure 4. Recognition rates for retrieval-practiced (Rp+) items, non-retrieval-practiced items for never-practiced categories (Nrp), and unpracticed items from practiced categories (Rp−) in the two Ugandan groups (PTSD and Non-PTSD).

no significant interaction between the two factors occurred ($F(1, 45) = .11; p > .70$).

The analysis of the false-alarm-corrected recognition data likewise produced no significant effects. We found neither a significant main effect for the factor item ($F(1, 45) < 1$), nor a main effect for the factor group ($F(1, 45) = 1.26; p > .20$) and no significant interaction between the two factors ($F(1, 45) < 1$). Recognition rates for the different item types in the two Ugandan groups are shown in Figure 4.

Retrieval-Induced Forgetting Effect

Using hit rates, a Group (Non-PTSD, PTSD) × Item type (Nrp, Rp−) ANOVA revealed no significant effects. The main effect for factor group ($F(1, 45) < 1$) and item type ($F(1, 45) = 2.35; p > .10$) as well as the interaction between both factors failed to reach significance ($F(1, 45) < 1$).

Figure 4 illustrates the results for false-alarm-corrected recognition rates. Statistical analysis revealed neither a main effect for factor group ($F(1, 45) = 3.01; p > .05$), nor a main effect for factor item type ($F(1, 45) < 1$) which would be indicative of retrieval-induced forgetting, or a Significant group × Item type interaction ($F(1, 45) < 1$) indicating different effects in the two groups.

Distractor Tasks

Raven's CPM

Since only 5 min of the Raven's CPM were used as a distractor task, performance was analyzed comparing between groups the number of items completed and the rate of correctly solved items during the time given. One-way ANOVAs with factor group (PTSD, Non-PTSD) revealed no group differences, Ugandan PTSD and Non-PTSD participants did not differ in the number of completed items ($F(1, 45) = 1.03; p > .30$) and performed equally well in terms of percentage correctly completed items on the Raven's CPM ($F(1, 45) < 1$). However, the German students, not surprisingly performed much better, they solved about twice as many items on average (32 vs. 16; $F(2, 75) = 154.24$) and were also more correct in selecting the proper missing item (95% correct vs. 65% correct; $F(2, 75) = 88.85$). Still, the Ugandans performed well above chance, because, given the six alternatives each CPM item offers, chance level is at about 16%.

Block Design

Ugandan participants turned out to have had conceptual difficulties understanding and performing the task within 5 min, therefore the data were not further analyzed.

Discussion

The present study investigated episodic memory performance in Ugandan IDPs with and without PTSD as well as in German students. The study was motivated by the fact that the incidence of traumatic events as well as the prevalence of PTSD is very high in Northern Uganda, whereas there is practically no empirical research on the cognitive effects on afflicted individuals and societies. Recently, mechanisms of retrieval-induced forgetting have been implicated in the formation and regulation of collective memories in social groups (Cuc et al., 2007). At the same time, both phenomenological evidence from PTSD patients' clinical symptoms and experimental evidence (Amir et al., 2009) suggested impaired retrieval-induced forgetting in trauma victims. A novel picture recognition memory-based retrieval-induced forgetting design was used to investigate recognition memory in general and the retrieval-induced forgetting effect in particular. The design was first tested in a German student population, where retrieval-induced forgetting, that is a negative effect of retrieval practice of parts of studied material on the later recall of related material, was found. A response bias partly contributed to the effect as retrieval-induced forgetting was attenuated for the false-alarm-corrected recognition performance compared to the hit rate.

The design was then used in Ugandan IDPs with and without PTSD. First, the impact of PTSD and traumatic stress on overall memory accuracy as evidenced by hit and false alarm rates was tested. Second, the effects of traumatic events and/or the presence of PTSD on retrieval-induced forgetting were analyzed. While a retrieval-induced forgetting effect was found in the healthy German comparison group, the Ugandan participants did not show retrieval-induced forgetting, either the ones with or the ones without a PTSD diagnosis. This result held both for hit rates and the false-alarm-corrected recognition rates. However, considerably elevated false alarm rates were particularly characteristic of the Ugandan PTSD group. Participants with a PTSD diagnosis had higher false alarms both in comparison with the Ugandan Non-PTSD group and, even more so, with the German group. The apparent retrieval-practice effect in the Ugandan group also proved to be mainly due to an elevated false alarm rate, perhaps indicative of a very global processing strategy in the Ugandans. Since targets and distractors in the recognition test stemmed from the same categories, poorer processing of pictorial detail in the stress-exposed Ugandans may contribute to the effect.

Regarding false alarms the results are consistent with previous reports of less accurate recognition with higher levels of commission errors in PTSD (Vasterling et al., 1998). Since in the present study the Ugandan PTSD and Non-PTSD group differed, it seems that exceptionally high false alarm rates are related to the PTSD diagnosis itself rather than the experience of traumatic events. On the other hand, since both Ugandan groups had much higher false alarm rates than the Germans, but had also experienced much more life stress and traumatic events, the impact of traumatic stress on recognition accuracy may not be entirely restricted to a PTSD diagnosis. This would also appear to be suggested by experimental studies demonstrating higher levels of false memory after stress induction (Payne, Nadel, Allen, Thomas, & Jacobs, 2002). From a neuropsychological perspective, high level of false alarms in recognition memory is particularly compatible with prefrontal (Butler, McDaniel, Dornburg, Price, & Roediger, 2004), but also with hippocampal dysfunction (Weiss et al., 2004). Both structures are densely populated with glucocorticoid receptors, making them prime target sites for stress effects (Joels, 2001; McEwen, 2003; Sanchez, Young, Plotsky, & Insel, 2000).

However, obviously the German group and the two Ugandan groups differed on many more aspects beside the presence and intensity of past and current life stress. There are huge cultural and educational differences between the groups and the performance on the distractor tasks reflects some of these differences: Although the two Ugandan groups did not differ in their Raven's CPM performance, not surprisingly, they performed much worse than German students, who solved nearly all the items within 5 min, the test having been designed for IQ testing in children. Likewise, while German students had no problems understanding the block design task, many Ugandan participants had difficulty understanding the task. Therefore, some of the considerable cultural and educational differences may have contributed to group differences in false alarm rates or retrieval-induced forgetting.

The lack of a retrieval-induced forgetting effect in both Ugandan groups is consistent with the thesis that the experience of traumatic events, even without the presence of a PTSD diagnosis, is enough to impair retrieval-induced forgetting (Amir et al., 2009). In Western societies retrieval-induced forgetting has been found in 7 year olds as well as in 70 year olds (e.g., Ford, Keating, & Patel, 2004; Gomez-Ariza et al., 2009), suggesting that education and age play a minor role in the occurrence of the effect. Still, this is the first study in an African population, leaving open the possibility that hitherto unknown cultural or educational factors rather than past or current stress levels impair retrieval-induced forgetting. Moreover, although successful recall in the retrieval-practice phase is not necessary for the suppression effect to occur, at least a retrieval attempt is necessary. It would thus be conceivable that the Ugandans for some reason did not try to recall the presented pictures, while the German students did, giving rise to the differential effects. Therefore, we further examined the occurrence of retrieval-induced forgetting and its elimination by traumatic stress in subgroups of the current population: If retrieval-induced forgetting really occurs in a Ugandan IDP population and if life-time stress as reflected by the number of traumatic events affects the pattern of results, at least the most stressed individuals should differ from the least stressed ones. We thus analyzed the retrieval-induced forgetting patterns within the Ugandans, comparing them in terms of number of traumatic events in the highest and the lowest quartiles. The highest quartile consisted of 11 people who had experienced on average 31 traumatic events (range 24–39). Ten of the people in the highest quartile had been diagnosed with PTSD. The lowest quartile consisted of 10 people who had experienced on average four traumatic events (range 0–7, internal displacement alone was not counted as a traumatic event). Two of the people in the lowest quartile had been diagnosed with PTSD. Comparison of the retrieval-induced forgetting patterns between these two extreme groups yielded a significant interaction ($F(1, 19) = 4.98$, $p < .05$). In the lowest quartile, a retrieval-induced forgetting effect was found in that recognition of non-practiced pictures from practiced categories (Rp−) was lower than recognition of control items (Nrp), whereas in the highest quartile the opposite pattern emerged with higher Rp− than control item recognition. The latter reflects the overall pattern when all Ugandan participants were analyzed. Thus, this analysis indicates that retrieval-induced forgetting can be found in Ugandans and that the intensity of traumatic stress as measured by the number of experienced events influences the retrieval-induced forgetting patterns in the present population. This result supports the thesis that, in line with Amir et al.'s results (2009), the absence of retrieval-induced forgetting in the Ugandan IDPs is at least partly related to previous exposure to traumatic stress. The presently studied population was much more severely traumatized than Amir et al.'s (2009) who recently reported an absence of retrieval-induced forgetting already in trauma-exposed and not just in PTSD diagnosed undergraduates. Moreover, the experience of an experimentally induced social stressor, the Trier Social Stress Test (TSST), presumably via activation of the HPA axis already transiently abolishes retrieval-induced forgetting (Koessler et al., 2009). In comparison with the events experienced by many of the present participants (both with and without PTSD), the TSST with its combination of public speaking and doing calculations in public seems a very mild treatment, although its experimental efficacy and its effects on memory measures other than retrieval-induced forgetting have been amply demonstrated (e.g., Kuhlmann, Piel, & Wolf, 2005). Recent research indicates that retrieval-induced forgetting, although replicable across very different situations (e.g., Ciranni & Shimamura, 1999; Cuc et al., 2007;

MacLeod & Macrae, 2001; Shaw, Bjork, & Handal, 1995) and different age groups (Aslan et al., 2007; Ford et al., 2004; Zellner & Bäuml, 2005), is very sensitive to manipulations of emotional well-being, experimental induction of negative mood eliminating the effect (Bäuml & Kuhbandner, 2007). Obviously, living conditions in an IDP camp alone are more conducive to negative mood than German undergraduate student life. Given this apparent susceptibility of retrieval-induced forgetting to individual mood states or stress, one may come to question the implications of the effect for such complex phenomena as collective memories. On the other hand, cross-cultural studies also show that mildly positive mood states are the default for people in many societies (Diener & Diener, 1996), perhaps supporting the formation of coherent collective memories. Stress on the other hand may hamper this process. While such considerations may prove relevant for future theorizing and empirical studies, answers are clearly beyond the scope of the present research.

The present study cross-culturally confirms poorer memory performance and higher false alarm rates in severely traumatized people diagnosed with PTSD compared to a demographically very similar trauma-exposed comparison group without PTSD. The findings are in line with the thesis that retrieval-induced forgetting is reduced in people who have been exposed to traumatic events, although, as detailed above, interpretation is complicated by the absence of a demographically and educationally matched Ugandan control group with no exposure to psychological trauma whatsoever. Since our initial hypothesis focused on the effects of a PTSD diagnosis, our primary aim was to compare memory performance within IDPs with and without PTSD, the German student sample having been primarily intended for validation of the experiment rather than as a true healthy control group. Given the present data, a major challenge for future studies of cognitive functioning in crisis regions will be to provide such a demographically and educationally matched sample within the studied culture. This proves to be a difficult enterprise, because of the profound effects of civil wars on the afflicted societies and because less afflicted groups often enjoy more formal education and better general living conditions than more afflicted portions of the population. Nevertheless, considering the implications for research and therapy, we believe this to be a worthwhile endeavor.

Acknowledgments

We thank the members of the nongovernmental organization vivo (The Victim's Voice) for their help during all phases of this study. Special thanks to Herbert Tumusiime, Esther, Lawrence, and Tony for invaluable local support. We would also like to thank all participants for taking part in this study. Research was supported by the Deutsche Forschungsgemeinschaft (Ki1286/1-1).

References

Amir, N., Badour, C. L., & Freese, B. (2009). The effect of retrieval on recall of information in individuals with posttraumatic stress disorder. *Journal of Anxiety Disorders, 23*, 535–540.

Anderson, M. C., Bjork, R. A., & Bjork, E. L. (1994). Remembering can cause forgetting: Retrieval dynamics in long-term memory. *Journal of Experimental Psychology. Learning, Memory, and Cognition, 20*, 1063–1087.

Anderson, M. C., Bjork, E. L., & Bjork, R. A. (2000). Retrieval-induced forgetting: Evidence for a recall-specific mechanism. *Psychonomic Bulletin and Review, 7*, 522–530.

Aslan, A., Bäuml, K. H., & Pastotter, B. (2007). No inhibitory deficit in older adults' episodic memory. *Psychological Science, 18*, 72–78.

Barnier, A. J., Hung, L., & Conway, M. A. (2004). Retrieval-induced forgetting of emotional and unemotional autobiographical memories. *Cognition & Emotion, 18*, 457–477.

Bäuml, K. H. (2006). Retrieval inhibition in episodic recall: Effects on feature binding. In H. Zimmer, A. Mecklinger, & U. Lindenberger (Eds.), *Binding in human memory: A neurocognitive approach* (pp. 545–568). Oxford, UK: Oxford University Press.

Bäuml, K. H., & Kuhbandner, C. (2007). Remembering can cause forgetting–but not in negative moods. *Psychological Science, 18*, 111–115.

Bremner, J. D. (2001). Hypotheses and controversies related to effects of stress on the hippocampus: An argument for stress-induced damage to the hippocampus in patients with posttraumatic stress disorder. *Hippocampus, 11*, 75–81. discussion 82-74.

Bulheller, S., & Häcker, H. (2006). *Manual für Raven's Progressive Matrices and Vocabulary Scales von J. Raven, J. C. Raven und J. H. Court. Deutsche Bearbeitung und Normierung von S. Bulheller und H. Häcker* [German version of the manual for Raven's Progressive Matrices and Vocabulary Scales]. Frankfurt, Germany: Harcourt.

Butler, K. M., McDaniel, M. A., Dornburg, C. C., Price, A. L., & Roediger, H. L. III. (2004). Age differences in veridical and false recall are not inevitable: The role of frontal lobe function. *Psychonomic Bulletin & Review, 11*, 921–925.

Carrier, M., & Pashler, H. (1992). The influence of retrieval on retention. *Memory & Cognition, 20*, 633–642.

Ciranni, M. A., & Shimamura, A. P. (1999). Retrieval-induced forgetting in episodic memory. *Journal of Experimental Psychology: Learning, Memory, and Cognition. 25*, 1403–1414.

Coman, A., Brown, A. D., Koppel, J., & Hirst, W. (2009). Collective memory from a psychological perspective. *International Journal of Politics, Culture and Society, 22*, 125–141.

Coman, A., Manier, D., & Hirst, W. (2009). Forgetting the unforgettable through conversation: Socially shared retrieval-induced forgetting of September 11 memories. *Psychological Science, 20*, 627–633.

Conway, M. A., & Fthenaki, A. (2003). Disruption of inhibitory control of memory following lesions to the frontal and temporal lobes. *Cortex, 39*, 667–686.

Cuc, A., Koppel, J., & Hirst, W. (2007). Silence is not golden: A case for socially shared retrieval-induced forgetting. *Psychological Science, 18*, 727–733.

Diener, E., & Diener, C. (1996). Most people are happy. *Psychological Science, 7*, 181–185.

Foa, E., Cashman, L., Jaycox, L., & Perry, K. (1997). The validation of a self-report measure of posttraumatic stress disorder: The Posttraumatic Diagnostic Scale. *Psychological Assessment, 9*, 445–451.

Ford, R. M., Keating, S., & Patel, R. (2004). Retrieval-induced forgetting: A developmental study. *British Journal of Developmental Psychology, 22*, 585–603.

Gates, A. I. (1917). Recitation as a factor of memorizing. *Archives of Psychology, 6*, 1–104.

Gilbertson, M. W., Shenton, M. E., Ciszewski, A., Kasai, K., Lasko, N. B., Orr, S. P., & Pitman, R. K. (2002). Smaller hippocampal volume predicts pathologic vulnerability to psychological trauma. *Nature Neuroscience, 5*, 1242–1247.

Gomez-Ariza, C. J., Pelegrina, S., Lechuga, M. T., Suarez, A., & Bajo, M. T. (2009). Inhibition and retrieval of facts in young and older adults. *Experimental Aging Research, 35*, 83–97.

Hautzinger, M., Bailer, M., Worall, H., & Keller, F. (1994). *Beck-Depressions-Inventar (BDI)*. Bern, Switzerland: Huber.

Henson, R. N., Shallice, T., & Dolan, R. J. (1999). Right prefrontal cortex and episodic memory retrieval: A functional MRI test of the monitoring hypothesis. *Brain, 122*, 1367–1381.

Hicks, J. L., & Starns, J. J. (2004). Retrieval-induced forgetting occurs in tests of item recognition. *Psychonomic Bulletin and Review, 11*, 125–130.

Hogan, R. M., & Kintsch, W. (1971). Differential effects of study and test trials on long-term recognition and recall. *Journal of Verbal Learning and Verbal Behavior, 10*, 562–567.

Joels, M. (2001). Corticosteroid actions in the hippocampus. *Journal of Neuroendocrinology, 13*, 657–669.

Karunakara, U. K., Neuner, F., Schauer, M., Singh, K., Hill, K., Elbert, T., & Burnha, G. (2004). Traumatic events and symptoms of post-traumatic stress disorder amongst Sudanese nationals, refugees and Ugandans in the West Nile. *African Health Sciences, 4*, 83–93.

Koenen, K. C., Driver, K. L., Oscar-Berman, M., Wolfe, J., Folsom, S., Huang, M. T., & Schlesinger, L. (2001). Measures of prefrontal system dysfunction in posttraumatic stress disorder. *Brain and Cognition, 45*, 64–78.

Koessler, S., Engler, H., Riether, C., & Kissler, J. (2009). No retrieval-induced forgetting under stress. *Psychological Science, 20*, 1356–1363.

Kuhl, B. A., Dudukovic, N. M., Kahn, I., & Wagner, A. D. (2007). Decreased demands on cognitive control reveal the neural processing benefits of forgetting. *Nature Neuroscience, 10*, 908–914.

Kuhlmann, S., Piel, M., & Wolf, O. T. (2005). Impaired memory retrieval after psychosocial stress in healthy young men. *Journal of Neuroscience, 25*, 2977–2982.

Laux, L., Glanzmann, P., Schaffner, P., & Spielberger, C. D. (1981). *Das State-Trait-Angstinventar. Theoretische Grundlagen und Handanweisungen* [Manual of the German version of the State Trait Anxiety Inventory]. Weinheim, Germany: Beltz.

MacLeod, M. D., & Macrae, C. N. (2001). Gone but not forgotten: The transient nature of retrieval-induced forgetting. *Psychological Science, 12*, 148–152.

McEwen, B. S. (1999). Stress and hippocampal plasticity. *Annual Review of Neuroscience, 22*, 105–122.

McEwen, B. S. (2003). Mood disorders and allostatic load. *Biological Psychiatry, 54*, 200–207.

Neuner, F., Schauer, M., Karunakara, U., Klaschik, C., Robert, C., & Elbert, T. (2004). Psychological trauma and evidence for enhanced vulnerability for posttraumatic stress disorder through previous trauma among West Nile refugees. *BMC Psychiatry, 4*, 34.

Odenwald, M., Lingenfelder, B., Schauer, M., Neuner, F., Rockstroh, B., Hinkel, H., & Elbert, T. (2007). Screening for Posttraumatic Stress Disorder among Somali ex-combatants: A validation study. *Conflict and Health, 1*, 10.

Payne, J. D., Nadel, L., Allen, J. J., Thomas, K. G., & Jacobs, W. J. (2002). The effects of experimentally induced stress on false recognition. *Memory, 10*, 1–6.

Roediger, H. L., & Karpicke, J. D. (2006). Test-enhanced learning: Taking memory tests improves long-term retention. *Psychological Science, 17*, 249–255.

Sanchez, M. M., Young, L. J., Plotsky, P. M., & Insel, T. R. (2000). Distribution of corticosteroid receptors in the rhesus brain: Relative absence of glucocorticoid receptors in the hippocampal formation. *Journal of Neuroscience, 20*, 4657–4668.

Sapolsky, R. M. (2002). Chickens, eggs and hippocampal atrophy. *Nature Neuroscience, 5*, 1111–1113.

Shaw, J. S. I., Bjork, R. A., & Handal, A. (1995). Retrieval-induced forgetting in an eyewitness-memory paradigm. *Psychonomic Bulletin & Review, 2*, 249–253.

Spitzer, B., Hanslmayr, S., Opitz, B., Mecklinger, A., & Bäuml, K. H. (2009). Oscillatory Correlates of Retrieval-Induced Forgetting in Recognition Memory. *Journal of Cognitive Neuroscience, 21*, 976–990.

Storm, B. C., Bjork, E. L., Bjork, R. A., & Nestojko, J. F. (2006). Is retrieval success a necessary condition for retrieval-induced forgetting?. *Psychonomic Bulletin & Review, 13*, 1023–1027.

Tewes, R. (1991). *Hamburg-Wechsler-Intelligenztest für Erwachsene – Revision 1991 (HAWIE – R)* [German version of the Wechster Adult Intelligence Scale – Revised (WAIS – R)]. Bern, Switzerland: Huber.

Twamley, E. W., Hami, S., & Stein, M. B. (2004). Neuropsychological function in college students with and without posttraumatic stress disorder. *Psychiatry Research, 126*, 265–274.

Vasterling, J. J., Brailey, K., Constans, J. I., & Sutker, P. B. (1998). Attention and memory dysfunction in posttraumatic stress disorder. *Neuropsychology, 12*, 125–133.

Weiss, A. P., Zalesak, M., DeWitt, I., Goff, D., Kunkel, L., & Heckers, S. (2004). Impaired hippocampal function during the detection of novel words in schizophrenia. *Biological Psychiatry, 55*, 668–675.

Wimber, M., Rutschmann, R. M., Greenlee, M. W., & Bäuml, K. H. (2009). Retrieval from episodic memory: Neural mechanisms of interference resolution. *Journal of Cognitive Neuroscience, 21*, 538–549.

Winer, B. J. (1971). *Statistical principles in experimental design*. New York: McGraw-Hill.

Yehuda, R. (2002). Post-traumatic stress disorder. *The New England Journal of Medicine, 346*, 108–114.

Zar, J. H. (1984). *Biostatistical analysis*. Englewood Cliffs, NJ: Prentice-Hall.

Zellner, M., & Bäuml, K. H. (2005). Intact retrieval inhibition in children's episodic recall. *Memory & Cognition, 33*, 396–404.

Johanna Kissler

Department of Psychology
Box D25
University of Konstanz
78457 Konstanz
Germany
Tel. +49 7531 884616
E-mail Johanna.Kissler@uni-konstanz.de

Original Article

Classical Conditioning in Borderline Personality Disorder With and Without Posttraumatic Stress Disorder

Jana Mauchnik,* Ulrich W. Ebner-Priemer,* Martin Bohus, and Christian Schmahl

Department of Psychosomatic Medicine and Psychotherapy, Central Institute of Mental Health, University of Heidelberg, Mannheim, Germany

Abstract. Conditioning studies in Borderline Personality Disorder (BPD) revealed intact acquisition and within-session extinction for patients with low acute dissociation and impaired acquisition for patients with high acute dissociation. In Posttraumatic Stress Disorder (PTSD) delayed short-term extinction as well as reduced discrimination learning was found. Controlling for acute dissociation, with a subgroup analysis of BPD patients with and without comorbid PTSD we aimed to further understand the influence of both disorders on altered conditioning processes. Aversive differential conditioning was assessed in 33 non-medicated female patients meeting DSM-IV criteria for BPD (15 with and 18 without co-occurring PTSD). An aversive sound served as unconditioned stimulus (US), and two neutral pictures as conditioned stimuli (CS+, CS−). Conditioning was assessed by skin conductance responses (SCRs) and ratings of valence and arousal. BPD patients without PTSD revealed a significant differentiation between CS+ and CS− during acquisition, early and late extinction in SCR. BPD patients with PTSD did not show differential responses during any of these phases. BPD patients without PTSD showed differential responses during acquisition, early and late extinction. This underpins intact learning regarding acquisition processes, but points to impaired within-session extinction. BPD patients with PTSD had difficulties in the acquisition of the differentiation between the danger and the safety signal, possibly indicating a discrimination problem.

Keywords: PTSD, Borderline Personality Disorder, learning, classical conditioning, extinction

Investigating classical conditioning in psychiatric disorders can help to understand how symptoms develop and persist due to pathological basic learning processes. Furthermore, behavioral therapy strongly refers to, and its successful accomplishment depends on, intact learning. Classical conditioning has been examined in several disorders, primarily in anxiety disorders as their models of etiology mainly include fear conditioning (panic disorder: Michael, Blechert, Vriends, Margraf, & Wilhelm, 2007; social phobia: Hermann, Ziegler, Birbaumer, & Flor, 2002). Posttraumatic Stress Disorder (PTSD), particularly reexperiencing the traumatic event, avoidance of stimuli associated with the trauma, and autonomic hyperarousal, can also be seen as a result of conditioning by the association of neutral stimulus (NS), for example sensory stimuli, with the traumatic event, the unconditioned stimulus (US; Michael, Ehlers, & Halligan, 2005; Pitman, 1989; Rothbaum & Davis, 2003). This association may lead to triggering the conditioned response (CR; i.e., symptoms of arousal, intrusions) to the former neutral, now conditioned stimulus (CS) in the absence of the US, here the traumatic event. Patients with PTSD show higher conditionability, that is, stronger CR and/or attenuated extinction (Orr et al., 2000), an inability to inhibit fear responses in the presence of safety cues (Grillon & Morgan, 1999; Rothbaum & Davis, 2003), or difficulties to discriminate between safety and danger signal (Grillon & Morgan, 1999).

Differential conditioning designs include a safety and a danger signal as CS and compare responses to stimuli that signal the presence (CS+) or absence (CS−) of an aversive event. These designs thereby allow the investigation of differential responding, inhibition, and discrimination learning. Orr et al. (2000) found stronger differential conditioning during acquisition and extinction in PTSD patients compared to traumatized subjects without PTSD. In contrast, Peri, Ben-Shakhar, Orr, and Shalev (2000) found stronger differential conditioning in PTSD patients compared to trauma exposed and healthy controls (HC) only during extinction and additionally enhanced responses to the CS− during acquisition and extinction. Blechert, Michael, Vriends, and Wilhelm (2007) found delayed extinction to the CS+ in PTSD compared to HC. Wessa and Flor

* Both authors contributed equally to this work.

DOI: 10.1027/0044-3409/a000015

(2007) found a failure of extinction of fear responses during second-order conditioning (pictures of the event served as US) in PTSD. In a differential fear conditioning paradigm in PTSD, Grillon and Morgan (1999) found differential responses measured by the fear-potentiated startle response only during a second conditioning session after 1 week in PTSD patients. Traumatized subjects, by contrast, acquired differential responses already during the first conditioning session. Another study underpinning impaired discrimination learning in PTSD was conducted in combat veterans with and without PTSD and HC (Ayers, White, & Powell, 2003): Investigating eye blink conditioning, they found differential responding only in HC.

Clinical (Feeny, Zoellner, & Foa, 2002) and the neurobiological findings (Schmahl & Bremner, 2006) point to impaired learning processes in Borderline Personality Disorder (BPD). In a study by Ebner-Priemer, Mauchnik, Kleindienst, Schmahl, and Peper (2008), classical conditioning was investigated in two groups of patients with BPD scoring low or high in acute dissociative features and HC. They found intact acquisition and within-session extinction in BPD patients with low levels of dissociative symptomatology. However, the differentiation between CS+ and CS− during late extinction nearly reached significance thereby pointing to delayed extinction in BPD. In BPD patients with high dissociation, a lack of differential acquisition was found. Furthermore, acute dissociation led to reduced physiological reactivity. Therefore, acute dissociation appears to impair basic learning processes in BPD.

In sum, only few data exist on conditioning processes in patients with BPD (i.e., Ebner-Priemer et al., 2008), whereas several studies were conducted in PTSD patients. For the latter, four studies found a higher conditionability, meaning they showed an increased difference between CS+ and CS− or delayed extinction (Blechert et al., 2007; Orr et al., 2000; Peri et al., 2000; Wessa & Flor, 2007) and two found support for a lack of discrimination learning with no (Ayers et al., 2003) or delayed (Grillon & Morgan, 1999) differential responses to CS+ and CS−.

Approximately 50% of BPD patients suffer from co-occurring PTSD (Zanarini, Frankenburg, Hennen, Reich, & Silk, 2004; Zimmermann, 1999). Therefore, and because of the differential findings in both disorders as mentioned above, we were interested in differential conditioning in BPD patients with and without co-occurring PTSD. In a conditioning paradigm, we investigated acquisition, early and late within-session extinction in BPD patients with and without co-occurring PTSD. We expected BPD patients without PTSD to show intact learning (differential responding during acquisition and early within-session extinction, *Hypothesis 1*) and impaired short-term extinction (prolonged differentiation between CS+ and CS− during late within-session extinction, *Hypothesis 2*) and patients with PTSD to show impaired inhibition (elevated responses to the CS−, *Hypothesis 3*) and impaired discrimination learning (smaller or even a lack of differential responses, *Hypothesis 4*). We included present-state dissociative experience as a covariate, as it has been demonstrated to impede conditioning processes (Ebner-Priemer et al., 2008) and diminish physiological responses (Ebner-Priemer et al., 2005).

Methods and Materials

Participants

The study was conducted at the Department of Psychosomatic Medicine and Psychotherapy, Central Institute of Mental Health, Mannheim, Germany. A total of 45 female BPD patients were recruited for this study (previous analyses of this study have been published elsewhere (Ebner-Priemer et al., 2008)). Due to technical problems, four participants (defective memory card, detached electrodes) had to be excluded. In addition, six participants (BPD) did not tolerate the US (aversive sound). Furthermore, two other patients did not show any SCR. Therefore, the final sample thus included 33 BPD patients, 15 with and 18 without co-occurring PTSD. BPD patients were recruited from consecutively admitted patients to a treatment program at the CIMH or via announcements on BPD-associated websites. We used the Structured Clinical Interview for DSM-IV Axis I Disorders (SCID-I) (Wittchen, Wunderlich, & Gruschwitz, 1997) and the International Personality Disorder Examination (IPDE) (Loranger, 1999). Trained psychologists administered all diagnostic instruments (inter-rater reliability for IPDE ($\kappa = .77$) and SCID-I ($\kappa = .69$)). All patients met full DSM-IV criteria for BPD. Patients with schizophrenia, bipolar disorder, current major depression, or current alcohol/drug abuse were excluded. All participants were between 18 and 45 years old and had been free of psychotropic medications for at least 4 weeks prior to the investigation. Demographic and psychometric measures for BPD patients with and without comorbid PTSD are presented in Table 1A–C.

Patients and HC did not significantly differ regarding age, education, sex (all female), and ethnicity (one Asian participant without PTSD) or any of the psychological measures. All subjects were paid for participating (10€) and gave written informed consent after receiving a description of the study. The study was approved by the ethical review committee of the University of Heidelberg, Germany, in accordance with the Declaration of Helsinki.

Psychometric Measures

We assessed present-state dissociative experience with the state version of the "Dissociation-Tension-Scale" (DSS; Stiglmayr, Braakmann, Haaf, Stieglitz, & Bohus, 2003; Stiglmayr, Shapiro, Stieglitz, Limberger, & Bohus, 2001). This self-rating scale consists of 20 items including psychological (e.g., depersonalization and amnesia) as well as somatic dissociation (e.g., reduced perception of pain). Trait dissociation was assessed by the German version of the Dissociative Experience Scale (FDS; Freyberger, Spitzer, & Stieglitz, 1999), state anxiety by the "State-Trait Anxiety Inventory" (STAI; Laux, Glanzmann, Schaffner, & Spielberger, 1981), depressive symptoms by the "Beck Depression Inventory" (BDI; Hautzinger, Bailer, Worall, & Keller, 1994), handedness by the Edinburgh Inventory of Handedness (EHI; Oldfield, 1971), and global borderline

Table 1. Demographic and psychometric measures for BPD patients with (N = 15) and without (N = 18) comorbid PTSD

	BPD mean (*SD*)	BPD + PTSD	BPD + PTSD vs. BPD (*t* tests)
A. Demographic data			
Age	28.2 (7.9)	27.3 (5.6)	t = .366; df = 31; p = .717
Years of education	12.4 (2.6)	12.4 (3.2)	t = .031; df = 30; p = .975
B. General psychopathology			
DSS	1.73 (1.80)	1.64 (1.80)	t = .144; df = 31; p = .886
FDS	21.93 (13.87)	26.07 (13.44)	t = .868; df = 31; p = .392
STAI	60.94 (7.94)	60.93 (7.49)	t = .003; df = 29; p = .997
BDI	25.33 (10.60)	29.29 (12.51)	t = .967; df = 30; p = .341
BSL	1.73 (.63)	1.94 (.41)	t = 1.064; df = 31; p = .295
Eating disorder current/lifetime	4/9	2/8	–
Anxiety disorder current/lifetime	11/10	9/11	–
Trauma lifetime	12	15	–
Sexual abuse	9	15	–
Major depression current/lifetime	0/15	0/14	–
PD Cluster A	2	2	–
PD Cluster B	1	2	–
PD Cluster C	6	11	–
C. Baseline reactivity	BPD mean (*SEM*)	BPD + PTSD	BPD + PTSD vs. BPD (*t* tests)
US valence	5.11 (.25)	5.40 (.34)	t = .699; df = 31; p = .490
US arousal	5.28 (.21)	5.00 (.28)	t = .813; df = 31; p = .422
CS+ valence	3.83 (.31)	3.93 (.33)	t = .222; df = 31; p = .826
CS– valence	4.17 (.27)	4.33 (.30)	t = .410; df = 3; p = .684
CS+ arousal	3.94 (.32)	4.00 (.32)	t = .122; df = 31; p = .904
CS– arousal	3.94 (.33)	3.73 (.33)	t = .450; df = 31; p = .656
US log(SCR+1)	.36 (.04)	.39 (.05)	t = .424; df = 31; p = .675
CS+ (habituation) log(SCR+1)	.08 (.02)	.06 (.02)	t = .179; df = 31; p = .859
CS– (habituation) log(SCR+1)	.09 (.02)	.06 (.02)	t = 1.140; df = 31; p = .263

BPD = Borderline Personality Disorder; PTSD = Posttraumatic Stress Disorder; anxiety disorders without PTSD; cluster B without BPD; *SD* = standard deviation; *SEM* = standard error; n.s. = not significant; DSS = Dissociation-Tension-Scale (Stiglmayr et al., 2001); FDS = German version of the Dissociative Experience Scale (Freyberger et al., 1999); STAI = State Trait Anxiety Inventory (Laux et al., 1981); BDI = Beck Depression Inventory (Hautzinger et al., 1994); BSL = Borderline Symptom List (Bohus et al., 2007); PD = personality disorder; valence (Likert scale 1–6; pleasant (1) vs. unpleasant (6)); arousal (Likert scale 1–6; relaxing (1) vs. exciting (6)); US = unconditioned stimulus; SCR = Skin conductance response; *SD* = standard deviation; SEM = standard error of the mean.

psychopathology by the Borderline Symptom List (BSL; Bohus et al., 2007). Hearing thresholds of all participants were assessed, using a simplified version of the published procedure from the Presentation Library (aud-rand-thresh-old.exp; Neurobehavioral Systems, San Francisco).

Experimental Design

In this aversive differential conditioning procedure, the dependent variables were SCR, valence, and arousal ratings. The CSs were two neutral ink blots (size: 7.5 × 5.5 on screen), which were already used in previous conditioning studies (Blechert et al., 2007; Michael et al., 2007). Stimulus duration was 0.6 s, the US lasted 3.5 s and was administered 0.5 s after CS onset. The intertrial interval lasted between 15 and 30 s, randomly generated. CS+ (CS paired with the US) and CS– (non-reinforced CS) were counterbalanced across participants and presented in pseudorandom order with the constraint of a maximum of two consecutive presentations of the CS+ (danger signal) or CS– (safety signal). A stressful/aversive sound (baby cry) (Peper & Karcher, 2001; Peper et al., 2001) rather than an electric shock was used as the US, in light of altered pain thresholds in BPD (Bohus et al., 2000; Schmahl & Bremner, 2006). The digitized acoustic stimulus was presented binaurally via headphones. Volume was calibrated and adjusted to 95 dB (sound level meter Bruel & Kjaer, type 2206/artificial ear).

The conditioning session started with habituation (4 CS+, 4 CS–). During acquisition, 12 CS+ paired with the US and 9 CS– never paired with the US were presented. Furthermore, 6 CS+ were presented but not paired with the US (catch trials). Catch trials were used to differentiate between the SCR to the CS+ and to the US. As the US followed the CS+ after only 0.5 s, SCR to CS+/US overlapped and catch trials allowed the measure of the SCR to the CS+ only. During extinction, 8 CS+ and 8 CS– were presented.

Procedure

Participants were seated in front of a computer in a sound-attenuated, temperature-controlled room. Camera and microphone served to observe the participant from the laboratory. Participants were seated in an armchair placed 0.6 m in front of a 19-in. monitor (refresh rate 75 Hz). In the conditioning session, after complete description of the study, electrodes were attached. Then demographic data were collected and state questionnaires (STAI, DSS) were administered. Before and after the procedure (before habituation and after within-session extinction), CSs were rated according to valence (6-point Likert scale; endpoints were labeled: pleasant (1) and unpleasant (6)) and arousal (relaxing (1) and exciting (6)). To mitigate the influence of instructions on conditioning (Baeyens, Eelen, & Van den Bergh, 1990), we neither obtained ratings during the experiment, nor announced different experimental phases. Ratings after each phase would have possible markers for the participants indicating the beginning of a different phase and pointing to the association between CS and US. However, we were interested in a natural course of learning. Therefore, we only obtained ratings before and after the procedure. Participants were told to keep their eyes open and not to move their hand with the SCR-electrodes attached. After the session, BSL, BDI, and DES (Dissociative Experience Scale) were administered.

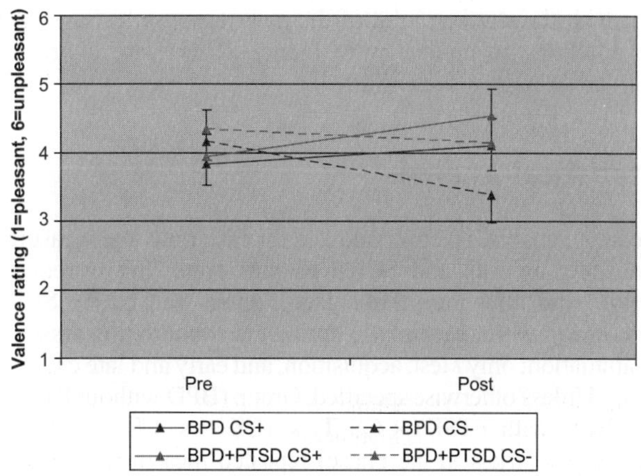

Conditioning session[a]

[a]Significant Time × CS Type interaction for all participants.

Figure 1a. Valence ratings for CS+ and CS− for BPD patients with ($N = 15$) and without ($N = 18$) comorbid PTSD for the conditioning session. Valence (Likert scale 1–6; pleasant (1) vs. unpleasant (6)); arousal (Likert scale 1–6; relaxing (1) vs. exciting (6)); CS+ = conditioned stimulus, sometimes paired with US during acquisition; CS− = conditioned stimulus, never paired with US; BPD = Borderline Personality Disorder; PTSD = Posttraumatic Stress Disorder.

Apparatus and Physiological Recordings

Stimulus delivery was controlled by a PC running Presentation Software (Neurobehavioral Systems, San Francisco). Physiological data acquisition was controlled by an ibook running Vitagraph version 4.61 (Becker Meditec, Karlsruhe, Germany). Physiological channels were recorded at a rate of 256 Hz in continuous mode using the Vitaport II system (Becker). SCR was obtained from 10-mm (sensor diameter) Ag/AgCl-electrodes (Marquette Hellige GmbH, Freiburg, Germany) filled with an isotonic EDR jelly TDE-246 (Steffens, Berlin, Germany) and placed on the thenar and hypothenar of the nondominant hand (constant voltage method with 0.5 V). Arm movement was assessed as a control measure using a two-dimensional accelerometer attached to the nondominant hand, since movement may trigger spurious SCRs.

Data Reduction

The electrodermal activity was determined according to published guidelines (Boucsein, 1992) with the program EDR-Para (Schäfer, Wuppertal). Phasic SCRs were defined as the response magnitude (maximum deflection) within a 1–4 s time frame (first interval response, FIR). SCRs lower than 0.05 μS were scored as zero. The FIR was counted as missing when the SCR was clearly initiated prior to CS onset. If such an anticipatory response was superimposed on a stimulus-related response, the scoring method (B) as described by Boucsein (1992, p. 136) was used, that is, the superimposed response was included in the analysis

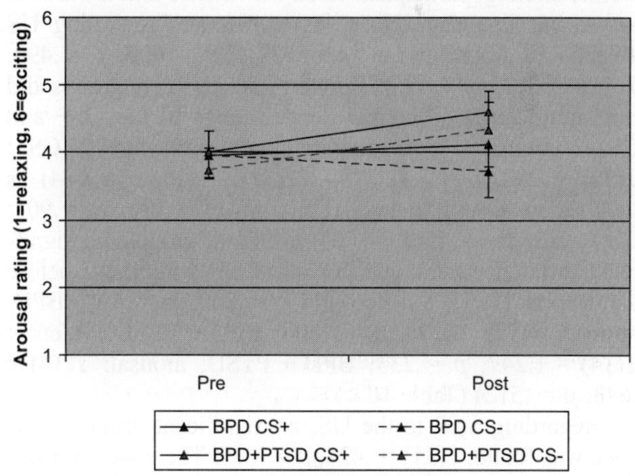

Conditioning session[a]

[a]Trend for the Time × CS Type interaction for the BPD patients without PTSD, significant effect for the BPD patients with PTSD.

Figure 1b. Arousal ratings for CS+ and CS− for BPD patients with ($N = 15$) and without ($N = 18$) comorbid PTSD for the conditioning session. Valence (Likert scale 1–6; pleasant (1) vs. unpleasant (6)); arousal (Likert scale 1–6; relaxing (1) vs. exciting (6)); CS+ = conditioned stimulus, sometimes paired with US during acquisition; CS− = conditioned stimulus, never paired with US; BPD = Borderline Personality Disorder; PTSD = Posttraumatic Stress Disorder.

but with the starting point of the new response as baseline. In addition, no outliers were found. SCRs were logtransformed to reduce skewness.

Statistical Analysis

Separate analyses were conducted for each outcome measure (valence, arousal, and SCR). Ratings were only assessed before and after the session (see Figures 1a and b). SCR was analyzed for each phase during the conditioning session (habituation: only *t* test, acquisition, and early and late extinction). Unless otherwise specified, Group (BPD without PTSD vs. BPD with PTSD) × CS Type (CS+ vs. CS−) × Time (number of trials in the phase) repeated measures analyses of covariance (ANCOVAs) were performed with present-state dissociative experience as covariate. A Greenhouse-Geisser correction was employed if the sphericity assumption was not met. Separate ANCOVAs for each group were also conducted as well as Group × Time repeated measures ANCOVAs with only the responses to the CS− as dependent variable to investigate impaired inhibition. Demographic and questionnaire data as well as baseline reactivity were compared by *t* tests. Statistical analysis was performed using SPSS 14.0 (SPSS Inc., Chicago, IL). An alpha level of < .05 determined statistical significance.

Results

Baseline Reactivity

Before starting, participants rated US *valence and arousal* to assess baseline data. No group differences regarding US valence or arousal were found ($T(31) = -.699$, $p = .490$; $T(31) = .813$, $p = .422$). Furthermore, the two groups did not significantly differ in valence ratings of the CS+ and CS− before the conditioning procedure (CS+: $T(31) = .222$, $p = .826$; CS−: $T(31) = .410$, $p = .684$) as well as in arousal ratings (CS+: $T(31) = .122$, $p = .904$; CS−: $T(31) = -.450$, $p = .656$). In both groups, no significant difference between CS+ and CS− was found before acquisition (BPD, valence: $T(17) = .860$, $p = .402$; BPD, arousal: $T(17) = .000$, $p = 1.000$; BPD + PTSD, valence: $T(14) = 1.247$, $p = .233$; BPD + PTSD, arousal: $T(14) = .673$, $p = .512$) (Table 1C).

Regarding *SCR* to the US, no significant group difference was found, $T(31) = .424$, $p = .675$. There were no significant group differences during habituation regarding baseline reactivity in SCR to CS+ and CS− (CS+: $T(31) = .179$, $p = .859$; CS−: $T(31) = 1.140$, $p = .263$). Both groups did not exhibit significant differences between CS+ and CS− before acquisition (BPD: $T(17) = .435$, $p = .669$; BPD + PTSD: $T(14) = 1.471$, $p = .163$).

Self-Report Measures: Valence

For the comparison of pre-habituation and post-extinction values, valence ratings showed a significant Time × CS Type interaction, $F(1, 30) = 10.521$, $p = .003$. After the conditioning process, CS+ was rated as more unpleasant, CS− as less unpleasant. No significant interaction with Group was found (× Time: $F(1, 30) = .802$, $p = .377$; × CS Type: $F(1, 30) = .380$, $p = .542$; × Time × CS Type: $F(1, 30) = .266$, $p = .610$). There was no significant effect of Group, $F(1, 30) = 1.414$, $p = .244$. Separate analyses revealed the significant Time × CS Type interaction for each group (BPD + PTSD: $F(1, 13) = 5.237$, $p = .039$; BPD: $F(1, 16) = 5.750$, $p = .029$) (Figure 1a).

Self-Report Measures: Arousal

For the arousal ratings, a significant Time × CS Type interaction, $F(1, 30) = 6.139$, $p = .019$, and a trend for the CS Type effect, $F(1, 30) = 3.419$, $p = .074$, were found. No significant interaction with Group appeared (× Time: $F(1, 30) = 1.466$, $p = .235$; × CS Type: $F(1, 30) = .000$, $p = .987$; × Time × CS Type: $F(1, 30) = .764$, $p = .389$). There was no significant effect of Group, $F(1, 30) = .771$, $p = .387$. BPD patients without PTSD showed a trend for the Time × CS Type interaction, $F(1, 16) = 4.236$, $p = .056$, while BPD patients with PTSD did not show any significant effect (Time: $F(1, 13) = .105$, $p = .752$; CS Type: $F(1, 13) = 1.022$, $p = .331$; Time × CS Type: $F(1, 13) = 1.936$, $p = .187$) (Figure 1b).

SCR

For *habituation*, there was no significant difference between CS+ and CS− for both groups (BPD: $T(17) = .435$, $p = .669$; BPD + PTSD: $T(14) = 1.471$, $p = .163$). Both groups did not differentiate between CS+ and CS− during habituation. There were no significant group differences during habituation (CS+: $T(31) = .179$, $p = .859$; CS−: $T(31) = 1.140$, $p = .263$) (Figures 2 and 3).

During *acquisition*, significant effects of Time, $F(5, 26) = 3.252$, $p = .021$) and CS Type, $F(1, 30) = 7.019$, $p = .013$, as well as a trend for the Time × Group interaction, $F(5, 26) = 2.323$, $p = .072$, were observed. No significant Group effect appeared, $F(1, 30) = .062$, $p = .805$. BPD patients without PTSD showed significant effects of Time, $F(5, 12) = 5.026$, $p = .010$, and CS Type, $F(1, 16) = 6.616$, $p = .020$, during acquisition, while BPD patients with PTSD did not show any significant effect (Time: $F(5, 9) = 1.052$, $p = .445$; CS Type: $F(1, 13) = 1.145$, $p = 304$). BPD patients with PTSD did not differentiate between CS+ and CS−. For the response to the US during acquisition, a significant effect of Time, $F(11, 20) = 7.108$, $p < .001$, but no Group effect, $F(1, 30) = .135$, $p = .716$, or interaction effects with Group, $F(11, 20) = .834$, $p = .611$, were found.

During *early within-session extinction*, a significant effect of CS Type, $F(1, 30) = 8.389$, $p = .007$, was found. No significant Group effect, $F(1, 30) = .233$, $p = .633$, and no significant interaction effects with Group were found

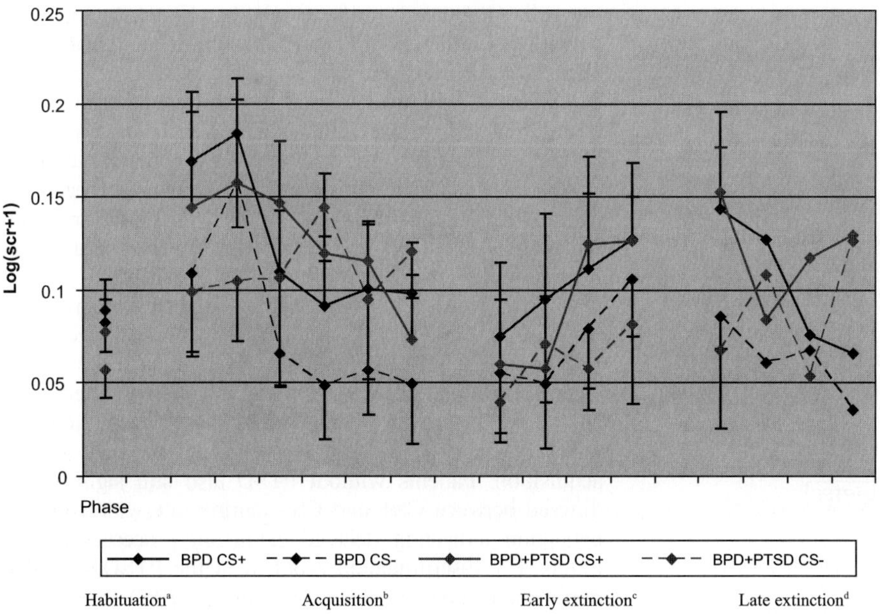

Figure 2. Conditioned SCR (mean, standard error (SEM)) during acquisition, early and late within-session extinction to CS+ (conditioned stimulus, sometimes paired with US during acquisition); here: only catch trials without US and CS− (conditioned stimulus, never paired with US) for BPD patients with (N = 15) and without (N = 18) comorbid PTSD.

[a]No significant differences between the two groups as well as no significant differentiation between responses to CS+ and to CS.

[b]Trend for the Group × Time interaction, significant Time and CS Type effects for the BPD patients without PTSD, no significant effects for the BPD patients with PTSD.

[c]Significant CS Type effect for the BPD patients without PTSD, no significant effect for the BPD patients with PTSD.

[d]Significant CS Type effect for the BPD patients without PTSD, no significant effect for the BPD patients with PTSD.

(× Time: $F(3, 28) = .068$, $p = .976$; × CS Type: $F(1, 30) = .039$, $p = .845$; × Time × CS Type: $F(3, 28) = .596$, $p = .623$). In separate analyses, the CS Type effect was found for the patients without PTSD, $F(1, 16) = 5.824$, $p = .028$, but not for the other patient group, $F(1, 13) = 2.893, p = 113$. BPD patients with PTSD did not differentiate between CS+ and CS−.

During *late within-session extinction*, a significant effect of CS Type, $F(1, 30) = 6.012$, $p = .020$, and a trend for Time, $F(3, 28) = 2.692$, $p = .065$, were found. No significant Group effect, $F(1, 30) = .286, p = .597$, and no significant interaction effects with Group were found (× Time: $F(3, 28) = 1.111$, $p = .361$; × CS Type: $F(1, 30) = .142$, $p = .709$; × Time × CS Type: $F(3, 28) = 1.668, p = .197$). In separate analyses, the CS Type effect was found for patients without PTSD, $F(1, 16) = 7.941$, $p = .012$, but not for the other patient group, $F(1, 13) = .864$, $p = .369$. BPD patients with PTSD did not differentiate between CS+ and CS−.

For the ANCOVAs with CS− as dependent variable no significant effect of Group appeared (data available upon request).

Discussion

Our study of conditioning processes in BPD patients with and without PTSD revealed two main findings: First, we found impaired differential acquisition in BPD patients with co-occurring PTSD. Second, we found impaired within-session extinction in borderline patients without PTSD.

During *acquisition*, a trend for a group difference regarding time course of SCRs was found. BPD patients with PTSD habituated more slowly than the patients without PTSD in their responses to CS+ and CS−. While BPD patients without PTSD differentiated between CS+ and CS− during acquisition, BPD patients with PTSD did not learn the differentiation. During *early* and *late within-session extinction*, BPD patients without PTSD showed a significant differentiation between responses to CS+ and CS−, but again, the other patient group did not. Therefore, as expected in Hypothesis 1, for BPD patients without PTSD intact acquisition (differentiation during acquisition and early within-session extinction) was found. Confirming Hypothesis 2, impaired within-session extinction (late within-session extinction) was found. Hypothesis 3, higher responses to the CS− in patients with PTSD (impaired inhibition), could not be confirmed as no group difference regarding responses to CS− appeared during any phase of the experiment. However, we found support for a lack of discrimination learning in BPD patients with PTSD (Hypothesis 4) since they could not differentiate between CS+ and CS− during acquisition and early within-session extinction. Descriptively, the lack of differentiation in the group with PTSD does not appear to emerge from similarly strong responses to CS+ and CS− but from oscillating between high and low responses to both stimuli. This may be due to insecurity of these patients about the significance of a stimulus as dangerous or safe. Interestingly, both groups showed increasing responses to CS+ and CS− during early

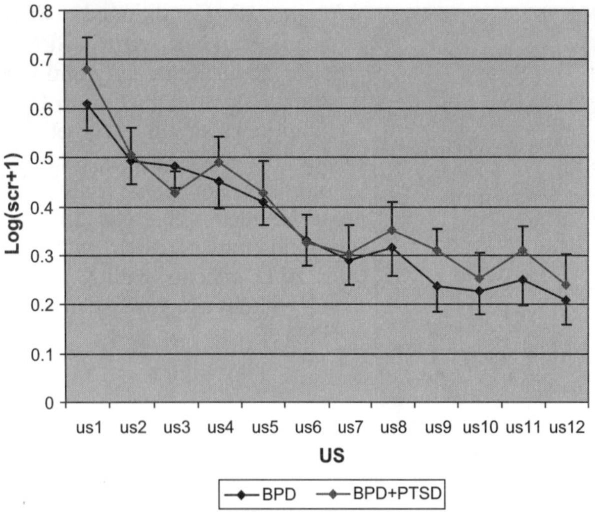

Acquisition[a]

[a]Significant time effect, no group effect or interaction effect with group.

Figure 3. Conditioned SCR (mean, standard error (SEM)) during acquisition to the US for BPD patients with (N = 15) and without (N = 18) comorbid PTSD.

extinction. This may be due to insecurity of these patients about the significance of a stimulus as dangerous or safe. Interestingly, both groups showed increasing responses to CS+ and CS− during early extinction. This phenomenon may be due to cognitive factors that play an important role in human conditioning (Beaver, Mogg, & Bradley, 2005). Here, due to partial reinforcement and no announcement of different phases, participants could expect another US presentation after some trials without the US. This may lead to increased responses before they learn that the US is no longer presented.

Regarding *subjective ratings*, we found a significant differentiation between CS+ and CS− after the conditioning session in the valence ratings of both groups. As the second rating took place after extinction, this pattern is not easy to understand. In contrast to the SCR findings, the differentiation after extinction may point to impaired or reduced extinction. However, due to the lack of comparing ratings after acquisition, it remains open if this differentiation is similar to an evaluative conditioning process that remains stable in spite of extinction and is thereby just underpinning acquisition effects. For the arousal ratings, a significant differentiation for BPD patients without PTSD was found, whereas the other patients again did not differentiate significantly. BPD patients without PTSD appear to show a stronger reduction of the unpleasantness rating regarding the CS−. This becomes even more apparent for the arousal ratings, as BPD patients with PTSD show a nearly parallel rise of unpleasantness ratings for both CSs.

In summary, BPD patients with co-occurring PTSD revealed a pattern similar to the PTSD patients in the studies of Grillon and Morgan (1999) during the first session and Ayers et al. (2003) who found a problem with discrimination as well. Compared to the study by Ebner-Priemer and coworkers (2008) on BPD patients with high and low dissociation scores, the lack of a significant CS Type effect in BPD patients with acute dissociation differed from the lack of differentiation in the PTSD-subgroup in the present study: Dissociative patients showed very low reactivity to both stimuli, also apparent in a significant Group effect regarding overall reactivity. BPD patients with PTSD showed oscillating reactions to CS+ and CS− which were not different from the BPD patients without PTSD regarding general reactivity. Thus, while dissociation led to similarly low responses to CS+ and CS− and a lack of associative learning, co-occurring PTSD might lead to high reactivity to both stimuli. BPD patients without PTSD showed a pattern similar to BPD patients without acute dissociation, however intact differential learning was already apparent during acquisition. Patients without PTSD also still significantly differed between CS+ and CS− during late within-session extinction indicating delayed extinction processes in this group. The discrimination problem of the PTSD-subgroup might have impeded this result for the BPD group with low acute dissociation. Therefore, after intact acquisition, new or extinction learning appears to be attenuated or even impaired. BPD patients with PTSD, in contrast, showed difficulties in learning the differentiation between a safety and a danger signal at all.

Both findings might have clinical implications. Learning mechanisms and extinction processes in particular can not only be seen as basic mechanisms in the perpetuation of adaptive and maladaptive behavior but also as the basis of psychotherapy in general and exposure therapy in specific. Our data suggest that extinction or new learning is impaired in BPD patients without PTSD. Therefore, a higher number of prolonged exposure sessions may be helpful for this group of patients. The focus of therapy for BPD patients with PTSD, in contrast, should be on discrimination learning.

Validity and strengths of study and paradigm have to be considered. The groups did not differ significantly regarding age or years of education as well as psychopathological measures. We controlled for acute dissociation and the differential conditioning paradigm made it possible to focus on different aspects of learning, that is, responses to danger and safety signals. This was important to find the main differences between the two subgroups. Another important aspect of this study is that it not only focuses on one psychiatric disorder without any comorbidity but also investigates the influence of a second, frequently comorbid disorder.

There are several limitations of this study. Since this was a female sample, the generalizability of the findings is constrained. However, the purely female sample also reduced heterogeneity, which may have been useful given the data suggesting differences between sexes in emotional responding (Fischer, 2000). Due to the subgroup analysis, we only had relatively small sample sizes and some results might have been different with more participants due to a power problem. This might also be the reason for a lack of significant group differences. Other limitations arise from the chosen design. The overlap between CS+ and US was very short with the US still present during the black screen. This unusual design might have influenced the association between CS+ and US. Furthermore, we presented the US only once before acquisition and not during habituation but did not impose SCR to the US as baseline, potentially mixing up acquisition of and habituation to the US. In addition, there was a strong habituation to the US in both groups explaining a decrease instead of an increase in learning during acquisition. Altogether, the number of stimuli in each phase, in particular four of each CS during habituation and only six catch trials during acquisition, might have been too low for habituation and learning. However, effects might have been even larger with more trials during the acquisition phase, above all in case of 100% reinforcement instead of 33%. The decision to only reinforce 33% of the trials allowed to neatly separate responses to the US from those to the CS+, thereby analyzing the CR already during acquisition. As a major problem it remains that we had different numbers of danger and safety signals, though at least the CS+ was presented more often, thus strengthening the habituation to this stimulus and not to the safety signal. Therefore, differential responses could have been even better with similar numbers of CS+ and CS− presentations. Finally, the timing of the valence and arousal ratings has to be discussed. As we aimed to investigate a natural course of conditioning/learning, we avoided any indicator for a new phase of the experiment, which ratings after each phase (habituation, acquisition) clearly would have been. On the other hand, we therefore do not have subjective ratings for each phase and the interpretation of the ratings we have is difficult.

To our knowledge, this is the first study comparing classical conditioning in subgroups of unmedicated BPD patients with and without PTSD. In addition, the differential paradigm made it possible to look into differences of two subgroups in more detail. In future research, our finding of impaired within-session extinction processes in BPD patients without PTSD and a problem of discriminating between danger and safety signal in BPD patients with PTSD should be replicated with a higher number of participants and related to treatment.

Financial Disclosures

Dr. Mauchnik discloses having received a travel grant by GlaxoSmithKline. Dr. Ebner-Priemer reports having received a travel grant from GlaxoSmithKline. Dr. Schmahl reports having received travel grants from Pfizer Pharma GmbH, Lilly Deutschland GmbH, and Lundbeck Research USA Inc. Dr. Bohus reports having received lecture fees from Astra, Lilly, and Pfizer.

Acknowledgments

We thank the Deutsche Studienstiftung for support (scholarship Jana Mauchnik) and Annegret Krause for data collection. This study was supported by the DFG (SFB 636/C2).

References

Ayers, E. D., White, J., & Powell, D. A. (2003). Pavlovian eyeblink conditioning in combat veterans with and without post-traumatic stress disorder. *Integrative Physiological and Behavioral Science, 38*, 230–247.

Baeyens, F., Eelen, P., & Van der Bergh, O. (1990). Contingency awareness in evaluative conditioning: A case for an aware affective-evaluative learning. *Cognition and Emotion, 4*, 3–18.

Beaver, J. D., Mogg, K., & Bradley, B. P. (2005). Emotional conditioning to masked stimuli and modulation of visuospatial attention. *Emotion, 5*, 67–79.

Blechert, J., Michael, T., Vriends, N., & Wilhelm, F. H. (2007). Fear conditioning in posttraumatic stress disorder: Evidence for delayed extinction of autonomic, experiential, and behavioural measures. *Behavior Research and Therapy, 45*, 2019–2033.

Bohus, M., Limberger, M., Ebner, U., Glocker, F. X., Schwarz, B., Wernz, M., & Lieb, K. (2000). Pain perception during self-reported distress and calmness in patients with borderline personality disorder and self-mutilating behavior. *Psychiatry Research, 95*, 251–260.

Bohus, M., Limberger, M. F., Frank, U., Chapman, A. L., Kuehler, T., & Stieglitz, R. D. (2007). Psychometric properties of the borderline symptom list (BSL). *Psychopathology, 40*, 126–132.

Boucsein, W. (1992). *Electrodermal activity.* New York, NY: Plenum.

Ebner-Priemer, U. W., Badeck, S., Beckmann, C. F., Wagner, A. W., Feige, B., Weiss, I., ... Bohus, M. (2005). Affective dysregulation and dissociative experience in female patients with borderline personality disorder: A startle response study. *Journal of Psychiatric Research, 39*, 85–92.

Ebner-Priemer, U. W., Mauchnik, J., Kleindienst, N., Schmahl, C., & Peper, M. (2008). Emotional learning during dissociative states in borderline personality disorder. *Journal of Psychiatry and Neuroscience, 34*, 214–222.

Feeny, N. C., Zoellner, L. A., & Foa, E. B. (2002). Treatment outcome for chronic PTSD among female assault victims with borderline personality characteristics: A preliminary examination. *Journal of Personality Disorders, 16*, 30–40.

Fischer, A. H. (2000). *Gender and emotion*. New York, NY: Cambridge University Press.

Freyberger, H. J., Spitzer, C., & Stieglitz, R. D. (1999). *Fragebogen zu dissoziativen Symptomen (FDS)* [German adaption of the Dissociative Experience Scale (DES; E. Bernstein & F. W. Putman)]. Bern, Switzerland: Huber.

Grillon, C., & Morgan, C. A. (1999). Fear-potentiated startle conditioning to explicit and contextual cues in Gulf War veterans with posttraumatic stress disorder. *Journal of Abnormal Psychology, 108*, 134–142.

Hautzinger, M., Bailer, M., Worall, H., & Keller, F. (1994). *Beck-Depressions-Inventar (BDI)*. Bern, Switzerland: Huber.

Hermann, C., Ziegler, S., Birbaumer, N., & Flor, H. (2002). Psychophysiological and subjective indicators of aversive Pavlovian conditioning in generalized social phobia. *Biological Psychiatry, 52*, 328–337.

Laux, L., Glanzmann, P., Schaffner, P., & Spielberger, C. D. (1981). *Das State-Trait-Angstinventar (STAI)*. Weinheim, Germany: Beltz.

Loranger, A. W. (1999). *International personality disorder examination (IPDE): DSM-IV and ICD-10 modules*. Odessa, Ukraine: Psychological Assessment Resources.

Michael, T., Blechert, J., Vriends, N., Margraf, J., & Wilhelm, F. H. (2007). Fear conditioning in panic disorder: Enhanced

resistance to extinction. *Journal of Abnormal Psychology, 116*, 612–617.
Michael, T., Ehlers, A., & Halligan, S. L. (2005). Enhanced priming for trauma-related material in posttraumatic stress disorder. *Emotion, 5*, 103–112.
Oldfield, R. C. (1971). The assessment and analysis of handedness: The Edinburgh inventory. *Neuropsychologia, 9*, 97–113.
Orr, S. P., Metzger, L. J., Lasko, N. B., Macklin, M. L., Peri, T., & Pitman, R. K. (2000). De novo conditioning in trauma-exposed individuals with and without posttraumatic stress disorder. *Journal of Abnormal Psychology, 109*, 290–298.
Peper, M., & Karcher, S. (2001). Differential conditioning to facial emotional expressions: Effects of hemispheric asymmetries and CS identification. *Psychophysiology, 38*, 936–950.
Peper, M., Karcher, S., Wohlfarth, R., Reinshagen, G., & LeDoux, J. E. (2001). Aversive learning in patients with unilateral lesions of the amygdala and hippocampus. *Biological Psychology, 58*, 1–23.
Peri, T., Ben-Shakhar, G., Orr, S. P., & Shalev, A. Y. (2000). Psychophysiologic assessment of aversive conditioning in posttraumatic stress disorder. *Biological Psychiatry, 47*, 512–519.
Pitman, R. K. (1989). Post-traumatic stress disorder, hormones, and memory. *Biological Psychiatry, 26*, 221–223.
Rothbaum, B. O., & Davis, M. (2003). Applying learning principles to the treatment of post-trauma reactions. *Annals of the New York Academy of Science, 1008*, 112–121.
Schmahl, C., & Bremner, J. D. (2006). Neuroimaging in borderline personality disorder. *Journal of Psychiatric Research, 40*, 419–427.
Stiglmayr, C., Braakmann, D., Haaf, B., Stieglitz, R. D., & Bohus, M. (2003). Construction and psychometric properties of the Dissoziations-Spannungs-Skala (DSS-akut), a self-rating scale assessing dissociative symptoms and aversive inner tensions. *Psychotherapie, Psychosomatik und Medizinische Psychologie, 53*, 287–294.
Stiglmayr, C., Shapiro, D. A., Stieglitz, R. D., Limberger, M. F., & Bohus, M. (2001). Experience of aversive tension and dissociation in female patients with borderline personality disorder – A controlled study. *Journal of Psychiatric Research, 35*, 111–118.
Wessa, M., & Flor, H. (2007). Failure of extinction of fear responses in posttraumatic stress disorder: Evidence from second-order conditioning. *American Journal of Psychiatry, 164*, 1684–1692.
Wittchen, H. U., Wunderlich, U., & Gruschwitz, S. (1997). *SKID. Strukturiertes Klinisches Interview für DSM-IV Achse I* [German Version of the SCID-I (Structured Clinical Interview for DSM-IV Axis I Disorders)]. Göttingen, Germany: Hogrefe.
Zanarini, M. C., Frankenburg, F. R., Hennen, J., Reich, D. B., & Silk, K. R. (2004). Axis I comorbidity in patients with borderline personality disorder: 6-year follow-up and prediction of time to remission. *American Journal of Psychiatry, 161*, 2108–2114.
Zimmermann, M. J. (1999). Axis I diagnostic comorbidity and borderline personality disorder. *Comprehensive Psychiatry, 40*, 245–252.

Jana Mauchnik

Department of Psychosomatic Medicine and Psychotherapy
Central Institute of Mental Health
Postfach 12 21 20
68072 Mannheim
Germany
Tel. +49 621 1703-4412
Fax +49 621 1703-4005
E-mail jana.mauchnik@zi-mannheim.de

Original Article

Non-Idiographic Emotional Script-Driven Imagery in Posttraumatic Stress Disorder

Impact of Priming of Episodic Recall and Self-Referential Processing

Paul A. Frewen and Ruth A. Lanius

The University of Western Ontario, London, ON, Canada

Abstract. Abnormal emotional responses to standardized emotional stimuli in posttraumatic stress disorder (PTSD) implicate problems in emotional processing less obviously linked to traumatic experiences. However, the personal meaningfulness and association of standardized emotional stimuli with specific episodic memories in PTSD participants has not been investigated. This paper takes the position that emotional processing of standardized stimuli cannot be divorced from the personal meaning these stimuli are ascribed, such as via the priming of episodic memory. Women with PTSD reported greater priming of episodic memories within the context of emotional imagery of standardized scripts, and episodic recall predicted emotional responses to script-driven imagery. Furthermore, greater priming of episodic recall during imagery of fear-anxiety scripts was associated with less response within the ventral medial prefrontal cortex. Clinical, theoretical, and methodological issues are discussed.

Keywords: autobiographical memory, semantic memory, episodic memory, emotion, fear, anxiety, script-driven imagery, self-referential processing, childhood abuse, medial prefrontal cortex (MPFC), posttraumatic stress disorder

The current diagnostic criteria for posttraumatic stress disorder (PTSD) include reexperiencing of traumatic memories as flashbacks and/or intrusive thoughts, images, emotions, and psychophysiological responses (American Psychiatric Association [APA], 2000). Individuals with PTSD also experience tonic hyperarousal, emotional numbing, and avoidance symptoms that theoretically are assumed to develop either directly in response to trauma exposure or indirectly as a consequence of reexperiencing symptoms (e.g., Brewin & Holmes, 2003; Dalgleish, 2004; Litz, 1992; Litz & Gray, 2002; Rosen & Lilienfeld, 2008). The neural correlates of acute reexperiencing as compared with normal episodic recall of traumatic memories have been the subject of several neuroimaging studies using a script-driven imagery paradigm (meta-analysis by Etkin & Wager, 2007). This paradigm entails exposing traumatized individuals with and without PTSD to verbal reminders of their own traumatic and other neutral memories. The most replicated findings of trauma script-driven imagery studies include deficient response of the anterior cingulate cortex (ACC) and medial prefrontal cortex (MPFC) during exposure to reminders of traumatic relative to neutral memories in traumatized individuals with as opposed to without PTSD (Etkin & Wager, 2007).

A somewhat independent line of research has investigated emotional processing of standardized (non-idiographic) stimuli in PTSD, such as via responses to facial expressions (Bryant et al., 2008; Rauch et al., 2000; Shin et al., 2005; Williams et al., 2006), pictures (New et al., 2009; Phan, Britton, Taylor, Fig, & Liberzon, 2006; but see Protopopescu et al., 2005), the emotional Stroop task (Bremner et al., 2004; Shin et al., 2001), and standardized emotional scripts (McTeague et al., 2010). Significantly, these studies evaluate whether the emotional processing disturbances associated with PTSD are specific to personalized trauma-related stimuli or extend to threatening-aversive stimuli more broadly (Liberzon & Martis, 2006). Strikingly, many of the most replicated findings distinguishing the PTSD response to personalized trauma-relevant stimuli also characterize PTSD individuals' responses to generally threatening-aversive stimuli, including a reduced ACC-MPFC response and altered (*increased*; Bryant et al., 2008; Rauch et al., 2000; Williams et al., 2006, or *decreased*; Phan et al., 2006) response within the amygdala. Similarly, Lanius et al. (2003) demonstrated reduced ACC-MPFC response during imagery of otherwise sad and anxious (although not patently traumatic) personal life events in individuals with PTSD. Collectively, findings of

DOI: 10.1027/0044-3409/a000016

disturbances in emotional processing of standardized stimuli in PTSD lend support to the theoretical contention that emotional processing disturbances in PTSD may be both diverse and pervasive (e.g., Frewen & Lanius, 2006), and to psychotherapeutic strategies that directly address skill deficits in emotional awareness and regulation in addition to traumatic memory reprocessing (e.g., Cloitre, Cohen, & Koenen, 2006).

Since classic cognitive theories of emotional processing (e.g., Oatley & Johnson-Laird, 1987) hold that emotional responses to events are determined by appraisal processes, one mediator of disturbed emotional processing of standardized stimuli in PTSD may be via cognitive appraisal (Ehlers & Clark, 2000). Significantly, a number of neuroimaging studies document that neural responses to emotional stimuli can be modulated by cognitive appraisals resulting either in the diminishment (e.g., Ochsner et al., 2002) or accentuation (e.g., Ochsner et al., 2004) of their emotional salience (for application to PTSD and psychological resilience, see Frewen & Lanius, 2006; Liberzon & Martis, 2006; New et al., 2009). One way in which individual differences in cognitive appraisal can influence individual differences in emotional processing of standardized stimuli is in terms of differential assignment of self-relevance (Lemogne et al., 2009; Northoff, 2007). Specifically, numerous studies have shown that when participants assess the degree to which stimuli are descriptive of themselves and/or when participants are presented with inherently self-descriptive stimuli, metabolic activity within the MPFC is increased (e.g., Moran, Heatherton, & Kelley, 2009; reviews by Gillihan & Farah, 2005; Legrand & Ruby, 2009; Northoff et al., 2006; Ochsner et al., 2004; Saxe, Moran, Scholz, & Gabrieli, 2006; Schmitz & Johnson, 2007). To illustrate, within the context of a study of emotional processing, Phan et al. (2004) presented participants with emotional pictures and asked them to determine their self-relevance (i.e., "How much do you relate to this picture?") or valence (i.e., "How does this picture make you feel?"). The ventral MPFC was significantly more metabolically active during self-relevance assessment relative to emotional valence judgment (Phan et al., 2004). Furthermore, during self-relevance assessment, response within both ventral and dorsal MPFC increased *as a function of* individual differences in the degree to which stimuli were determined to be self-relevant across study participants (Phan et al., 2004).

The results of Phan et al. (2004) are particularly interesting in considering that the stimulus set they used (International Affective Picture System; Lang, Bradley, & Cuthbert (1997)) was apparently the same as that utilized in their study of emotional perception in PTSD (Phan et al., 2006) and similar to that used in New et al.'s (2009) study of emotion regulation (cognitive reappraisal) in PTSD (Lang, Bradley, & Cuthbert, 2005). Thus findings of increased ventral MPFC response during self-relevance in healthy individuals (Phan et al., 2004) may be relevant to findings regarding emotional processing of non-traumatic visual stimuli in PTSD, where non-trauma exposed healthy controls more greatly activated the ventral MPFC than did individuals with PTSD when viewing non-traumatic threatening-aversive relative to neutral pictures (Phan et al., 2006). In other words, reduced response within the ventral MPFC in PTSD during non-traumatic visual processing, although consistent with a model emphasizing deficient regulatory control over amygdala-based primary emotional appraisals in PTSD (Etkin & Wager, 2007; Phan et al., 2006), may also indirectly implicate disturbances in self-referential processing in PTSD (Liberzon & Martis, 2006). The latter interpretation may provide partial explanation as to why individuals with PTSD failed to show an expected increased amygdala response to standardized threatening-aversive pictures (PTSD participants revealed significantly *reduced* amygdala responses relative to healthy controls; Phan et al., 2006). These considerations motivated the present research to assess the potential influence of self-referential processing in mediating differences in emotional responses to a standardized emotional imagery task in PTSD.

As an effort to integrate the trauma memory, emotional processing, and self-referential processing literatures toward a better understanding of the psychology and neurobiology of PTSD, the present study sought to investigate the personalized processing of standardized emotional scripts comparing women with versus without PTSD (see also McTeague et al., 2010). In pilot testing of emotional responses to imagining oneself involved in various standardized emotional vignettes, it became clear that participants not only differed in terms of their emotional responses to the scripts, but they also varied in terms of the frequency with which their engaging in the imagery task primed their spontaneously recalling a real lived event of a congruent theme or description to that of the standardized script. In other words, in the context of spontaneous priming of episodic memory, the task of imagining oneself in a standardized but make-believe scenario essentially became the experience of episodically recalling an actually lived event for some participants.

We reasoned that such spontaneous episodic recall could be utilized as an indirect marker of the degree of self-relevance of the vignette, and thereafter sought to assess the significance of this response in determining subjective emotional and functional neural responses to the standardized imagery task. Our hypotheses for this study were the following: (1) Scripts that primed episodic recall would be associated with increased self-reported emotional responses, such that primed recall occurring during negatively valenced scripts would be associated with increased self-reported negative emotional responses, and primed recall occurring during positively valenced scripts would be associated with increased self-reported positive emotional responses; and (2) Scripts that participants reported primed episodic recall would be associated with altered response within the MPFC in considering the involvement of the MPFC in self-referential processing (Gillihan & Farah, 2005; Legrand & Ruby, 2009; Northoff et al., 2006; Ochsner et al., 2004; Saxe et al., 2006; Schmitz & Johnson, 2007). We also investigated whether women with versus without PTSD would differ in their disposition toward being primed to recall actual life events within the context of imagining a standardized set of emotional vignettes, and how such recall might inform interpretations of the significance of differences in self-reported emotional responses to the vignettes in individuals with versus without PTSD.[1]

Method

Participants

Fifty-seven women who were aged 22–55 years (M = 39.85, SD = 8.03) and who had a primary diagnosis of PTSD as established by the *Clinician Administered PTSD Scale* (Blake et al., 1995; score $\geq$ 50, F1-S2 scoring rule) participated in this study. These subjects were included in a previous report; see Frewen et al. (in press) for data pertinent to clinical severity and psychiatric comorbidity. Subjects were recruited through newspaper advertisements, posters presented within local hospitals, and an outpatient service for treatment of trauma-related disorders. All women did not note any lifetime history of severe head injury during interviews. Comorbid diagnoses were established by administration of the *Structured Clinical Interview for DSM-IV Research Version* (First, Gibbon, Spitzer, & Williams, 1996). All research diagnoses were made by trained masters or doctoral level psychology students with immediate consultation from investigators P.F. and R.L., a clinical psychologist and psychiatrist, respectively, with considerable experience conducting diagnostic assessments in individuals with PTSD. Participants either completed emotional imagery tasks (described below) in an fMRI scanner (n = 14) or a standard hospital office setting (n = 43) depending on MRI exclusionary criteria (i.e., standard safety precautions for MRI assessment and absence of current psychotropic medication use). Women without any reported history of psychiatric disturbance served as a control group (participants took part either in the fMRI (n = 20) or non-fMRI (n = 29) study). Within-group results for the control groups will be reported elsewhere (Frewen et al., in press).

Behavioral Task Description and Procedure

Affective response tests – Negative and positive versions (ART-N and ART-P, respectively). We refer the reader to another report (Frewen et al., in press) for a more detailed description of the ART-N and ART-P used in this study. These tasks entailed participants listening to and imagining twenty-four 30-s audio-scripted vignettes happening to themselves in the present tense while attending to their emotional responses to the vignettes. Participants continued to imagine the effects of these scripts for a 12-s silent period following the script-listening period. Participants then rated their emotional responses to each script in terms of positive emotional states and negative emotional states; participants also rated avoidance responses and their ability to imagine each script as described elsewhere (Frewen et al., in press). Twelve of the scripts described emotional experiences of moderate to strong intensity, with the scripts divided into categories of three scripts encompassing each of the following themes: (1) social rejection (negative valence), (2) non-social fear-anxiety (negative valence), (3) social praise or affection (positive valence), and (4) non-social relaxation (positive valence). Thus scripts were categorized in terms of valence and sociality in a 2 × 2 within-group design. The remaining 12 scripts described less emotional situations (i.e., more emotionally insignificant or "neutral" events). Participants answered questions about their emotional responses to the script-imagery task using standard intensity questions.

As the focus of the present report, participants were asked whether imagining the script "*caused them to recall a specific memory from their own life*." A binary response rating to this question was collected (yes or no answer, scored 1 and 0, respectively), as this was determined to be most understandable to participants during the piloting of the task. The dependent measure for the memory recall was therefore a frequency score of up to 3 (0–3) per emotional script-type indicating the number of scripts that resulted in priming of episodic recall.

Statistical Analysis

Analyses of self-report responses were conducted within the non-fMRI participant groups who, due to their larger sample size, were considered more likely to provide reliable results. Imaging data were analyzed only for the PTSD group using Statistical Parametric Mapping 2 (SPM2) and employed standard preprocessing procedures. Unfortunately, self-report data from 2 of the 14 PTSD participants who completed the fMRI study were lost due to technical error; thus only a sample of 12 was available for analyses. Response to script-driven imagery was calculated as the BOLD signal change during the combined 42 s script-listening and script-imagining period relative to signal observed during an "implicit baseline period" of 30 s prior to the onset of each script. Emotion-scripts were then contrasted with neutral scripts, and memory recall scores (also differences scores; frequency of primed episodic recall during the emotional script minus that occurring during the neutral script) were regressed as predictors of the resulting contrast maps (i.e., SPM2 simple-correlation analysis). Fixed-effects analyses determined areas of significant effect at the individual-subject level, which were then taken forward into mixed effects analyses (subjects as random factor) to afford population-based inference. Correlations were only investigated within the MPFC as consistent with hypotheses. Voxels were considered significantly correlated with BOLD response in the contrast *Emotional Script minus Paired-Neutral Script* if they met all of the following criteria:

[1] The primary outcomes of this study comparing group differences in emotional processing as a function of script-types will be reported elsewhere, with the present report being specific to spontaneous primed episodic memory retrieval as a dependent measure. To avoid redundancy in the Method sections between reports, the present article includes only the most pertinent methodological material. Please consult Frewen et al. (in press) for further discussion.

(1) $p < .005$ uncorrected, (2) cluster-size (SPM k-statistic) ≥ 10, and (3) $p < .05$ small-volume corrected (p_{SVC}) for the family-wise error rate (FWE) and/or false-discovery rate (FDR). Regions of interest were based on the following previously published coordinates for the ventral MPFC (spherical search region with radius = 10 mm) as emphasized in the introduction: (1) Phan et al. (2004; self-referential processing effect: Montreal Neurological Institute (MNI) coordinates −6 +39 −9), and (2) Etkin and Wager (2007; PTSD meta-analysis: MNI coordinates +2 +38 −14).

Results

Group Differences in Priming of Episodic Recall During Standardized Emotional Imagery

A within-subject repeated measures analysis of variance was conducted on responses collected from the non-fMRI participants with emotional-script type (four categories) as the within-subject factor and the spontaneous recall rating as the dependent measure. See Table 1 for descriptive statistics. Significant effects were determined for group, $F(1, 70) = 9.19$, $p < .01$, and emotion, $F(3, 210) = 17.32$, $p < .001$, but not their interaction, $F(3, 210) = 1.44$, *ns*. The within-group effect could be attributed to increasing reported primed episodic recall in the context of non-social relaxation events as compared with all other script-types (all p's $< .001$ vs. non-social fear-anxiety scripts: $t(71) = 5.75$ vs. social rejection-criticism scripts: $t(71) = 6.12$ vs. social affection-praise scripts: $t(71) = 4.55$). There was also a trend for greater self-reported primed episodic recall when imagining social affection-praise scripts in comparison with social rejection-criticism scripts, $t(71) = 1.73$, $p = .09$. Follow-up of the between-group effect indicated that women with PTSD endorsed greater priming of episodic recall when compared with the control group across all script-types.

Correlations Between Priming of Episodic Recall and Self-Reported Emotional Response

Table 2 reports the results of correlations between the frequency of self-reported priming of episodic recall and affect ratings in women with PTSD. Greater negative affect ratings were correlated with greater priming of episodic recall during imagery of social rejection-failure scripts, and a trend for the same effect was determined for imagery of non-social fear-anxiety scripts. Recall was positively correlated with positive affect ratings during imagery of both non-social relaxation scripts and social affection-praise scripts.

Neural Correlates of Priming of Episodic Recall During Imagery of Fear-Anxiety Scripts

Within the PTSD group, during imagery of non-social fear-anxiety scripts, greater self-reported primed episodic recall was correlated with lesser response within the ventral MPFC (maximum at MNI 0 +44 −14, $k = 189$ voxels, $t(18) = 3.59$, $p = .002$; see Figure 1). This effect remained significant after correcting for multiple comparisons (spherical

Table 1. Mean incidence of self-reported primed episodic recall during standardized emotional imagery

	Non-social fear-anxiety	Social rejection-criticism	Non-social relaxation	Social affection-praise
PTSD (n = 43)	0.61 (0.32)	0.60 (0.32)	0.66 (0.36)	0.82 (0.22)
Non-PTSD (n = 29)	0.43 (0.36)	0.38 (0.35)	0.51 (0.38)	0.79 (0.24)

Note. Non-fMRI participants only. Means represent average number of scripts out of three per script-type that were reported to prime episodic recall in each group. Therefore possible scores ranged from 0 to 3. Standard deviations in brackets.

Table 2. Correlation between self-reported primed episodic recall and emotional response during standardized emotional imagery

	Non-social fear-anxiety	Social rejection-criticism	Non-social relaxation	Social affection-praise
Negative emotion	+.23^	+.30*	–	–
Positive emotion	–	–	+.45**	+.28*

Note. Non-fMRI participants only. ^$p = .08$. *$p < .05$. **$p < .01$. Negative emotion ratings were averaged across the following individual ratings: (1) anger, (2) fear, (3) anxiety, (4) sadness, (5) disgust, and (6) shame. Positive emotion ratings were similarly averaged across the following: (1) happiness, (2) physical-bodily pleasure (defined as "feeling good, enjoying oneself, and/or being aroused in a physical-bodily based way, such as, for example, involved in feelings of sensuality"), (3) relaxation, and (4) momentary increased self-esteem/pride. Each individual emotion rating was given on the following (0–3 scale): "No increase in emotion" (0), "felt slightly/somewhat" (1), "felt moderately strong" (2), and "felt strongly or very strongly" (3).

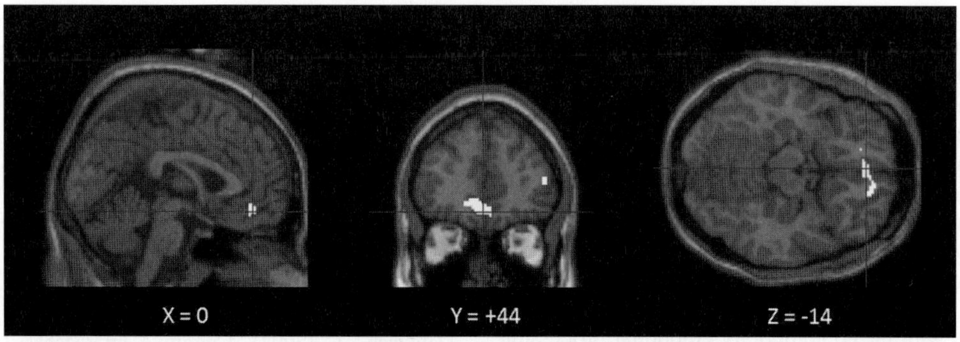

Figure 1. Negative Correlation between Self-Reported Primed Episodic Recall and Emotional Response during Standardized Emotional Imagery of Non-Social Fear-Anxiety Scripts.
Note. Negative correlation indicates increasing self-reported priming of episodic recall was associated with less BOLD response within the Ventral MPFC during Standardized Emotional Imagery of Non-Social Fear-Anxiety Scripts (contrasted with paired neutral scripts) in 12 women with PTSD. $p_{SVC} < .05$. Coordinates are in MNI space.

search region, 10 mm radius) within the ventral MPFC relative to the independent observations of Phan et al. (2004; MNI −6 +39 −9; FWE-corrected $p_{SVC} = .041$ and FDR-corrected $p_{SVC} = .015$), and Etkin and Wager (2007; MNI +2 +38 −14; FWE-corrected $p_{SVC} = .041$ and FDR-corrected $p_{SVC} = .014$). No similar findings were observed in response to the other script-types.

Discussion

This study assessed the frequency of occurrence of primed episodic memory recall within the context of an emotional script-driven imagery study using standardized (non-idiographic) scripts in individuals with and without PTSD. Women with PTSD more often reported standardized emotional script-driven imagery primed episodic memory recall. Furthermore, within women with PTSD, primed episodic memory recall was associated with greater valence-congruent affective responses. Specifically, primed episodic memory recall occurring during imagery of positive-valence scripts was associated with greater self-reported positive affective response, whereas primed episodic memory recall occurring during imagery of negative-valence scripts was associated with greater self-reported negative affective response. Finally, individuals with PTSD who reported more frequent priming of episodic recall during imagery, specifically of non-social fear-anxiety scripts, evidenced lesser response within the ventral MPFC during script-driven imagery. Each of these findings is intriguing but open to interpretation. We discuss each in turn with an aim toward establishing future productive research directions.

The first finding that women with PTSD recalled a greater number of episodic memories within the context of a standardized (non-idiographic) emotional script-driven imagery study may reflect a previously unidentified specific memory-emotional bias associated with PTSD influencing episodic memory retrieval processes. Specifically, this bias may promote novel social and non-social life events being processed directly in relation to past events, and/or facilitate the reexperiencing of past life events via episodic recall when presented with new salient emotional events in the present. These findings may significantly relate to often clinically noted dysfunctional behaviors such as repetition compulsion in traumatized individuals. Limiting this interpretation, however, is that it is possible that women with PTSD simply had actually experienced (i.e., in their previous lives before the study) a greater number of the events used in the current standardized imagery task, relative to women without PTSD. While perhaps a reasonable assumption for the negative event scripts, women with PTSD demonstrated increased episodic recall priming for both positive and negative events in the present study, thus making this interpretation less likely. Furthermore, while on the surface one might expect the PTSD group to have actually lived through a greater number of the events described in the fear-anxiety scripts, this too is not necessarily the case since such events did not reflect the dominant theme of these women's trauma-based concerns and were scripted so as to involve events reasonably encountered by anyone at random (i.e., the non-social fear-anxiety script content described the following events: (i) Participant is potentially being followed by another individual; (ii) Near drowning; and (iii) Job application test). Future studies should therefore further evaluate the tendency to respond with a greater priming of episodic memory during emotional-processing tasks in PTSD. Explicit assessments of the degree to which stimuli used in such experiments have been actually experienced before by participants as well as the degree to which experimental stimuli not only prime episodic recall but are rated to be personally meaningful more generally are warranted (Phan et al., 2004). The fundamental message of this study along these lines is that, although all participants were presented with the same standardized (non-idiographic) stimuli, the *meaning ascribed to such events was not equivalent across individuals*, with women with PTSD more likely to report being led to interpret the scripted vignettes directly within the context of their own life history. The second finding of this study for scripts that primed recall of episodic memories to be responded with greater valence-congruent affective responses also deserves further consideration. These findings, as hypothesized, suggest that when standardized stimuli are assigned personal meaning, such as when the processing of experimental stimuli primes episodic recall, they may also be deemed more emotionally significant. This finding significantly bears on the future design of studies of response to standardized stimuli in PTSD.

Finally, the third finding of this study that women with PTSD who recalled more episodic memories during imagery of non-social fear-anxiety memories less activated the ventral MPFC fits with the contemporary emotional processing framework relating to fear-anxiety regulation in PTSD (Etkin & Wager, 2007). Specifically, the ventral MPFC may be less active to the extent that a threatening-aversive stimulus is deemed more personally and emotionally significant (e.g., via the amygdala). This can be at least indirectly indexed by assessing the degree to which traumatic events explicitly prompt reexperiencing symptoms (Hopper, Frewen, van der Kolk, & Lanius, 2007). Nevertheless, autobiographical memories may be episodic or semantic, with each distinctive informational code theoretically maintained by at least partly dissociable neural systems (Levine, 2004; McKinnon, Svoboda, & Levine, 2007; Svoboda, McKinnon, & Levine, 2006). Unfortunately, the single question inquired of participants post-imagery in this study fails to disambiguate these systems. However, differential response was mediated within the ventral MPFC, suggesting episodic rather than semantic autobiographical retrieval (Levine, 2004; McKinnon et al., 2007; Svoboda et al., 2006). As the present investigation had several limitations including small sample size and little depth regarding investigations relating to the occurrence of spontaneous episodic recall, future studies are clearly indicated. It is hoped that the significance of self-referential and memory-based processing in PTSD during exposure to standardized emotional stimuli will be more fully explored in future investigations of the personalized processing of non-idiographic stimuli in trauma-related psychiatric disorders.

Acknowledgments

For M. S. Special thanks to Suzy Southwell, Stephanie Nevill, Melodie Chow, and Maria Densmore for their assistance with data collection and analysis, and for the support of the London Health Sciences Centre Traumatic Stress Service.

References

American Psychiatric Association (APA). (2000). *Diagnostic and statistical manual of mental disorders* (4th ed.). Washington, DC: Author.

Blake, D. D., Weathers, F. W., Nagy, L. M., Kaloupek, D. G., Gusman, F. D., Charney, D. S., & Keane, T. M. (1995). The development of a clinician-administered PTSD scale. *Journal of Traumatic Stress, 8*, 75–90.

Bremner, J. D., Vermetten, E., Vythilingam, M., Afzal, N., Schmahl, C., Elzinga, B., & Charney, D. S. (2004). Neural correlates of the classic color and emotional Stroop in women with abuse-related posttraumatic stress disorder. *Biological Psychiatry, 55*, 612–620.

Brewin, C. R., & Holmes, E. A. (2003). Psychological theories of posttraumatic stress disorder. *Clinical Psychology Review, 23*, 1041–1065.

Bryant, R. A., Felmingham, K., Kemp, A., Das, P., Hughes, G., Peduto, A., & Williams, L. M. (2008). Amygdala and ventral anterior cingulated activation predicts treatment response to cognitive behaviour therapy for posttraumatic stress disorder. *Psychological Medicine, 38*, 555–561.

Cloitre, M., Cohen, L. R., & Koenen, K. C. (2006). *Treating survivors of childhood abuse: Psychotherapy for the interrupted life*. New York, NY: Guilford Press.

Dalgleish, T. (2004). Cognitive approaches to posttraumatic stress disorder: The evolution of multi-representational theorizing. *Psychological Bulletin, 130*, 228–260.

Ehlers, A., & Clark, D. M. (2000). A cognitive model of posttraumatic stress disorder. *Behaviour Research & Therapy, 38*, 319–345.

Etkin, A., & Wager, T. D. (2007). Functional neuroimaging of anxiety: A meta-analysis of emotional processing in PTSD, social anxiety disorder, and specific phobia. *American Journal of Psychiatry, 164*, 1476–1488.

First, M. B., Gibbon, M., Spitzer, R. L., & Williams, J. B. W. (1996). *Structured clinical interview for DSM-IV axis I disorders – Research version (SCID-I, version 2.0, February, 1996, final version)*. New York, NY: Biometrics Research.

Frewen, P. A., Dozois, D. J. A., Neufeld, R. W. J., Densmore, M., Stevens, T., & Lanius, R. A. (in press). Social emotions and emotional valence during imagery in women with PTSD: Affective and neural correlates. *Psychological Trauma: Theory, Research, Practice & Policy.*

Frewen, P. A., & Lanius, R. A. (2006). Toward a psychobiology of posttraumatic self-dysregulation: Re-experiencing, hyperarousal, dissociation, and emotional numbing. *Annals of the New York Academy of Sciences, 1071*, 110–124.

Gillihan, S. J., & Farah, M. J. (2005). Is self special? A critical review of evidence from experimental psychology and cognitive neuroscience. *Psychological Bulletin, 131*, 76–97.

Hopper, J. W., Frewen, P. A., van der Kolk, B. A., & Lanius, R. A. (2007). Dimensional analysis of responses to script-driven trauma imagery in PTSD: Neural correlates of re-experiencing, avoidance, and dissociation. *Journal of Traumatic Stress, 20*, 713–725.

Lang, P. J., Bradley, M. M., & Cuthbert, B. N. (1997). *International affective picture system (IAPS): Technical manual and affective ratings*. Gainesville, FL: NIMH Center for the Study of Emotion and Attention, University of Florida.

Lang, P. J., Bradley, M. M., & Cuthbert, B. N. (2005). *International affective picture system (IAPS): Technical report A-6*. Gainesville, FL: University of Florida.

Lanius, R. A., Williamson, P. C., Hopper, J., Densmore, M., Boksman, K., & Gupta, M. A., ... Menon, R. S. (2003). Recall of emotional states in posttraumatic stress disorder: A fMRI investigation. *Biological Psychiatry, 53*, 204–210.

Legrand, D., & Ruby, P. (2009). What is self-specific? Theoretical investigation and critical review of neuroimaging results. *Psychological Review, 116*, 252–282.

Lemogne, C., le Bastard, G., Mayberg, H., Volle, E., Bergouignan, L., & Lehéricy, S., ... Fossati, P. (2009). In search of the depressive self: Extended medial prefrontal network during self-referential processing in major depression. *Social Cognitive & Affective Neuroscience, 4*, 305–312.

Levine, B. (2004). Autobiographical memory and the self in time: Brain lesion effects, functional neuroanatomy, and lifespan development. *Brain & Cognition, 55*, 54–68.

Liberzon, I., & Martis, B. (2006). Neuroimaging studies of emotional responses in PTSD. *Annals of the New York Academy of Sciences, 1071*, 87–109.

Litz, B. T. (1992). Emotional numbing in combat-related posttraumatic stress disorder: A critical review and reformulation. *Clinical Psychology Review, 12*, 417–432.

Litz, B. T., & Gray, M. J. (2002). Emotional numbing in posttraumatic stress disorder: Current and future research directions. *Australian & New Zealand Journal of Psychiatry, 36*, 198–204.

McKinnon, M. C., Svoboda, E., & Levine, B. (2007). The frontal lobes and autobiographical memory. In B. L. Miller & J. L. Cummings (Eds.), *The human frontal lobes: Functions and disorders* (2nd ed., pp. 227–248). New York, NY: Guilford Press.

McTeague, L. M., Lang, P. J., Laplante, M.-C., Cuthbert, B. N., Shumen, J. R., & Bradley, M. M. (2010). Aversive imagery in posttraumatic stress disorder: Trauma recurrence, comorbidity, and physiological reactivity. *Biological Psychiatry, 67*, 346–356.

Moran, J. M., Heatherton, T. F., & Kelley, W. M. (2009). Modulation of cortical midline structures by implicit and explicit self-relevance. *Social Neuroscience, 4*, 197–211.

New, A. S., Fan, J., Murrough, J. W., Liu, X., Liebman, R. E., & Guise, K. G., ... Charney, D. S. (2009). A functional magnetic resonance imaging study of deliberate emotion regulation in resilience and posttraumatic stress disorder. *Biological Psychiatry, 66*, 656–664.

Northoff, G. (2007). Psychopathology and pathophysiology of the self in depression: Neuropsychiatric hypothesis. *Journal of Affective Disorders, 104*, 1–14.

Northoff, G., Heinzel, A., de Greck, M., Bermpohl, F., Dobrowolny, H., & Panksepp, J. (2006). Self-referential processing in our brain: A meta-analysis of imaging studies on the self. *NeuroImage, 31*, 440–457.

Oatley, K., & Johnson-Laird, P. N. (1987). Towards a cognitive theory of emotions. *Cognition & Emotion, 1*, 29–50.

Ochsner, K. N., Knierim, K., Ludlow, D. H., Hanelin, J., Ramachandran, T., Glover, G., & Mackey, S. C. (2004). Reflecting upon feelings: An fMRI study of neural systems supporting the attribution of emotion to self and other. *Journal of Cognitive Neuroscience, 16*, 1746–1772.

Ochsner, K. N., Bunge, S. A., Gross, J. J., & Gabrieli, J. D. E. (2002). Rethinking feelings: An fMRI study of the cognitive regulation of emotion. *Journal of Cognitive Neuroscience, 14*, 1215–1229.

Phan, K. L., Britton, J. C., Taylor, S. F., Fig, L. M., & Liberzon, I. (2006). Corticolimbic blood flow during nontraumatic emotional processing in posttraumatic stress disorder. *Archives of General Psychiatry, 63*, 184–192.

Phan, K. L., Taylor, S. F., Welsh, R. C., Ho, S.-H., Britton, J. C., & Liberzon, I. (2004). Neural correlates of individual ratings of emotional salience: A trial-related fMRI study. *NeuroImage, 21*, 768–780.

Protopopescu, X., Pan, H., Tuescher, O., Cloitre, M., Goldstein, M., & Engelien, W., ... Stern, E. (2005). Differential time courses and specificity of amygdala activity in posttraumatic stress disorder subjects and normal control subjects. *Biological Psychiatry, 57*, 464–473.

Rauch, S. L., Whalen, P. J., Shin, L. M., McInerny, S. C., Macklin, M. L., & Lasko, N. B., ... Pitman, R. K. (2000). Exaggerated amygdala response to masked facial stimuli in posttraumatic stress disorder: A functional MRI study. *Biological Psychiatry, 47*, 769–776.

Rosen, G. M., & Lilienfeld, S. O. (2008). Posttraumatic stress disorder: An empirical evaluation of core assumptions. *Clinical Psychology, 28*, 837–868.

Saxe, R., Moran, J. M., Scholz, J., & Gabrielli, J. (2006). Overlapping and non-overlapping brain regions for theory of mind and self-reflection in individual subjects. *Social Cognitive and Affective Neuroscience, 1*, 229–234.

Schmitz, T. W., & Johnson, S. C. (2007). Relevance to self: A brief review and framework of neural systems underlying appraisal. *Neuroscience and Biobehavioral Reviews, 31*, 585–596.

Shin, L. M., Whalen, P. J., Pitman, R. K., Bush, G., Macklin, M. L., & Lasko, N. B., ... Rauch, S. L. (2001). An fMRI study of anterior cingulate function in posttraumatic stress disorder. *Biological Psychiatry, 50*, 932–942.

Shin, L. M., Wright, C. L., Cannistraro, P. A., Wedig, M. M., McMullin, K., & Martis, B., ... Rauch, S. L. (2005). A functional magnetic resonance imaging study of amygdala and medial prefrontal cortex responses to overtly presented fearful faces in posttraumatic stress disorder. *Archives of General Psychiatry, 62*, 273–281.

Svoboda, E., McKinnon, M. C., & Levine, B. (2006). The functional neuroanatomy of autobiographical memory: A meta-analysis. *Neuropsychologia, 44*, 2189–2208.

Williams, L. M., Kemp, A. H., Felmingham, K. L., Barton, M., Olivieri, G., & Peduto, A. S., ... Bryant, R. A. (2006). Trauma modulates amygdala and medial prefrontal responses to consciously attended fear. *NeuroImage, 29*, 347–357.

Paul A. Frewen

Departments of Psychiatry & Psychology
The University of Western Ontario
South St. Hospital
375 South Street
London, ON N6A 4G5
Canada
Tel. +519 685 8500 x77760
E-mail pfrewen@uwo.ca

Review Article

Searching for the Anatomy of Dissociative Amnesia

Angelica Staniloiu[1] and Hans J. Markowitsch[1,2]

[1]Physiological Psychology, University of Bielefeld, Germany, [2]Institute for Advanced Study, Alfried-Krupp Wissenschaftskolleg, Greifswald, Germany

Abstract. Brain damage was traditionally seen as the product of a neurological disease or injury. Nevertheless, modern brain imaging techniques have provided increasing evidence for alterations in brain tissue and metabolism for a number of psychiatric disorders. Though for a while "dissociated" (Spiegel, 2006) from the clinical and scientific arena, dissociative disorders have in the last several years received a renewed interest among several groups of researchers, who embarked on the work of disentangling their neural correlates. We review data from our own research as well as others, which point to distinct changes in brain regions underlying dissociative amnes(t)ic disorders. These changes may consist of overall reductions in brain metabolism or more selective alterations primarily in the right temporo-frontal cortices. Recent evidence with refined magnetic resonance imaging techniques furthermore reveals selective fiber degenerations in these regions. While these changes may persist and probably even intensify in some patients, they may be reversible in others – especially if treatment is carried out successfully within short time after onset. Implications of these findings for the pathogenetic conceptualization of dissociative amnes(t)ic disorders are outlined.

Keywords: psychogenic amnesia, temporo-frontal cortex, positron-emission tomography, white matter

The quest for the brain correlates of human intellectual functions, behavior, and emotions has taken a new dimension since increasingly sophisticated neuroimaging techniques have been incorporated into the cognitive neuroscience armamentarium. The employment of these techniques has provided evidence that the environment may have a lasting effect on organization and function of nervous system and that structural brain changes or brain metabolic alterations underlie a variety of mental disorders such as schizophrenia, major depression, obsessive-compulsive disorder (Bao, Meynen, & Swaab, 2008; Gur et al., 2000; Lange & Irle, 2004; Nakamura et al., 2007; Szeszko et al., 1999; van Erp et al., 2004), post-traumatic stress disorder (PTSD) (Nardo et al., 2010; Woodward et al., 2006), dissociative identity disorders (Vermetten, Schmahl, Lindner, Loewenstein, & Bremner, 2006), and even severe deviances in social behavior, such as violent behavior (Boccardi et al., 2010; Glenn & Raine, 2008).

These findings have led to the questioning of old strict distinctions between organic and psychogenic. In the field of memory disorders, an initial challenge to the dichotomy between organic and psychogenic amnesia came from observing that the two conditions may at times overlap. Furthermore it was noted that deliberately feigned amnesia (for primary or secondary gains) could also accompany both of the previously described forms of amnesia. "An epileptic, who also has hysteria and is a malingerer, may have periods of amnesia which exhibit features of all three types ("pathological [organic]," "psychological," and "feigned"; Lennox, 1943, p. 741)." Cases of psychogenic amnesia occurring on a forensic background were reported by several authors. Heine (1911) in his publication on the forensic significance of amnesia listed more than a dozen conditions for amnesia, most of which had a nonorganic origin. Ganser syndrome (see below) – a condition that is, presently less frequently diagnosed (e.g., Cocores, Santa, & Patel, 1984; Staniloiu et al., 2009) – had initially been linked to a forensic context (cf. Hey, 1904; Jung, 1902; Meyer, 1904; Pick, 1905; Stertz, 1910) and is still occasionally so nowadays. At the turn to the 20th century fugue states were also frequently considered to have "forensic relevance" (Zingerle, 1912).

Despite the possibility of these simultaneous occurrences, most researchers and clinicians (including ourselves) would, however, agree with keeping and discussing malingering as much as possible separately, outside of the psychogenic-organic "conundrum" (Lucchelli & Spinnler, 2002).

The most recent debate over the validity of a sharp organic-psychogenic distinction in amnesia has been fueled by findings from brain functional imaging. These yielded evidence for a long searched biological link between the two forms of amnesia, by demonstrating brain functional and metabolic alterations in psychogenic amnesia, which involve anatomical structures that are agreed upon to exert a crucial role in memory processing. Furthermore, these findings have provided proof that successful therapy could reinstate a normal brain metabolism and an almost normal level of cognitive abilities after a previously measured and documented reduction in brain metabolism and cognitive capacities (Markowitsch, Kessler, Weber-Luxenburger, Van der Ven, & Heiss, 2000).

The neural correlates of "psychogenic" amnesia – as evidenced by functional brain imaging – and the putative neurobiological mechanisms underlying them – constitute the main topics that will be outlined in this contribution.

We named the current paper "Searching for the anatomical basis of psychogenic amnesia" after two previous writings – a paper entitled "Searching for the anatomical basis of retrograde amnesia" (Markowitsch, Calabrese, Haupts, et al., 1993) and a book subchapter with the title "The Search for the Anatomical Bases of Chronic Alcoholism and Korsakoff's Syndrome" (Markowitsch, 1992). These writings, which were produced at a time of fascination with psychogenic amnesia, but only little knowledge about its brain underpinnings, are witnesses of the long, but unfinished journey for disentangling the neural correlates of psychogenic memory loss.

Dissociative Amnes(t)ic Conditions

The term amnesia refers to an inability to learn new information or recall previously learned information or past events, in an otherwise alert, non-delirious individual, which is out of proportion in comparison to dysfunctions in other cognitive domains. It could describe a disorder, a syndrome, or a symptom of another disorder. The diagnosis of an amnestic disorder requires (according to the DSM-IV-TR, 2000) that amnesia does not occur exclusively during the course of delirium. In addition such a diagnosis is not made in the presence of neuropsychological and neurological deficits suggestive of dementia.

Given that various memory systems have different degrees of susceptibility to insults and therefore are most of the time unevenly affected by environmental injuries, the use of the term amnesia requires a clear description of the type and severity of the memory problems involved.

Amnesia without direct evidence of brain damage (as detected by conventional structural imaging techniques) has over the years been captured by different terminologies, including hysterical, psychogenic, dissociative, functional, or medically unexplained.

In the present official nomenclatures (DSM-IV-TR and ICD-10) the earlier designations of hysterical amnesia have preponderantly been subsumed to the categories of dissociative disorders (DSM-IV-TR, 2000) and dissociative (conversion) disorders (ICD-10, 1992), but also to several other subcategories such as somatization disorder (DSM-IV-TR), PTSD, and acute stress disorder (DSM-IV-TR).

Echoing Janet's (1907) superior view of hysteria as "*désagrégation mentale*," DSM-IV-TR describes dissociative disorders as disturbances of the integrated organization of memory, perception, consciousness, or identity. Among dissociative disorders in DSM-IV-TR (2000), dissociative amnesia has as the central symptom the inability to recall important personal information, often of stressful or traumatic nature. The symptoms are not better explained by normative forgetfulness or other psychiatric or medical conditions (such as traumatic brain injury). Deliberate feigning which is consciously motivated by external gains (such as malingering) or is prompted by psychological motivations in the absence of identifiable external incentives (such as in factitious disorder) has to be ruled out. The symptoms of dissociative amnesia cause significant impairment of functioning or distress. The degree of experienced distress may, however, depend on many variables, including the cultural views of dissociative experiences, selfhood, and past. While in DSM-IV-TR the preponderant contribution of psychological mechanisms to the emergence of dissociative amnesia is conveyed in a more implicit way, the ICD-10 explicitly spells out as a criterion for the diagnosis of dissociative amnesia (as well as for the other dissociative disorders) the existence of "convincing associations in time between the symptoms of the disorder and stressful events, problems or needs." The presence of amnesia might, however, pose a significant difficulty to the clinicians and researchers who try to identify the precipitating stressful events. Furthermore we encountered cases of dissociative (psychogenic) amnesia that did not occur as a result of an objectively major psychological stressor, but they were recorded after a seemingly objectively minor stress. In most of the latter cases, a careful history taking and collateral information gathering provided evidence for a series of stressful events often occurring since childhood or early adulthood. These observations are consistent with pathogenetic models of kindling sensitization (Post, Weiss, Smith, Rose, & Frye, 1995), or protracted effects of early life stressful events, due to an incubation phenomenon (Lupien, McEwen, Gunnar, & Heim, 2009). Another factor that may hinder the unearthing of convincing associations between stressful events and onset of dissociative amnesia is the presence in some patients with dissociative (psychogenic) amnesic disturbances of an altered capacity for emotional processing (impaired emotional awareness and clarity) in the face of ongoing stress or recurrent stressful events (Staniloiu et al., 2009).

According to most studies (including our own data) dissociative amnesia affects both genders roughly equally. Dissociative amnesia tends to preponderantly occur in younger people, being most frequently diagnosed in the third and fourth decade of life (Coons & Milstein, 1992; Kanzer, 1939). The younger age distribution of dissociative amnesia on one hand mirrors the findings of increased scores on dissociation scales among the younger age group (Ross, Joshie, & Currie, 1990). On the other hand it may partly reflect developmental differences in windows of vulnerability to stress of key brain structures that are involved in memory processes (Lupien et al., 2009).

Dissociative amnesia typically occurs as a single episode, not uncommonly after a mild traumatic brain injury, although – similarly to dissociative fugue – recurrent episodes have been reported (Coons & Milstein, 1992). Some cases of dissociative amnesia follow a chronic course, in spite of treatment. Comorbidities of dissociative amnesia with major depressive disorder, personality disorders, and bulimia nervosa and somatoform disorders have been reported (Maldonado & Spiegel, 2008). Alterations in personality after the onset of dissociative amnesia in the form of changes in eating preferences, smoking habits, or other previously rewarding activities (such as car driving) have also been reported (Fujiwara et al., 2008; Thomas Antérion, Mazzola, Foyatier-Michel, & Laurent, 2008; Tramoni et al., 2009).

Dissociative amnesia could be differentiated according to the degree and time frame of impairment (global vs. selective, anterograde vs. retrograde) of autobiographical-episodic memory and the coexistence of deficits in autobiographical-semantic memory and general semantic knowledge (cf. Serra, Fadda, Buccione, Caltagirone, & Carlesimo, 2007). The most frequent types of dissociative (psychogenic) amnesias are retrograde. DSM-IV-TR (2000) distinguishes between localized amnesia, selective amnesia, generalized amnesia, continuous amnesia, and systematized amnesia, while in the psychological literature several other forms of amnesia are found as well (e.g., Markowitsch, 2000a).

A particular form of retrograde dissociative (psychogenic) amnesia has been coined the "mnestic block syndrome" (Markowitsch, Kesseler, Russ, et al., 1999). This form is defined by an episodic-autobiographical block, which may encompass the whole past life. Affected patients otherwise have largely preserved semantic memories; they can read, write, calculate, and *know* how to behave in social situations. Furthermore, they can lay down new long-term autobiographic-episodic memories, though the acquisition of these new events may be less emotionally flavored in comparison to normal subjects (Brand & Markowitsch, 2009; Reinhold & Markowitsch, 2009).

Data about the frequency of dissociative amnesia are still limited and at times difficult to interpret, though Johnson et al. (2006) reported a 12 month prevalence of 1.8% of dissociative amnesia in a USA community of 658 adults. Similarly to other dissociative disorders, cases of dissociative amnesia are likely not accurately reported (Foote, Smolin, Kaplan, Legatt, & Lipschitz, 2006). One possible reason for this is related to the challenges clinicians face when searching for convincing evidence of stressful events or trauma. Another reason is the fact that dissociative amnesia can occur as a symptom of other dissociative disorders such as dissociative identity disorder (DSM-IV-TR) or multiple personality disorder (ICD-10), dissociative fugue, Ganser syndrome, and dissociative trance disorder and possession trance, as well as a symptom of certain anxiety disorders, such as acute stress disorder and PTSD or DSM-IV-TR described somatoform disorders (somatization disorder) or personality disorders, such as borderline personality disorder, but under these circumstances it is not recorded as a separate diagnostic entity.

When retrograde dissociative amnesia is accompanied by suddenly leaving the customary environment – home and city – and compromised knowledge about personal identity – the condition is named dissociative fugue (Markowitsch, Fink, Thöne, Kessler, & Heiss, 1997). Fugues have been reported for over a century (e.g., Woltär, 1906), though they were frequently erroneously associated with epilepsy (e.g., Burgl, 1900; Donath, 1899; Raecke, 1908). A century ago, these conditions were named *Wanderlust* in Germany; cf. e.g., Burgl, 1900. Fugue states were described to be preponderant in children and young adults (Bregman, 1899; Dana, 1874; Donath, 1908; Heilbronner, 1903, 1905; Hey, 1904). They were thought to increase in frequency during wartimes and be more frequent among men, although some studies conducted in the nonwar periods found no gender differences. Identified precipitants included rape, sexual assault, combat, marital distress, and financial problems. Presentations similar to fugues have also been described in certain cultures, where they represent idioms of distress (Maldonado & Spiegel, 2008). Most fugues were not found to involve the formation of a new identity and were usually reported to be brief, but some prolonged courses were also described (Hennig-Fast et al., 2008). Franz (1933) gave a detailed description of a subject, named Jack, who ostensibly traveled between Europe, Africa, and the United States and whom he described as being captured and held as a prisoner during World War I in East Africa. Associations between fugues and Ganser syndrome were also found.

Ganser syndrome is a condition that has been submitted to several diagnostic revisions and debates over the years. In comparison to previous DSM editions, where Ganser syndrome was presented as a Factitious Disorder, Ganser syndrome is currently included under the category of Dissociative Disorders Not Otherwise Specified in DSM-IV-TR and it is simply defined by giving approximate answers to questions (*vorbeireden*). Ganser's (1894, 1904) original description of the syndrome was, however, much broader than the current DSM-IV-TR one. It included a hysterical semitrance or twilight state, characterized by a tendency to give approximate answers, impairments of consciousness, amnesia, and hallucinations, being more consistent with the later views of this disorder as a brief reactive psychosis to stress. Though initially linked to forensic background, Ganser syndrome was also reported in non-forensic contexts. The syndrome was found to affect preponderantly young men with a mean age of 35 years, although there were some case reports in women and children as well (Miller, Bramble, & Buxton, 1997; Nardi & Di Scipio, 1977). Both a transient, limited course and a chronic course have been recorded.

In spite of its current categorization under dissociative disorders in DSM-IV-TR Ganser syndrome has continued to be a diagnostic puzzle for clinicians and a challenge for formal diagnostic classifications. Not infrequently its clinical presentation suggests a mixture of underlying psychological mechanisms, such as dissociative mechanisms intimately interwoven with psychologically motivated exaggeration of symptoms. In the face of such cases it is not surprising that several authors (including the present writers) have continued to employ terminologies such as psychogenic amnesia (McKay & Kopelman, 2009), while acknowledging its imperfections. As opposed to the category of dissociative amnesia that only captures a part of the dissociative amnesic disorders and carries a specific theoretical load, psychogenic amnesia is more comprehensive. It also has the advantage that it emphasizes the preponderant contribution of psychological factors to the emergence of the amnesic episode, without defining from the start the nature of the psychological mechanisms involved.

In comparison to psychogenic amnesia, functional amnesia is a broader category, which encompasses not only "clear-cut" psychogenic amnesic disturbances, but also forms of amnesia with no yet (readily) identifiable psychological or medical precipitants.

Dissociative Amnes(t)ic Disorders and Trauma

Dissociative (psychogenic) amnesic disorders have been linked to psychological trauma or stress in a variety of cultures (Bremner, Steinberg, Southwick, Johnson, & Charney, 1993; Draijer & Langeland, 1999; Jones, Fear, & Wessely, 2007; Kaszniak, Nussbaum, Berren, & Santiago, 1988; Kiersch, 1962; Seligman & Kirmayer, 2008; Spiegel & Cardena, 1991; Thom & Fenton, 1920; Xiao et al., 2006). Although connections between trauma (especially early traumatic experiences) and psychiatric symptomatology were suggested by other psychiatrists or scientists in the 19th century (van der Kolk & van der Hart, 1989), including Freud in his first approach to psychopathology (Breuer & Freud, 1895), it is Janet (1898) who claimed dissociation as a mechanism related to traumatic experiences that accounted for the various manifestations of hysteria (including hysterical amnesia). Janet is credited by several authors (Maldonado & Spiegel, 2008) with a superior view of dissociation that anticipated contemporary theories and involved not just separation or compartmentalization but a failure of integration of various functions. He underlined the importance of memory for a healthy personality, especially of those memories that were accompanied by a particular type of awareness (that seems to resemble what we presently name autonoetic self-awareness). "It is not enough to be aware of a memory that occurs automatically in response to particular current events: It is also necessary that the personal perception 'knows' this image and attaches it to other memories" (p. 135, cited by van der Kolk & van der Hart, 1989). Furthermore, Janet suggested that the impact of trauma on a particular individual may be dependent on a variety of factors (such as the person's characteristics, prior experiences, and the severity, duration, and recurrence of the trauma) and might not become evident immediately, but after a certain latency period (van der Kolk & van der Hart, 1989). Many of Janet's ideas have later received corroboration from both clinical observations (including our own data on dissociative amnesia) and neurobiological investigations and have subsequently been incorporated in current pathogenetic models of dissociative disorders. We describe below our proposed model to account for the findings in patients with dissociative amnesia, which is shown in Figure 1.

As depicted in this model, traumatic situations (especially the ones with an early onset) may change the brain's activation of certain neurotransmitters and may lead to an altered processing of incoming information. The nature and magnitude of these changes depend on the (sometimes synergistic) interaction of these early traumatic experiences with genetic dispositions (with protective or deleterious effect) (Becker-Blease et al., 2004) and other environmental factors (with buffering or exacerbating effects) and the time frame (the developmental window) when this interaction takes place (Lupien, McEwen, Gunnar, & Heim, 2009; McCarthy et al., 2009). If the person subsequently fails to acquire appropriate coping strategies, the appearance of further stress events may result in a dissociation between the processing of emotional and cognitive portions of new information with the result of a full-blown stress reaction (Reinhold & Markowitsch, 2007, 2009). That is, the usual synchronization between emotion-processing regions of the brain (limbic system, in particular the amygdala and the septal region/basal forebrain) (MacLean, 1970) and fact-processing regions is no longer possible with the consequence that one or the other region takes dominance. This then leads to the block of autobiographical information processing, either in general or specific with respect to time-epochs or material. Our model is consistent with accumulating evidence that shows that early life experiences can lead to changes in stress responses, neurotransmitters, synaptic plasticity, brain connectivity, and brain structures, including microstructural changes in the uncinate fascicle (Bluhm et al., 2009; Govindan, Behen, Helder, Makki, & Chugani, 2010; Lupien et al., 2009; Mehta et al., 2009). The latter is highly relevant for the processes of episodic-autobiographical memory (EAM) retrieval (see below). Its changes in children exposed to early trauma are of particular interest, especially when corroborated with findings from other studies that point to reduced autobiographical memory specificity (overgeneral memory effect) in children with a history of abuse or neglect (Valentino, Toth, & Cicchetti, 2009). An optimum balance of glucocorticoids (stress hormones) is essential for the neuronal survival and learning and memory processes (Du et al., 2009). Enduring alterations in stress hormone responses in response to early life experiences might occur via epigenetic mechanisms, which act during windows of heightened vulnerability (McGowan et al., 2009). The effects of stress on mental health might be observed clinically after a lag period. This may be accounted for by the fact that the early stress effects on synaptic organization only emerge after the completion of synaptic organization (Lupien et al., 2009).

Alternatively, this phenomenon might be explained by a mechanism of kindling sensitization (Post et al., 1995). Stressful events could lead to the release of a variety of hormones and initiate a neurotoxicity cascade (Joels & Baram, 2009; O'Brien, 1997; Ulrich-Lai & Herman, 2009). As Figure 1 implies, it is assumed that the release of stress hormones – in particular glucocorticoids – is principally responsible for the block in the function of brain structures essential for the encoding or retrieval of information. In fact, it is known that several key brain structures involved in memory processing show especially during their periods of development or regression (Lupien et al., 2009) an increased susceptibility to the hormonal effects of stress and aside from limbic brain regions, temporo-frontal regions are engaged in triggering the retrieval of already stored information. With respect to the retrieval of memory, it was proposed that a regional combination of inferolateral prefrontal and anterior temporal regions is essential (Fink et al., 1996; Kroll, Markowitsch, Knight, & von Cramon, 1997; Markowitsch, Calabrese, Liess, et al., 1993). LaBar and Cabeza wrote in 2006 that "studies of retrograde amnesia support Markowitsch's proposal that retrieval of remote personal memories involves interactions between the inferior PFC [prefrontal cortex] and its connections with the anteriormedial temporal lobe that course through the

Usually early psychological or biological trauma

↓

Biological priming

Change in receptor structure of "second messenger"-cascade

↓

Supersensitivity for excitatory neurotransmitters

↓

1st latency phase

↓

(Re-)Activation
via
psychological mechanisms

(e.g., sorrow, role change, role conflict, deprivation)

or

biological events

(e.g., viral infection, surgery, accident)

↓

absence of an adequate emotional-cognitive processing

↓

2nd latency phase

↓

Dissociation between emotion and cognition

↓

Psychobiological stress reaction

↓

(CRH-overdrive, change in cortisol level, increase in the number of β-receptors)

↓

Depression?

↓

Mnestic block syndrome (dissociative amnesic state)

Figure 1. Proposed model of possible changes in brain-behavior interrelations induced by stress conditions (after Aldenhoff, 1997; Markowitsch, 2000b).

uncinate fasciculus." In fact it was established by histological methods that the uncinate fascicle (Figure 2) has 33% more fibers in the right than in the left hemisphere (Highley, Walker, Esiri, Crow, & Harrison, 2002) and that it is the only fiber bundle that may continue to develop beyond the age of 30 years (Lebel, Walker, Leemans, Phillips, & Beaulieu, 2008). As we and others found, the regional combination of inferolateral prefrontal and polar temporal areas is essential for retrieving two forms of memory, which will be explained in the next section – episodic-autobiographical and semantic memory. EAM is in our experience related to the right hemisphere (i.e., the emotion-processing hemisphere) and semantic memory to the left hemisphere (where also the Broca and Wernicke language areas are situated).

The Nature of Memory Loss in Dissociative Amnes(t)ic Disorders

Our experience with dissociative amnesias confirms other authors' findings, which is that in most cases only one memory system is affected, namely the EAM, while information processing via the other memory systems either is preserved or is easily regained after a significant stressful event. In particular, those memory systems, acting on a subconscious level, like procedural memory and the priming memory system, are intact and even the so-called noetic (conscious reflection requiring) memory systems could remain intact – that is, perceptual and semantic memory.

On the other side, with respect to memory loss there are apparently two forms of dissociative (psychogenic) amnesia, the common form in which retrograde EAM is impaired and an anterograde form where anterograde EAM is impaired. Although anterograde memory deficits could occasionally accompany retrograde dissociative (psychogenic) amnesia, cases of dissociative (psychogenic) anterograde amnesia with preserved retrograde EAM are a much rarer occurrence. Up to now we have studied about three dozen patients with the common, retrograde form, but only three patients with the anterograde form (cf. Markowitsch, Kessler, Kalbe, & Herholz, 1999). Also from other groups reports on patients with psychogenic anterograde amnesia are very rare (Kumar, Rao, Sunny,

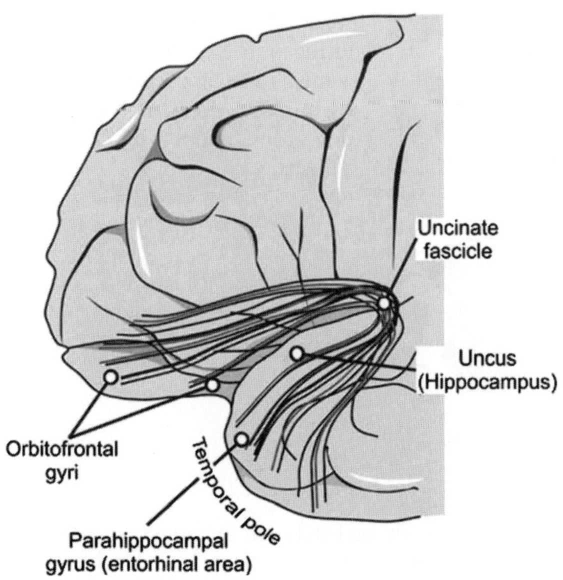

Figure 2. The location of the ventral branch of the uncinate fascicle, interconnecting the inferior lateral prefrontal cortex and the temporopolar cortex. It is assumed that these regions are essential for triggering the retrieval of semantic (left hemisphere) and episodic-autobiographical information (right hemisphere) (cf. Markowitsch & Welzer, 2009).

& Gangadhar, 2007). The differences in the susceptibility to insults among memory systems are mirrored by Tulving's (2002, 2005) classification of memory systems, which corresponds to an ontogenetic and phylogenetic hierarchy. The EAM, which is situated at the top of this hierarchy, entails an ability for flexible mental time traveling in the past and future and a superior capacity for reflection upon oneself in relation to the others (his or her social and biological environment). Furthermore, EAM possesses an intimate link to emotions. The recall of EAMs is usually accompanied by appraisals of their emotional meaning for the individual – whether an event was a happy or a sad one, for example. As emotions might play a motivational role, the ability to access emotionally laden episodic memories of personal experience is important for the maintenance of an enduring sense of personal identity in the face of a changing environment.

The flexible handling of EAMs becomes apparently no longer possible in dissociative amnesic conditions. In the following we briefly review cases with dissociative amnesic conditions in which one or several forms of brain imaging were performed before we provide more general conclusions on possible neuroanatomical correlates of amnesia in dissociative amnesic patients. As neuroimaging methods we typically either measured the glucose metabolism with positron-emission tomography (PET) or applied a paradigm with several conditions under water PET. In addition static magnetic resonance imaging (MRI) was used in all patients. In one patient single photon emission computed tomography (SPECT) was applied in addition to PET and MRI. Furthermore functional magnetic resonance imaging (fMRI) paradigms were employed in the last few years.

Patient NN

NN's case was described in Markowitsch, Fink, et al. (1997). He was a 37-year-old man with low self-esteem. He was the single child of alcohol-dependent parents and had been maltreated by them since birth. He was dressed as a girl until starting elementary school because his mother wanted to have a daughter instead of a son. Later his mother frequently criticized him as being weak and as behaving in a girlish manner. She predicted that he never would become successful in life and instead would ruin their business. Indeed, N.N. grew up with very low self-esteem and was easily frustrated. In his early 20s, he married a woman who apparently was similar in behavior to his mother and possessed the self-confidence he was missing. He took her family name also for himself and she directed his way of life. Reportedly, she one day decided that they will leave with their car for a vacation the following week. Though he knew that they would not have enough financial resources for that, he did not want to object.

Three days prior to the intended start of the holidays NN was supposed to get rolls from the bakery for breakfast. He took his bicycle, but instead of returning home he continued biking for the next days from North to South Germany until reaching the center of a large city. At the central station of this city he was asked about his well-being by a person from the Salvation Army who then suggested to him to enter the city's psychiatric university hospital, what he actually did. All the days he did not remember who he was nor why he was biking – he simply had the drive to do so. As described above, this combination of losing the autobiographical memories and leaving the usual place of living is named *dissociative fugue* in psychiatry.

In the clinic, NN felt quite happy, made friends, and appeared not to care about his condition of having no access to his past – a presentation which has been noted in other patients with dissociative amnesia and has been termed *belle indifférence* by Janet (1907). After a police search, initiated by his wife, NN was found and visited by her after about 10 days. Contrary to the old teaching lore that stated that a confrontation with reality leads to immediate reinstatement of memories, this did not happen to him. He did not recognize his wife and instead believed that the doctors wanted to couple him with a woman, unknown to him. He nevertheless returned with his wife to their home – complaining however at arrival about how one could live with the existing furniture and tapestry. He also failed to recognize his children. Interestingly, he changed his habits (e.g., while having been an avid car driver prior to the onset of his amnesia, he now barely dared to enter a car), and his job, and even ceased having allergy and asthma attacks. He relearned his past and then could

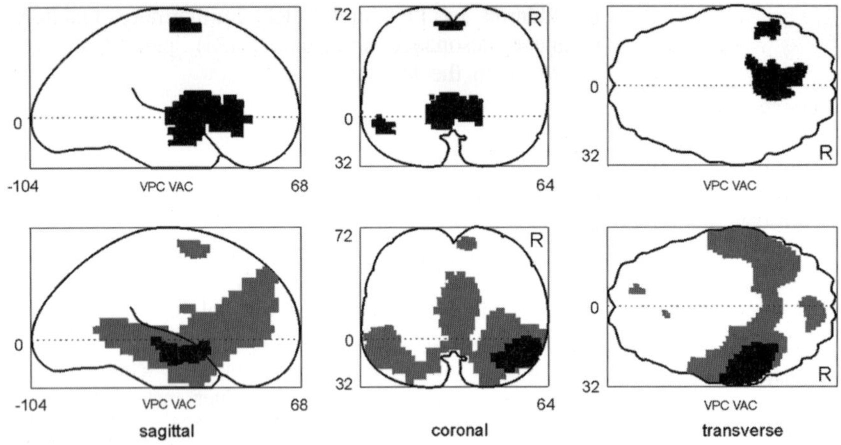

Figure 3. "Glass brain" activations during retrieval of autobiographic events. The top row shows the activations in patient N.N., the bottom row those of comparison subjects.

retrieve portions of it in a neutral, affectless manner. Other cognitive functions were largely spared or regained within weeks.

We tested him neuropsychologically and performed a water-PET where we used the design of Fink et al. (1996) and confronted him with events from his personal past. However, as it can be seen from the outcome illustrated in Figure 3, he was apparently unable to relate events he had experienced in the past to himself: While the normal subjects activated in the water-PET study predominantly the fronto-temporal region of the right hemisphere, he activated largely the left hemisphere which is considered to be relevant for the retrieval of neutral, impersonal facts (De Renzi, Liotti, & Nichelli, 1987; Grossi, Trojano, Grasso, & Orsini, 1988; Markowitsch, Calabrese, Neufeld, Gehlen, & Durwen, 1999).

Patient AD

Another patient appeared to have had a dissociative fugue condition with a forensic background (Markowitsch, Calabrese, et al., 1997). He had burned a house and left with a high amount of money across the border to a foreign country. When he was brought back to his home country, he did not know anything about his personal past. In a neurological university clinic, he was investigated neuropsychologically, with SPECT, glucose-PET, and MRI. A significant finding was a reduction in his right fronto-temporal cortex, that is, in exactly that area that was active in functional brain imaging when normal subjects were asked to recall their personal events from the past (Figure 4). Aside from persistent retrograde amnesia in the autobiographic domain, his memories and other cognitive functions were largely intact. Lumbar puncture did not yield any evidence of infection.

Patient AMN

While both patients described above showed evidence of a change in the right temporo-frontal cortex, patient AMN was somewhat different. This 23-year-old young man one afternoon witnessed the outbreak of an open fire in the cellar of his house. He immediately left the house, shouting "fire, fire" and was apparently shaken up by what he saw. His friend, who had also been present in the house at that time, called the fire-workers who immediately extinguished the fire. AMN then went to bed that night, but when awakening the next morning, he had lost access to the last six years of his life and was also anterogradely amnesic. His semantic memory was quickly regained. Any medical or neurological causation (e.g., hypoxia) was ruled out by a thorough medical workup. We examined this patient neuropsychologically and with glucose-PET a few weeks after the accident (Markowitsch, Kessler, Van der Ven, Weber-Luxenburger, & Heiss, 1998).

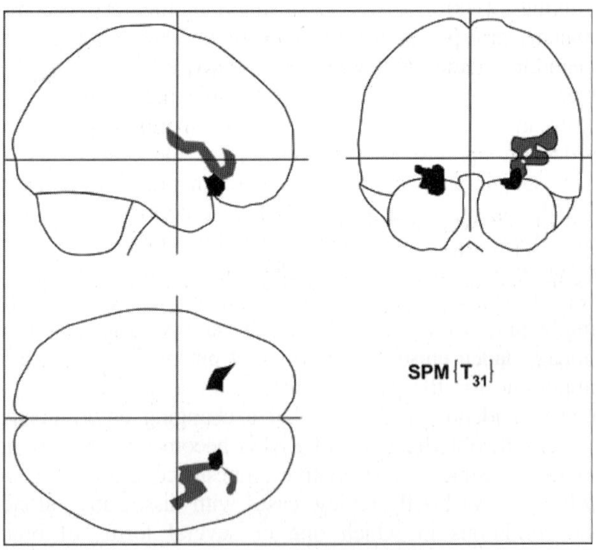

Figure 4. Schematic reconstructions of two horizontal brain sections of two patients. The left brain section represents the brain metabolism (perfusion) of a patient with herpes encephalitis and consequently neurological brain damage (darker shaded areas). The right one represents the brain perfusion of a patient with dissociative amnesia (after PLATE 2 of Markowitsch, Kessler, Kalbe, et al., 1999).

In the course of psychotherapeutic explorations, AMN revealed that when he was 4 years old he witnessed with his mother the death of a man in a burning car. He recalled that that man shouted, cried, and hammered against the windows, but was unable to escape the fire. Since that time, open fire situations were perceived as life-threatening by the patient. We propose that the witnessing of the first fire situation represented the initial traumatic event that likely initiated already subtle biological changes as described in Figure 1, and that the later witnessing of the fire outbreak in his own house resulted in a magnified biological response in the form of a cascade-like release of stress hormones (glucocorticoids; cf. O'Brien, 1997), which led to the mnestic block. The time span covered by memory loss for personal events (the last 6 years) could be related to the negative emotional loading of the life events that happened during that time frame (such as significant conflicts with parents, leaving both home and school) (De Kloet, Joels, & Holsboer, 2005; Lupien, Maheu, Tu, Fiocco, & Schramek, 2007). A number of findings, in fact, support the idea that especially traumatic conditions in young age may lead to a later vulnerability to stress-related events (Fries, Ziegler, Kurian, Jacoris, & Pollak, 2005; Weinstock, 2008).

PET revealed an overall reduction in AMN's brain's glucose metabolism. In addition, there was a more severe reduction in his anterior and medial temporal lobes and the diencephalon (cf. Bluhm et al., 2009; Gianaros et al., 2007; Szeszko et al., 2006). Treating the patient psychopharmaceutically and with psychotherapy resulted in a reinstatement of most of his old memories and a reinstatement of his ability to encode new episodic events long term (Markowitsch et al., 2000). This patient therefore resembles one of the few cases with severe autobiographical retrograde amnesia who regained his memories within roughly a year (see also Thomas Antérion et al., 2008).

Patient KP

Patient KP was already over 50 years old when he was found sitting helplessly on a bench in a park of a big city. As he had no papers for identification and did not know who he was, he was brought into a psychiatric hospital. After a press conference, the media revealed his identity. He nevertheless did not recognize his long-term partner, nor did he regain any other personal memory. Only after psychotherapy and an intensive visiting and confrontation with places and persons from his childhood and youth, patient KP regained access to single events while he still does not remember much of his later decades of life. Brain imaging again revealed temporo-frontal glucose reductions (Reinhold, Kühnel, Brand, & Markowitsch, 2006).

Patient CD

Another patient with typical dissociative amnesia was a 33-year-old skilled worker who had been found unconscious in his bathroom by his wife. He had lost access to the last 14 years of life and glucose-PET revealed a significant reduction in glucose metabolism in his fronto-temporal brain areas.

Patient DO

Patient DO had been severely maltreated by her father as a child with the consequence that she still – at age 55 – was undergoing psychotherapy, because she had no access to her personal memories from the epoch between age 10 and 16 years (Markowitsch, Thiel, Kessler, von Stockhausen, & Heiss, 1997). Her therapist suggested to her to draw paintings representing events from her past and DO replied that she could do so when she was in a particular affective state. These pictures could be divided into those representing concrete scenes – usually showing a small, sad, or suffering looking child with or without an adult male person – and those with abstract content. The colors were largely dark, purple or black, or white. DO perceived these abstract paintings as emotionally more negatively arousing than the ones showing concrete scenes. Scanning her brain with water-PET while she viewed her paintings resulted in right temporopolar activations, pointing to a deficiency in integrating emotional and factual components of memory (Reinhold & Markowitsch, 2007, 2009).

Patient KL

A woman of 35 years of age came to our attention because of a peculiar loss of memory affecting the last 14 years of her life. When she awoke from surgery, KL gave as the present date a date that was 14 years back in time compared to the real one. She exactly remembered events and facts until then, but not thereafter. This implied that she still considered the German Democratic Republic to exist as well as Deutschmarks as currency. She was astonished by the existence of small cars (Smarts) on the streets or by what was available in supermarkets. Scanning her brain with water-PET (as she had a heart pacemaker we could not do fMRI) and a paradigm where the brain activity during presentation of events from her last 14 years of life versus the life thereafter was compared revealed activations in the right temporo-frontal zone for recently acquired and properly retrieved events, but not for those of the inaccessible past.

Patient MN

A special variant of dissociative disorder is the Ganser syndrome (Cocores et al., 1984; Ganser, 1898, 1904; Staniloiu et al., 2009), which is sometimes associated with a forensic background. A family father in his middle thirties was suddenly accused of having sexually abused two women years ago. The patient immediately became unable to work and developed very severe changes in cognition and affect. He apparently could no longer perform simple tasks and spent the whole day sitting or lying around without doing anything. He became totally dependent on his wife. He developed significant difficulties urinating and subsequently his wife had to catheterize him. Glucose-PET revealed significant overall changes in his brain metabolism.

Cases of Dissociative (Psychogenic) Amnesia or Possible Dissociative (Psychogenic) Amnesia Investigated with Brain Imaging Reported by Other Authors

In recent years several other groups have performed static and functional brain imaging in patients with dissociative (psychogenic) amnesia or functional amnesia. Most studies employed fMRI within a task paradigm; these studies have therefore limited relevance with respect to the question of possible neuroanatomical changes as a consequence of the dissociative state and will consequently not be reviewed here, although they specifically point to similar brain mechanisms in "organic" and psychogenic (or functional or dissociative) forms of amnesia (e.g., Botzung, Denkova, & Manning, 2007; Brandt & Van Gorp, 2006; Glisky et al., 2004; Ouellet, Rouleau, Labrecque, Bernier, & Scherzer, 2008; cf. Markowitsch, 1996).

There is, however, one pertinent new case report in which a 34-year-old patient with functional amnesia is described (Tramoni et al., 2009). He was investigated neuropsychologically and with various brain imaging methods. He fell from a ladder and became unconscious. Thereafter he presented with extensive retrograde amnesia in the autobiographical domain, while other cognitive skills were preserved. Investigating his brain with MRI methods sensitive to microstructural and metabolic brain damage (density and magnetization transfer ratio; MR spectroscopic imaging) revealed damage in the right prefrontal white matter involving parts of the superior longitudinal fasciculus, the fronto-occipital fasciculus, and the genu of the corpus callosum. These results reflect subtle focal tissue damage with concomitant neural dysfunction or demyelination. They are consistent with ideas on brain regions relevant for processing of old autobiographical memories (Markowitsch, 1995) and point to a kind of disconnection syndrome, similar to what we had described before (Brand & Markowitsch, 2009; Markowitsch, 2002; Markowitsch, Kessler, Russ, et al., 1999).

Relations Between Dissociative Amnesias and Neuroanatomical Changes

The findings from various brain imaging methods converge in demonstrating that environmental influences such as psychological trauma or stressful experiences could induce alterations on the brain level (Markowitsch, 1999a, 1999b).

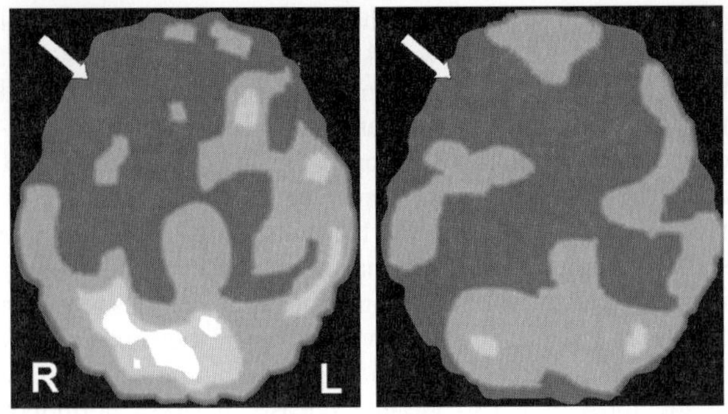

Figure 5. Schematic sagittal (top left), horizontal (bottom left), and frontal sections through the human brain. Areas of relative decrease in regional cerebral glucose metabolism in 14 patients with dissociative amnesia relative to 19 control subjects are shown as "glass brains" (after Figure 1 of Brand et al., 2009).

These changes may be long-lasting, if treatment remains unsuccessful or they have already followed a prolonged course prior to being diagnosed and treated. They can broadly be classified as changes in brain metabolism and changes in brain tissue volume and in brain structure itself.

Changes in brain metabolism are observed most universally and persist weeks to months after the occurrence of the psychotraumatic situation leading to the dissociative condition (Reinhold et al., 2006). Aside from affecting the cerebrum as a whole these seem to be targetable especially in the right-hemispheric temporo-frontal region (Brand et al., 2009; Piolino et al., 2005; Tramoni et al., 2009), though some SPECT data in patients with unclear etiology or diagnosis (traumatic brain injury, post-traumatic retrograde amnesia) also point to changes in other cortical regions (Cantagollo, Grassi, & Della Sala, 1999; Stracciari, Ghidoni, Guarino, Poletti, & Pazzaglia, 1994). Our search for the neural signature of psychological stress in dissociative (psychogenic) amnesia in a relatively large sample of 14 patients with dissociative (psychogenic) amnesia characterized by severe retrograde EAM deficits and no overt structural abnormalities as detected by conventional imaging methods found evidence of functional changes (hypometabolism) during resting state in the right temporo-frontal region with a significant decrease in the inferolateral prefrontal cortex (Figure 5) (Brand et al., 2009). These changes are in striking agreement with the findings of Tramoni et al. (2009), based on a different methodology (see above).

We therefore can conclude that there is accumulating evidence from several sources for the existence of significant brain alterations in patients with dissociative (psychogenic) amnes(t)ic disorders. These changes reflect most likely more subtle fiber damage and/or reductions in functionality in the regions of the right anterior hemisphere, in particular in right fronto-temporal areas and their interconnecting fiber tracts. As it was stated previously, these findings point to similar neurobiological mechanisms underlying the "organic" and "psychogenic" memory loss conditions. They suggest that it might indeed be the case that these conditions represent two sides of the same coin (Markowitsch, 1996) and the gap that we still perceive between the two is mainly a consequence of technological limitations.

We end by citing Pietro Pietrini, who stated in 2003 in the *American Journal of Psychiatry* (p. 1908): "It was not long ago that psychiatric disorders were grossly classified as 'organic' and 'functional' according to whether there was a known brain structural alteration (e.g., dementia) or not (e.g., depression or schizophrenia). This merely reflected our inability to go beyond what could be visible to the naked eye in the brain. Functional brain studies ... have given us a powerful microscope to dissect the intimate molecular aspects of brain function."

Acknowledgment

HJM thanks the Institute of Advanced Study, Alfried-Krupp Wissenschaftskolleg, for hosting him as Senior Fellow.

References

Aldenhoff, J. (1997). Überlegungen zur Psychobiologie der Depression [Reflections on the psychobiology of depression]. *Nervenarzt, 68*, 379–389.

Bao, A. M., Meynen, G., & Swaab, D. F. (2008). The stress system in depression and neurodegeneration: Focus on the human hypothalamus. *Brain Research Review, 57*, 531–553.

Becker-Blease, K. A., Deater-Deckard, K., Eley, T., Freyd, J. J., Stevenson, J., & Plomin, R. (2004). A genetic analysis of individual differences in dissociative behaviors in childhood and adolescence. *Journal of Child Psychology and Psychiatry, 45*, 522–532.

Bluhm, R. L., Wiliamson, P. C., Osuch, E. A., Frewen, P. A., Stevens, T. K., Boksman, K., ... Lanius, R. A. (2009). Alterations in default network connectivity in posttraumatic stress disorder related to early-life trauma. *Journal of Psychiatry and Neuroscience, 34*, 187–194.

Boccardi, M., Ganzola, R., Rossi, R., Sabattoli, F., Laakso, M. P., Repo-Tiihonen, E., ... Tiihonen, J. (2010). Abnormal hippocampal shape in offenders with psychopathy. *Human Brain Mapping, 31*, 438–447.

Botzung, A., Denkova, E., & Manning, L. (2007). Psychogenic memory deficits associated with functional cerebral changes: an FMRI study. *Neurocase, 13*, 378–384.

Brand, M., Eggers, C., Reinhold, N., Fujiwara, E., Kessler, J., Heiss, W.-D., & Markowitsch, H. J. (2009). Functional brain imaging in fourteen patients with dissociative amnesia reveals right inferolateral prefrontal hypometabolism. *Psychiatry Research: Neuroimaging Section, 174*, 32–39.

Brand, M., & Markowitsch, H. J. (2009). Environmental influences on autobiographical memory: The mnestic block syndrome. In L. Bäckman & L. Nyberg (Eds.), *Festschrift in honor of Lars-Göran Nilsson* (pp. 229–264). Hove, UK: Psychology Press.

Brandt, J., & Van Gorp, W. G. (2006). Functional ("psychogenic") amnesia. *Seminars in Neurology, 26*, 331–340.

Bregman, L. E. (1899). Ueber den "Automatisme ambulatoire" ("Fugues", "Dromomania") [On the "automatisme ambulatoire" ("fugues", "dromomania")]. *Neurologisches Centralblatt, 18*, 776–781.

Bremner, J. D., Steinberg, M., Southwick, S. M., Johnson, D. R., & Charney, D. S. (1993). Use of the Structured Clinical Interview for DSM-IV Dissociative Disorders for systematic assessment of dissociative symptoms in posttraumatic stress disorder. *American Journal of Psychiatry, 150*, 1011–1014.

Breuer, J., & Freud, S. (1895). *Studien über Hysterie* [Studies on hysteria]. Wien, Austria: Deuticke.

Burgl, G. (1900). Eine Reise in die Schweiz im epileptischen Dämmerzustande und die transitorischen Bewusstseinsstörungen der Epileptiker vor dem Strafrichter [A journey to Switzerland done in epileptic somnolence and the transitory disturbances of consciousness before the criminal judge]. *Münchener medizinische Wochenschrift, 37*, 1270–1273.

Cantagollo, A., Grassi, L., & Della Sala, S. (1999). Dissociative disorder after traumatic brain injury. *Brain injury, 13*, 219–288.

Cocores, J. A., Santa, W. G., & Patel, M. D. (1984). The Ganser syndrome: Evidence suggesting its classification as a dissociative disorder. *International Journal of Psychiatry in Medicine, 14*, 47–56.

Coons, P. M., & Milstein, V. (1992). Psychogenic amnesia: A clinical investigation of 25 cases. *Dissociation, 5*, 73–79.

Dana, C. L. (1874). The study of a case of amnesia or "double consciousness". *Psychological Review, 1*, 570–580.

De Kloet, E. R., Joels, M., & Holsboer, F. (2005). Stress and the brain: From adaptation to disease. *Nature Reviews Neuroscience, 6*, 463–475.

De Renzi, E., Liotti, M., & Nichelli, P. (1987). Semantic amnesia with preservation of autobiographic memory. A case report. *Cortex, 23*, 575–597.

Donath, J. (1899). Der epileptische Wandertrieb (Poriomanie) [The epileptic drive to wander (poriomania)]. *Archiv für Psychiatrie und Nervenkrankheiten, 32*, 335–355.

Donath, J. (1908). Ueber hysterische Amnesie [On hysterical amnesia]. *Archiv für Psychiatrie und Nervenkrankheiten, 44*, 559–575.

Draijer, N., & Langeland, W. (1999). Childhood trauma and perceived parental dysfunction in the etiology of dissociative symptoms in psychiatric inpatients. *American Journal of Psychiatry, 156*, 379–385.

DSM-IV-TR. (2000). *Diagnostic and statistical manual of mental disorders* (4th ed.). Washington, DC: American Psychiatric Association.

Du, J., Wang, Y., Hunter, R., Wei, Y., Blumenthal, R., Falke, C., ... Manji, H. K. (2009). Dynamic regulation of mitochondrial function by glucocorticoids. *Proceedings of the National Academy of Sciences of the United States of America, 106*, 3543–3548.

Fink, G. R., Markowitsch, H. J., Reinkemeier, M., Bruckbauer, T., Kessler, J., & Heiss, W.-D. (1996). Cerebral representation of one's own past: Neural networks involved in autobiographical memory. *Journal of Neuroscience, 16*, 4275–4282.

Foote, B., Smolin, Y., Kaplan, M., Legatt, M. E., & Lipschitz, D. (2006). Prevalence of dissociative disorders in psychiatric outpatients. *American Journal of Psychiatry, 163*, 623–629.

Franz, S. I. (1933). *Persons one and three. A study in multiple personalities*. New York, NY: Whittlesey House.

Fries, A. B. W., Ziegler, T. E., Kurian, J. R., Jacoris, S., & Pollak, S. D. (2005). Early experience in humans is associated with changes in neuropeptides critical for regulating social behavior. *Proceedings of the National Academy of Sciences of the United States of America, 102*, 17237–17240.

Fujiwara, E., Brand, M., Kracht, L., Kessler, J., Diebel, A., Netz, J., & Markowitsch, H. J. (2008). Functional retrograde amnesia: A multiple case study. *Cortex, 44*, 29–45.

Ganser, S. J. (1898). Ueber einen eigenartigen hysterischen Dämmerzustand [On a peculiar hysterical state of somnolence]. *Archiv für Psychiatrie und Nervenkrankheiten, 30*, 633–640.

Ganser, S. J. (1904). Zur Lehre vom hysterischen Dämmerzustande [On the theory of the hysterical state of somnolence]. *Archiv für Psychiatrie und Nervenkrankheiten, 38*, 34–46.
Gianaros, P. J., Jennings, J. R., Sheu, L. K., Greer, P. J., Kuller, L. H., & Matthews, K. A. (2007). Prospective reports of chronic life stress predict decreased grey matter volume in the hippocampus. *NeuroImage, 35*, 795–803.
Glenn, A. L., & Raine, A. (2008). The neurobiology of psychopathy. *Psychiatric Clinics of North America, 31*, 463–475.
Glisky, E. L., Ryan, L., Reminger, S., Hardt, O., Hayes, S. M., & Hupbach, A. (2004). A case of psychogenic fugue: "I understand, aber ich verstehe nichts". *Neurospsychologia, 42*, 1132–1147.
Govindan, R. M., Behen, M. E., Helder, E., Makki, M. I., & Chugani, H. T. (2010). Altered water diffusivity in cortical association tracts in children with early deprivation identified with tract-based spatial statistics. *Cerebral Cortex 20*, 561–569.
Grossi, D., Trojano, L., Grasso, A., & Orsini, A. (1988). Selective "semantic amnesia" after closed-head injury. A case report. *Cortex, 24*, 457–464.
Gur, R. E., Cowell, P. E., Latshaw, A., Turetsky, B. I., Grossman, R. I., Arnold, S. E. ... Gur, R. C. (2000). Reduced dorsal and orbital prefrontal gray matter volumes in schizophrenia. *Archives of General Psychiatry, 57*, 761–768.
Heilbronner, K. (1903). Ueber Fugues und fugue-ähnliche Zustände [On fugues and fugue-related states]. *Jahrbücher für Psychiatrie und Neurologie, 23*, 107–206.
Heilbronner, K. (1905). Studien über eine eklamptische Psychose [Studies on an eclampsic psychosis]. *Monatschrift für Psychologie, 17*, 277–287. and 367-460.
Heine, R. (1911). Die forensische Bedeutung der Amnesie [The forensic significance of amnesia]. *Vierteljahresschrift für gerichtliche Medicin (3. Folge), 42*, 51–93.
Hennig-Fast, K., Meister, F., Frodl, T., Beraldi, A., Padberg, F., Engel, R. R., ... Meindl, T. (2008). A case of persistent retrograde amnesia following a dissociative fugue: Neuropsychological and neurofunctional underpinnings of loss of autobiographical memory and self-awareness. *Neuropsychologia, 46*, 2993–3005.
Hey, J. (1904). *Das Gansersche Symptom und seine klinische und forense Bedeutung* [The Ganser symptom and its clinical and forensic importance]. Berlin, Germany: Hirschwald.
Highley, J. R., Walker, M. A., Esiri, M. M., Crow, T. J., & Harrison, P. J. (2002). Asymmetry of the uncinate fasciculus: A post-mortem study of normal subjects and patients with schizophrenia. *Cerebral Cortex, 12*, 1218–1224.
ICD-10. (1992). *Classification of mental and behavioral disorders: Clinical descriptions and diagnostic guidelines*. Geneva, Switzerland: World Health Organization.
Janet, P. (1898). *Nevroses et idees fixes* (Vols. 1 and 2): Paris, Felix Alcan [cited after van der Kolk & van der Hart, 1989].
Janet, P. (1907). *The major symptoms of hysteria: Fifteen lectures given in the Medical School of Harvard University.* New York, NY: Macmillan.
Joels, M., & Baram, T. Z. (2009). The neuro-symphony of stress. *Nature Reviews Neuroscience, 10*, 459–466.
Johnson, J. G., Cohen, P., Kasen, S., & Brook, J. S. (2006). Dissociative disorders among adults in the community, impaired functioning, and axis I and II comorbidity. *Journal of Psychiatric Research, 40*, 131–140.
Jones, E., Fear, N. T., & Wessely, S. (2007). Shell shock and mild traumatic brain injury: A historical review. *American Journal of Psychiatry, 164*, 1641–1645.
Jung, C. G. (1902). Ein Fall von hysterischem Stupor bei einer Untersuchungsgefangenen [A case of hysteric stupor in a prisoner on trial]. *Journal für Psychologie und Neurologie, 1*, 110–122.
Kanzer, M. (1939). Amnesia, a statistical study. *American Journal of Psychiatry, 96*, 711–716.
Kaszniak, A. W., Nussbaum, P. D., Berren, M. R., & Santiago, J. (1988). Amnesia as a consequence of male rape: A case report. *Journal of Abnormal Psychology, 97*, 100–104.
Kiersch, T. A. (1962). Amnesia: A clinical study of ninety-eight cases. *American Journal of Psychiatry, 119*, 57–60.
Kroll, N., Markowitsch, H. J., Knight, R., & von Cramon, D. Y. (1997). Retrieval of old memories – the temporo-frontal hypothesis. *Brain, 120*, 1377–1399.
Kumar, S., Rao, S. L., Sunny, B., & Gangadhar, B. (2007). Widespread cognitive impairment in psychogenic amnesia. *Psychiatry and Clinical Neurosciences, 61*, 583–586.
LaBar, K. S., & Cabeza, R. (2006). Cognitive neuroscience of emotional memory. *Nature Reviews Neuroscience, 7*, 54–64.
Lange, C., & Irle, E. (2004). Enlarged amygdala volume and reduced hippocampal volume in young women with major depression. *Psychological Medicine, 34*, 1059–1064.
Lebel, C., Walker, L., Leemans, A., Phillips, L., & Beaulieu, C. (2008). Microstructural maturation of the human brain from childhood to adulthood. *NeuroImage, 40*, 1055–1055.
Lennox, W. G. (1943). Amnesia, real and feigned. *American Journal of Psychiatry, 99*, 732–743.
Lucchelli, F., & Spinnler, H. (2002). The "psychogenic" versus "organic" conundrum of pure retrograde amnesia: Is it still worth pursuing? *Cortex, 38*, 665–669.
Lupien, S. J., Maheu, F., Tu, M., Fiocco, A., & Schramek, T. E. (2007). The effects of stress and stress hormones on human cognition: Implications for the field of brain and cognition. *Brain and Cognition, 65*, 209–237.
Lupien, S. J., McEwen, B. S., Gunnar, M. R., & Heim, C. (2009). Effects of stress throughout the lifespan on the brain, behaviour and cognition. *Nature Reviews Neuroscience, 10*, 434–445.
MacLean, P. D. (1970). The triune brain, emotion, and the scientific bias. In F. O. Schmitt (Ed.), *The neurosciences: Second study program* (pp. 336–349). New York, NY: Rockefeller University Press.
Maldonado, J. R., & Spiegel, D. (2008). Dissociative disorders. In E. Hales, S. C. Yudofsky, & G. O. Gabbard (Eds.), *The American psychiatric publishing textbook of psychiatry* (5th ed.). Arlington, VA: American Psychiatric Publishers.
Markowitsch, H. J. (1992). *Intellectual functions and the brain. An historical perspective*. Toronto, ON: Hogrefe & Huber Publishers.
Markowitsch, H. J. (1995). Which brain regions are critically involved in the retrieval of old episodic memory? *Brain Research Reviews, 21*, 117–127.
Markowitsch, H. J. (1996). Organic and psychogenic retrograde amnesia: Two sides of the same coin? *Neurocase, 2*, 357–371.
Markowitsch, H. J. (1999a). Neuroimaging and mechanisms of brain function in psychiatric disorders. *Current Opinion in Psychiatry, 12*, 331–337.
Markowitsch, H. J. (1999b). Functional neuroimaging correlates of functional amnesia. *Memory, 7*, 561–583.
Markowitsch, H. J. (2000a). Anatomical bases of memory disorders. In M. S. Gazzaniga (Ed.), *The new cognitive neurosciences* (2nd ed., pp. 781–795). Cambridge, MA: MIT Press.
Markowitsch, H. J. (2000b). Repressed memories. In E. Tulving (Ed.), *Memory, consciousness, and the brain: The Tallinn conference* (pp. 319–330). Philadelphia, PA: Psychology Press.
Markowitsch, H. J. (2002). Functional retrograde amnesia – mnestic block syndrome. *Cortex, 38*, 651–654.

Markowitsch, H. J., Calabrese, P., Fink, G. R., Durwen, H. F., Kessler, J., Härting, C., ... Gehlen, W. (1997). Impaired episodic memory retrieval in a case of probable psychogenic amnesia. *Psychiatry Research: Neuroimaging Section, 74*, 119–126.

Markowitsch, H. J., Calabrese, P., Haupts, M., Durwen, H. F., Liess, J., & Gehlen, W. (1993). Searching for the anatomical basis of retrograde amnesia. *Journal of Clinical and Experimental Neuropsychology, 15*, 947–967.

Markowitsch, H. J., Calabrese, P., Liess, J., Haupts, M., Durwen, H. F., & Gehlen, W. (1993). Retrograde amnesia after traumatic injury of the temporo-frontal cortex. *Journal of Neurology, Neurosurgery and Psychiatry, 56*, 988–992.

Markowitsch, H. J., Calabrese, P., Neufeld, H., Gehlen, W., & Durwen, H. F. (1999). Retrograde amnesia for famous events and faces after left fronto-temporal brain damage. *Cortex, 35*, 243–252.

Markowitsch, H. J., Fink, G. R., Thöne, A. I. M., Kessler, J., & Heiss, W.-D. (1997). Persistent psychogenic amnesia with a PET-proven organic basis. *Cognitive Neuropsychiatry, 2*, 135–158.

Markowitsch, H. J., Kessler, J., Kalbe, E., & Herholz, K. (1999). Functional amnesia and memory consolidation. A case of persistent anterograde amnesia with rapid forgetting following whiplash injury. *Neurocase, 5*, 189–200.

Markowitsch, H. J., Kessler, J., Russ, M. O., Frölich, L., Schneider, B., & Maurer, K. (1999). Mnestic block syndrome. *Cortex, 35*, 219–230.

Markowitsch, H. J., Kessler, J., Van der Ven, C., Weber-Luxenburger, G., & Heiss, W.-D. (1998). Psychic trauma causing grossly reduced brain metabolism and cognitive deterioration. *Neuropsychologia, 36*, 77–82.

Markowitsch, H. J., Kessler, J., Weber-Luxenburger, G., Van der Ven, C., & Heiss, W.-D. (2000). Neuroimaging and behavioral correlates of recovery from "mnestic block syndrome" and other cognitive deteriorations. *Neuropsychiatry, Neuropsychology, and Behavioral Neurology, 13*, 60–66.

Markowitsch, H. J., Thiel, A., Kessler, J., von Stockhausen, H.-M., & Heiss, W.-D. (1997). Ecphorizing semi-conscious episodic information via the right temporopolar cortex – a PET study. *Neurocase, 3*, 445–449.

Markowitsch, H. J., & Welzer, H. (2009). *The development of autobiographic memory.* Hove, UK: Psychology Press.

McCarthy, M. M., Auger, A. P., Bale, T. L., De Vries, G. J., Dunn, G. A., Forger, N. G., ... Wilson, M. E. (2009). The epigenetics of sex differences in the brain. *Journal of Neuroscience, 29*, 12815–12823.

McGowan, P. O., Sasaki, A., D'Alessio, A. C., Dymov, S., Labonte, B., Szyf, M., ... Meany, M. J. (2009). Epigenetic regulation of the glucocorticoid receptor in human brain associates with childhood abuse. *Nature Neuroscience, 12*, 342–348.

McKay, G. C. M., & Kopelman, M. D. (2009). Psychogenic amnesia: When memory complaints are medically unexplained. *Advances in Psychiatric Treatment, 15*, 152–158.

Mehta, M. A., Golembo, N. I., Nosarti, C., Colvert, E., Mota, A., Williams, S. C., ... Sonuga-Barke, E. J. (2009). Amygdala, hippocampal and corpus callosum size following severe early institutional deprivation: The English and Romanian adoptees study pilot. *Journal of Child Psychology and Psychiatry, 50*, 943–951.

Meyer, A. (1904). The anatomical facts and clinical varieties of traumatic insanity. *American Journal of Insanity, 60*, 373–441.

Miller, P., Bramble, D., & Buxton, N. (1997). Case study: Ganser syndrome in children and adolescents. *Journal of the American Academy of Child and Adolescent Psychiatry, 36*, 112–115.

Nakamura, M., Paul, G., McCarley, R. O., Levitt, J. J., Hsu, L., Kawashima, T., ... Shenton, M. E. (2007). Altered orbitofrontal sulcogyral pattern in schizophrenia. *Brain, 130*, 693–707.

Nardi, T. J., & Di Scipio, W. J. (1977). The Ganser syndrome in an adolescent Hispanic-black female. *American Journal of Psychiatry, 134*, 453–454.

Nardo, D., Högberg, G., Looi, J. C. L., Larsson, S., Hällström, T., & Pagani, M. (2010). Gray matter density in limbic and paralimbic cortices is associated with trauma load and EMDR outcome in PTSD patients. *Journal of Psychiatric Research, 44*, 477–485.

O'Brien, J. T. (1997). The "glucocorticoid cascade" hypothesis in man. *British Journal of Psychiatry, 170*, 199–201.

Ouellet, J., Rouleau, I., Labrecque, R., Bernier, G., & Scherzer, P. B. (2008). Two routes to losing one's past life: A brain trauma, an emotional trauma. *Behavioural Neurology, 20*, 27–38.

Pick, A. (1905). Zur Psychologie des Vergessens bei Geistes- und Nervenkranken [The psychology of forgetting in psychiatric and neurological patients]. *Archiv für kriminologische Anthropologie, 18*, 251–261.

Pietrini, P. (2003). Toward a biochemistry of the mind? *American Journal of Psychiatry, 160*, 1907–1908.

Piolino, P., Hannequin, D., Desgranges, B., Girard, C., Beaunieux, H., Gittard, B., ... Eustache, F. (2005). Right ventral frontal hypometabolism and abnormal sense of self in a case of disproportionate retrograde amnesia. *Cognitive Neuropsychology, 22*, 1005–1034.

Post, R. M., Weiss, S. R., Smith, M., Rosen, J., & Frye, M. (1995). Stress, conditioning, and the temporal aspects of affective disorders. *Annals New York Academy of Sciences, 771*, 677–696.

Raecke, J. (1908). Ueber epileptische Wanderzustände (Fugues, Poriomanie) [On epileptic states of wandering (fugues, poriomania)]. *Archiv für Psychiatrie und Nervenkrankheiten, 43*, 398–423.

Reinhold, N., Kühnel, S., Brand, M., & Markowitsch, H. J. (2006). Functional neuroimaging in memory and memory disturbances. *Current Medical Imaging Reviews, 2*, 35–57.

Reinhold, N., & Markowitsch, H. J. (2007). Emotion and consciousness in adolescent psychogenic amnesia. *Journal of Neuropsychology, 1*, 53–64.

Reinhold, N., & Markowitsch, H. J. (2009). Retrograde episodic memory and emotion: A perspective from patients with dissociative amnesia. *Neuropsychologia, 47*, 2197–2206.

Ross, C. A., Joshi, S., & Currie, R. (1990). Dissociative experiences in the general population. *American Journal of Psychiatry, 147*, 1547–1552.

Seligman, R., & Kirmayer, L. J. (2008). Dissociative experience and cultural neuroscience: Narrative, metaphor and mechanism. *Culture, Medicine and Psychiatry, 32*, 31–64.

Serra, L., Fadda, L., Buccione, I., Caltagirone, C., & Carlesimo, G. A. (2007). Psychogenic and organic amnesia: A multidimensional assessment of clinical, neuroradiological, neuropsychological and psychopathological features. *Behavioural Neurology, 18*, 53–64.

Spiegel, D. (2006). Recognizing traumatic dissociation. *American Journal of Psychiatry, 163*, 4.

Spiegel, D., & Cardena, E. (1991). Disintegrated experience: The dissociative disorders revisited. *Journal of Abnormal Psychology, 100*, 366–378.

Staniloiu, A., Bender, A., Smolewska, K., Ellis, J., Abramowitz, C., & Markowitsch, H. J. (2009). Ganser syndrome with work-related onset in a patient with a background of immigration. *Cognitive Neuropsychiatry, 14*, 180–198.

Stertz, G. (1910). Über psychogene Erkrankungen und Querulantenwahn nach Trauma nebst ihrer Bedeutung für die

Begutachtungspraxis [On psychogenic diseases and delusions of querulous persons after trauma and their importance for the practice of expert reports]. *Zeitschrift für ärztliche Fortbildung* (pp. 201–211).

Stracciari, A., Ghidoni, E., Guarino, M., Poletti, M., & Pazzaglia, P. (1994). Post-traumatic retrograde amnesia with selective impairment of autobiographical memory. *Cortex, 30*, 459–468.

Szeszko, P. R., Betensky, J. D., Mentschel, C., Gunduz-Bruce, H., Lencz, T., Ashtari, M., ... Bilder, R. M. (2006). Increased stress and smaller anterior hippocampal volume. *Neuroreport, 17*, 1825–1828.

Szeszko, P. R., Robinson, D., Alvir, J. M. J., Bilder, R. M., Lencz, T., Ashtari, M., ... Bogerts, B. (1999). Orbital frontal and amygdala volume reductions in obsessive-compulsive disorder. *Archives of General Psychiatry, 56*, 913–919.

Thom, D. A., & Fenton, N. (1920). Amnesias in war cases. *American Journal of Psychiatry, 76*, 437–448.

Thomas Antérion, C., Mazzola, L., Foyatier-Michel, N., & Laurent, B. (2008). À la recherche de la mémoire perdue: Nature des troubles et mode de récupération d'un cas d'amnésie rétrograde pure. *Revue Neurologique, 164*, 271–277.

Tramoni, E., Aubert-Khalfa, S., Guye, M., Ranjeva, J. P., Felician, O., & Ceccaldi, M. (2009). Hypo-retrieval and hyper-suppression mechanisms in functional amnesia. *Neuropsychologia, 47*, 611–624.

Tulving, E. (2002). Episodic memory: From mind to brain. *Annual Reviews of Psychology, 53*, 1–25.

Tulving, E. (2002). Episodic memory and autonoesis: Uniquely human? In H. S. Terrace & J. Metcalfe (Eds.), *The missing link in cognition: Self-knowing consciousness in man and animals* (pp. 3–56). New York, NY: Oxford University Press.

Ulrich-Lai, Y. M., & Herman, J. P. (2009). Neural regulation of endocrine and autonomic stress responses. *Nature Reviews Neuroscience, 10*, 397–409.

Valentino, K., Toth, S. L., & Cicchetti, D. (2009). Autobiographical memory functioning among abused, neglected, and nonmaltreated children: The overgeneral memory effect. *Journal of Child Psychology and Psychiatry, 50*, 1029–1038.

van der Kolk, B. A., & van der Hart, O. (1989). Pierre Janet and the breakdown of adaptation in psychological trauma. *American Journal of Psychiatry, 146*, 1530–1540.

van Erp, T. G. M., Saleh, P. A., Huttunen, M., Lönnqvist, J., Kaprio, J., Salonen, O., ... Cannon, T. D. (2004). Hippocampal volumes in schizophrenic twins. *Archives of General Psychiatry, 61*, 346–353.

Vermetten, E., Schmahl, C., Lindner, S., Loewenstein, R. J., & Bremner, J. D. (2006). Hippocampal and amygdalar volumes in dissociative identity disorder. *American Journal of Psychiatry, 163*, 630–636.

Weinstock, M. (2008). The long-term behavioural consequences of prenatal stress. *Neuroscience and Biobehavioral Reviews, 32*, 1073–1086.

Woltär, O. (1906). Über den Bewusstseinszustand während der Fugue [On the state of consciousness during a fugue state]. *Jahrbücher für Psychiatrie und Neurologie, 27*, 125–143.

Woodward, S. H., Kaloupek, D. G., Streeter, C. C., Kimble, M. O., Reiss, A. L., Eliez, S., ... Arsenault, N. J. (2006). Hippocampal volume, PTSD, and alcoholism in combat veterans. *American Journal of Psychiatry, 163*, 674–681.

Xiao, Z., Yan, H., Wang, Z., Zou, Z., Xu, Y., Chen, J. ... Keyes, B. B. (2006). Trauma and dissociation in China. *American Journal of Psychiatry, 163*, 1388–1391.

Zingerle, H. (1912). *Über transitorische Geistesstörungen und deren forensische Beurteilung. Juristisch-psychiatrische Grenzfragen* [On transitory mental disturbances and their forensic evaluation. Borderline or minor juridical-psychiatric cases]. Jena, Germany: Gustav Fischer.

Angelica Staniloiu

Physiological Psychology
University of Bielefeld
PO Box 100131
D-33501 Bielefeld
Germany
Tel. +49 521 106 4488
Fax +49 521 106 6049
E-mail Astaniloiu@uni-bielefeld.de

Review Article

Dissociation Following Traumatic Stress

Etiology and Treatment

Maggie Schauer and Thomas Elbert

Department of Psychology, University of Konstanz, Germany

Abstract. We postulate that the cascade "Freeze-Flight-Fight-Fright-Flag-Faint" is a coherent sequence of six fear responses that escalate as a function of defense possibilities and proximity to danger during life-threat. The actual sequence of trauma-related response dispositions acted out in an extremely dangerous situation therefore depends on the appraisal of the threat by the organism in relation to her/his own power to act (e.g., age and gender) as well as the perceived characteristics of threat and perpetrator. These reaction patterns provide optimal adaption for particular stages of imminence. Subsequent to the traumatic threats, portions of the experience may be replayed. The actual individual cascade of defense stages a survivor has gone through during the traumatic event will repeat itself every time the fear network, which has evolved peritraumatically, is activated again (i.e., through internal or external triggers or, e.g., during exposure therapy).When a parasympathetically dominated "shut-down" was the prominent peri-traumatic response during the traumatic incident, comparable dissociative responses may dominate responding to subsequently experienced threat and may also reappear when the traumatic memory is reactivated. Repeated experience of traumatic stress forms a fear network that can become pathologically detached from contextual cues such as time and location of the danger, a condition which manifests itself as posttraumatic stress disorder (PTSD). Intrusions, for example, can therefore be understood as repetitive displays of fragments of the event, which would then, depending on the dominant physiological response during the threat, elicit a corresponding combination of hyperarousal and dissociation. We suggest that trauma treatment must therefore differentiate between patients on two dimensions: those with peritraumatic sympathetic activation versus those who went down the whole defense cascade, which leads to parasympathetic dominance during the trauma and a corresponding replay of physiological and dissociative responding, when reminded. The differential management of dissociative stages ("fright" and "faint") has important treatment implications.

Keywords: dissociation, complex trauma, PTSD, sexual abuse, borderline personality disorder, tonic immobility, fainting

A coherent mental structure requires organized and interconnected representations of salient external and internal events, including sensory perceptions, affective and behavioral responding, and the conscious implications of a given context in terms of meaning (Marmar, Weiss, & Metzler, 1998; Van der Hart, Nijenhuis, Steele, & Brown, 2004; Schauer, Neuner, & Elbert, 2005). Experience of overwhelming threat may interfere with the process of integrating active elements of sensation, emotion, and cognition into the particular declarative memory of the event and thus result in disorders of the trauma spectrum (Brewin, 2001; Conway & Pleydell-Pearce, 2000; Ehlers & Clark, 2000; Elbert, Rockstroh, Kolassa, Schauer, & Neuner, 2006; Schauer et al., 2005; Van der Kolk, McFarlane, & Weisaeth, 1996). When later confronted with trauma reminders, survivors typically "replay" their original response of the traumatic event (e.g., Keane, Zimering, & Caddell, 1985). When a parasympathetically dominated "shut-down" was the prominent peritraumatic response to the traumatic incident, comparable dissociative responses may dominate responding to subsequently experienced threat and may also reappear when the traumatic memory is reactivated, such as during script-driven imagery (Lang, Bradley, & Cuthbert, 1998) or trauma-focused treatment (Schauer & Elbert, 2008). Strong dissociative reactions that may even include fainting obviously prevent the success of therapeutic measures that attempt to integrate the trauma memory into the autobiographic narrative and hence pose a serious obstacle to successful treatment of disorders of the trauma spectrum. Instead of trauma-focused therapy, these patients therefore typically receive skill-training, for example, how to identify and avoid potential triggers that induce detachment or how to end dissociative responding once it has been triggered. Current clinical practice adds to a varying degree elements from dialectic behavior therapy (Hunter et al., 2005; Linehan, 1993). Unfortunately, these strategies are not sufficient remedies for patients with trauma-related dissociative symptoms (Dyer, Priebe, Steil, Krüger, & Bohus, 2009) and clinical trials have identified dissociative symptoms as predictive for a negative treatment outcome (Spitzer, Barnow, Freyberger, & Grabe, 2007). This is not surprising, since dissociation prevents emotional processing and learning (Ebner-Priemer et al., 2009) due to the "shut-down" symptomatology typically characteristic of dissociative states (Simeon, Guralnik, Knutelska, Yehuda, & Schmeidler, 2003, p. 93).

The current concept of posttraumatic stress disorder (PTSD) does not distinguish whether the reminder of the traumatic experiences results in a fight-flight alarm response

DOI: 10.1027/0044-3409/a000018

or in a dissociative block of sympathetic arousal with a subsequent excessive vagal tone. However, Foa, Riggs, and Gershuny (1995) noted that different PTSD symptoms such as intense hyperarousal versus numbing may represent distinct pathological processes and that grouping PTSD subjects with different symptom patterns in the same diagnostic category may interfere with our understanding and treatment of post-trauma psychopathology. Bremner et al. (1999) suggested that there might be two subtypes of trauma responses, one characterized by intrusive memories and hyperarousal and the other predominately dissociative. Results reviewed by Lanius, Bluhm, Lanius, and Pain (2006) indicate that comparable patterns may indeed be seen in the neuroimaging laboratory: Key brain areas involved in the hyperarousal response include the anterior cingulate and surrounding medial prefrontal cortex, the amygdala and possibly the thalamus, while higher-order sensory association cortices are active during dissociative responses. Based on our own observations (Kolassa & Elbert, 2007; Kolassa et al., 2007; Ray et al., 2006), we assume that these abnormal activation patterns in parietal and occipital cortex might be driven by abnormalities in the temporal cortex and possibly limbic structures. In a meta-analysis of psychophysiological findings in PTSD, Pole (2007) acknowledges the weak consistency of psychophysiological responding and suggests that greater consideration be given to subtyping of PTSD.

Understanding Dissociation Within an Evolutionary-Based Framework of Mental Disorders

Dissociation was introduced as a term into psychiatry already at the end of the 19th century (Janet, 1889; Putnam, 1989), however, a conclusive, coherent conceptualization has not yet been eved. Experts note that "conceptual clarity regarding trauma-related dissociation is urgently needed" (Van der Hart, Nijenhuis, Steele, & Brown, 2004). Despite the appreciated clinical significance of dissociation, there is an ongoing controversy about its theoretical foundation. It "lacks a single, coherent referent ... that all investigators in the field embrace" (Cardena, 1994), and it still does today: "there is no consistent agreement about precisely what dissociation 'is' ... dissociation represents a semantically open term leading to conceptual confusions which – in turn – might restrict its value" (Spitzer, Barnow, Freyberger, & Grabe, 2006). The field is obviously hampered by a missing etiological model (Dutra, Bureau, Holmes, Lyubchik, & Lyons-Ruth, 2009). We propose that an evolutionary-based understanding of mental disorders (Brune, 2002; Jones & Blackshaw, 2000; Wakefield, 1992, 1999) permits to sort different theoretical approaches and thus facilitates the etiological modeling of such behavior. Such progress would especially be helpful for the development of effective therapeutic interventions; it would guide the therapist's measures when confronted with a client with the potential of severe dissociative responding, and it thus would overcome the dissociation-related obstacles during the course of trauma-focused therapy.

An evolutionary perspective suggests that dissociation, albeit hazarding the consequences of physical injury, is an adaptive, and when strike is close, final remaining survival response to specific types of life-threats that include nearness of a superior perpetrator or other situations dominated by helplessness. Dissociation enables survival in the following situations:

- when the organism is in direct and close encounter with a dangerous perpetrator, for example, when there is skin contact;
- in the presence of body fluids with danger of contamination, for example, blood or sperm;
- when bodily integrity is already injured, for example, invasion, penetration, sharp objects (e.g., teeth and knife) at the skin.

These situations require physiological adaptations, including immobility, pain tolerance and with it "switches" in consciousness, information processing, and behavior that are perceived as strange, because they are outside the range of ordinary experiences.

Evolution has equipped us with a defense armament to imminent threat. A coherent sequence of defense responses that escalate as a function of proximity to danger and threat has been established by evolutionary biology and psychophysiology alike. It seems that the defense process is a chain-linking sequence of steps that build on each other like a cascade. Obviously the animal and human organism is able to orchestrate its survival strategy according to the specific situation and along a staged process, called "defense cascade" (Lang, Davis, & Öhman, 2000). During life-threat, not every stage of the defense cascade is necessarily passed through by the individual. The actual sequence of trauma-related response dispositions carried out in an extremely dangerous situation is dynamic and depends on several factors. It is known that defensive reflex reactivity is organized sequentially to allow optimal responding depending on the proximity of the threat (Bradley, Codispoti, Cuthbert, & Lang, 2001; Fanselow & Lester, 1988) and with it its speed of approach. In addition, a particular response may be classically conditioned and thus depends on previous experiences with threatening events (Adenauer, Catani, Keil, Aichinger, & Neuner, 2009). Moreover, we propose that defense reactivity is organized to account for battlesomeness (chances to win a fight) of the threatened individual, that is, the appraisal of the threat by the organism in relation to its own power to counteract (age, gender, physical condition, defensive abilities, etc.) and, not least, for the threat-specifics (type of threat, type and speed of approach, context, threat involving blood loss, etc.). Whereas the dynamics of the defense cascade progresses in gradients of alternating ascending and descending activation, the various defense responses can be categorized into two general forms, namely active defense and immobility (Vila et al., 2007).

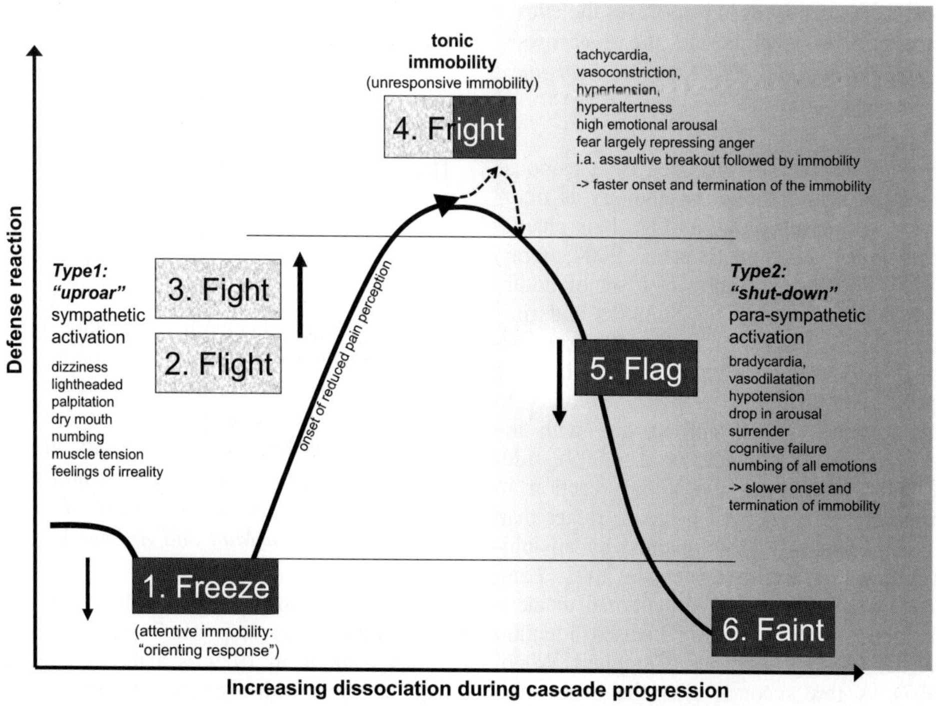

Figure 1. Schematic illustration of the defense cascade as it progresses along the 6-F course of action. The "uproar" sympathetic arousal reaches a maximum at the fright stage, eventually superseded by the onset of dissociative "shut down" (gray area).

The different suggestions for a defense cascade model consist of the following components: "freezing" in case of a large distance between subject and threat; "flight" when the distance is reduced; "fight" when the distance is eliminated; and "immobility" in case of prolonged elimination of distance (Ogden, Minton, & Pain, 2006). More recently, a model has integrated "faint" as another response possibility (Alboni, Alboni, & Bertorelle, 2008; Bracha, 2004; Lang et al., 2000; Moore & Amstey, 1962).

First, the freezing (orienting response – OR) facilitates a "stop-look-listen" perception of the threat. Pavlov (1927) referred to it as "Shto Eta/What is it?" – reflex that turns the sensory systems to the source of stimulation. This can be viewed as a collection of bodily responses that assist in processing the stimulus further, such as pupillary dilation, and a transient drop in heart rate. Then, having identified the danger and calculated the best means to escape, the mammal typically flees. If it is unable to successfully flee and the predator is upon it, it will initially fight. However, when there is clearly no chance of successfully fleeing or fighting, the animal may resort to immobility, in the hope that the predator will lose interest. Should the opportunity then present itself, the animal might make a final attempt to escape.

"Dissociation" as a defense disposition, however, has not been systematically included in the model of the defense cascade, although it accounts in large parts for an aggravated symptom spectrum of human survivors of life-threat and has immense treatment implications. Peri-traumatic dissociation is a set of subjective experiences, which includes alterations in perception of time, place, and self during and immediately after trauma exposure. Evidence has shown the predictive value of reported peritraumatic dissociation for the development of mental health problems including PTSD (Birmes et al., 2003; Bryant, 2007; Breh & Seidler, 2007), especially peritraumatic tonic immobility is a risk factor (Fusé, Forsyth, Marx, Gallup, & Weaver, 2007; Fiszman et al., 2008).

Our model wants to fill the missing link and suggests six defense responses, notably *Freeze, Flight, Fight, Fright, Flag,* and eventually *Faint,* whereby during the two Fs *Flight* and *Fight* bodily responses are mainly regulated via the sympathetic branch ("uproar reactions") and the following three Fs, the second half of the cascade, are dominated by parasympathetic arousal, determining the spectrum of dissociative responding ("shut-down" reactions: *Fright, Flag,* and *Faint*). We thus may arrange the stages of the defense cascade in form of an inverted u-shaped arousal function with the alarming flight-fight responses on the ascent of the curve and the set of dissociative variants on the descent (see Figure 1). In the next section, we discuss this evolutionary repertoire of armament step by step.

Stage 1 = *Freeze (Attentive Immobility)* – The OR

"Fear is often preceded by astonishment, and is so far akin to it, that both lead to the senses of sight and hearing being instantly aroused. In both cases the eyes and mouth are widely opened, and the eyebrows raised. . . ." (Charles Darwin, *The Expression of the Emotions in Man and Animals*).

The fight or flight response is preceded by a response with a varying period of time known in ethology as freezing behavior or in psychophysiology as OR. It is characterized by information gathering (Bracha, 2004; Gray, 1987; Pavlov, 1927) and the activation of a set of bodily responses that assist in processing the stimulus and may prepare for further stages (Rockstroh et al., 1987), sometimes referred to as hypervigilance or hyperarousal: being on guard, watchful, alert, ready to respond. Contrary to the classic stress response model and in line with the defense cascade perspective (Adenauer et al., 2009), studies have consistently found that the initial reaction to aversive stimuli is characterized by a decrease rather than an increase of heart rate and is accompanied by an inhibition of the startle response (Bradley et al., 2001; Lang et al., 2000). This "fear bradycardia" (attentional or alerting response) includes motor inhibition, focused attention to the threat, and decelerating heart rate (Campbell, Wood, & McBride, 1997). A few seconds after the onset of a threatening stimulus, the direction of the physiological response reverses toward cardiac acceleration and an increase of the startle reflex. The transient pause before action mobilization is associated with heightened sensory perception and processing of contextual details and has been interpreted as the human counterpart of the freezing state in animals (Graham, 1979; Sokolov, 1963).

Ethological research has demonstrated that prey that remain "frozen" during potential threat are more likely to avoid detection because the visual cortex and the retina of mammalian carnivores primarily detect shapes through moving objects rather than color (Nesse, 1999; Page, 1994). This freezing might play a role in survival if it helps a hunted animal to blend in with its surroundings by remaining as motionless as an inanimate object, thereby allowing the shift of attention of predators to other moving or noisy stimuli in the neighborhood. Interestingly, in human subjects, who have survived several traumatic events and suffer from PTSD with hyperarousal as a consequence, the OR is passed by in the defense cascade (Adenauer et al., 2009) and the alarm response is immediately initiated, that is, the defense cascade is adjusted to allow for a rapid flight response to threatening cues without any further exploration of the stimulus. This finding is consistent with the observation that PTSD patients react to threatening cues and trauma reminders with a hypersensitive alarm system (Rauch et al., 2000). In contrast to fright, as a measure to eliminate aggression and prevent attack, "freezing" actually means the initial orienting response at the beginning of the defense cascade, which is important to achieve concentrated attentiveness to focus on the signs of threat. This attentive immobility is primarily a transient defense strategy, preliminary to fighting or fleeing, in which the animal stops moving to avoid detection and shifts resources to perceptual and executive functions to better locate the predator and plan escape.

Stages 2 and 3 = *Flight* and *Fight*: Toward the Arousal Peak of the Alarm Response

". . . The heart beats quickly and violently, so that it palpitates or knocks against the ribs . . .. That the skin is much affected under the sense of great fear, we see in the marvellous manner in which perspiration immediately exudes from it . . .. The hairs also on the skin stand erect; and the superficial muscles shiver. In connection with the disturbed action of the heart, the breathing is hurried. The salivary glands act imperfectly; the mouth becomes dry, and is often opened and shut . . ." (Charles Darwin, *The Expression of the Emotions in Man and Animals*).

The long known "fight or flight" response, also called the "acute stress response," physiologically detailed by Walter Cannon in 1929 as a theory suggests that animals react to threat with a general discharge of the sympathetic nervous system, and has subsequently been advanced by evolutionary psychologists (Bracha, 2004). If a stimulus is perceived as a major threat, a more intense and prolonged discharge of the locus coeruleus activates the sympathetic division of the autonomic nervous system (ANS). The initial OR is followed by attempts to flee, and, if not successful, by attempts to fight. The organism becomes extremely aroused. An "alarm response" is initiated, with sympathetic arousal and sympathetically modulated adrenal release that enables the organism to counterstrike (heart rate acceleration, blood pressure elevation, and vasoconstriction). At the central level endorphins are released to reduce pain and with it somatosensory perception and awareness is dampened.

The activation of the sympathetic branch at this point enables a reorganization of blood supply (vasoconstriction of peripheral vessels – cold skin, dilatation of certain organ supply vessels) in order to increase blood flow to the heart and muscles while decreasing the likelihood of blood loss after injury through peripheral vasoconstriction. Blood pressure is rising through increased cardiac output. Preparedness for aggressive engagement increases. Faster and deeper breath facilitates increased oxygenation of important organs and muscles and increased perspiration can cool the body. Moist palms at the same time allow a better grip to flee, lowering the chances for injury. Activity not acutely needed is halted, for example, digestion reduces, bowel mobility halts to a point of emptying out.

At the height of arousal, the adaptivity to flee or fight begins to turn: General fear symptoms are experienced, including dizziness, nausea, palpitation, drowsiness, lightheadedness, tension, blurred vision, feelings of irreality, numbing, and tingling appear (prodromal period before "shut-down"/pre-syncope; see European Society of Cardiology guidelines, 2009). At the extreme apex, when the organism experiences a climaxing activation, parasympathetic activation sets in. The acute response to extreme stress becomes a peritraumatic "panic-like" dual autonomic activation. Stage 4 is reached, which we detail below. Moreover, a "*shut-down*" reaction and with it the various forms of dissociation appear. At this stage, sensation, perception, motor abilities, and speech behavior are dramatically altered. Before we continue in the characterization of the stages, we therefore discuss principles of the shut-down.

The Onset of Dissociative Shut-Down: Functional Sensory Deafferentation, Motor Paralysis, and Loss of Language Functions

DSM-IV characterizes dissociation as disruption of the usually integrated functions of consciousness, memory, identity, or perception of the environment. ICD-10 acknowledges that it may also involve the sensory and motor systems, leading to symptoms, which are subsumed under the term of conversion: "partial or complete loss of the normal integration, ... immediate sensations, and control of bodily movements".[1] In general, dissociation can be understood in three distinct ways: (1) as a lack of integration of mental modules or systems, (2) as an altered state of consciousness, and (3) as defense mechanism. All of these are partial or even complete failures to deliberately control processes and take actions that can normally be influenced by an act of volition, for example, the ability to bring accessible information into conscious awareness or move voluntary muscles. Furthermore, memory retrieval deficits appear (e.g., amnesia, conversion, somatoform disorders, "detachment," out-of-body/depersonalization, and derealization) as subjective experiences of an altered state of consciousness characterized by alienation of oneself or the external world, with a flattening of emotional experiences (Allen, 2001; Holmes et al., 2005). It is well known that dissociation involves dysregulation of the visual and somatosensory modalities (Bernstein and Putnam, 1986; Bremner et al., 1998). Nijenhuis et al. have also found a loss of normal integration of somatoform components of experience, bodily reactions and functions (Nijenhuis, Spinhoven, Vanderlinden, Van Dyck, & Van der Hart, 1998). The fact that dissociative symptoms also pertain to functions of movement, sensation, and perception has been largely overlooked for quite some time (Van der Hart et al., 2004). Previously, this was called "deficit symptom": loss of somatic function that has no evident organic basis, for example, numbness, or loss of sensory function like "hysterical blindness" (Nijenhuis, Van Engen, Kusters, & Van der Hart, 2001; Nijenhuis et al., 1998). Accordingly, we have found that in stages of shut-down as well as during later reappearance of dissociative states, reality construction becomes more difficult. These typical behavioral features include that threatened individuals cannot hear, see, or perceive well any more. They move less – obviously due to excessive muscle tension – until motility stops. Furthermore, they have difficulties to understand language and are unable to produce speech. Functional interruption of afferent and efferent nerve impulses is taking place. Thoughts and reasoning no longer make sense. The mind is confused. Time perception changes dramatically.

To summarize, we postulate that dissociation is adaptive and manifests itself behaviorally on three dominant levels as life-threat escalates: (1) rise of and finally complete functional sensory deafferentation, (2) decline of and finally absence of efferent motor commands, and (3) decline of and finally absence of speech perception and production. If motionlessness of a human organism is of crucial importance in such moments of life-threat, nature needs to take care of systems that might corrupt adaptive behavior – sensation, movement, and speech. As long as the victim can feel pain and anger and is able to act, he or she will attempt to move away from the aversive stimulus or fight it off. When the organism is about to be attacked, immobility tends to be combined with analgesia, which is functional in that perception of pain would divert attention of the prey from defensive concerns (Bolles & Fanselow, 1980). Furthermore, tonic immobility is combined with numbing for anger affect, whilst at the same time fear emotions reach their maximum. In order to enable a maximal defensive and "dead" appearance ("as if dead," "playing possum"), which provides survival advantage by complete giving in, and cessation of fighting, and moving, perceptions and later emotions need to be switched off or deactivated. To guarantee motionlessness in these highly perilous situations, the organism should be unable and unwilling to use voluntary muscles and should feel neither anger nor pain, be finally emotionally numb, as if anesthetized. During this cascade numbing of sensations, analgesia and anger inhibition are followed, at a later stage, by numbing of fear as well. These effects inhibit reactions, which would compromise optimal protection in this stage of imminence. For example, grooming and licking wounds would attract attention and would elicit further attack (Siegfried, Frischknecht, & Nunez de Souza, 1990). It is biologically important at that point not to show any recuperative behavior or to care for injuries. This is only possible through reduction of panic and fear (Siegfried et al., 1990; Van der Kolk, 1994), suppression and delay of emotional and panic escape behavior, and inhibition of the production of sounds (Kalin, 1993; Kalin & Shelton, 1989). Suarez and Gallup describe an inability to call out and scream as a consequence of suppressed vocal behavior (Suarez & Gallup, 1979). The loss of capacity to communicate, sometimes described as mutism (Porges, 1995), or "*et vox faucibus hœsit*" (and my voice stuck in my throat) as Vergil has put it, seems adaptive at this stage. Whereas movement and vocalization must be put on complete hold during contact with the offender, on termination of threat imminence, pain perception returns and instigates

[1] World Health Organization. The ICD-10 classification of mental and behavioural disorders. Clinical descriptions and diagnostic guidelines. Geneva: World Health Organization, 1991.

recuperative behavior (Bolles & Fanselow, 1980), including behaviors directed at injuries, grooming behavior, and resting behavior serving to promote healing. The recuperative stage may be considered mainly as a response to nociceptive stimulation arising from injury and tissue damage. While stimuli predicting aversive events come to elicit analgesia, the presentation of a safety signal produced an abrupt change in pain sensitivity, essentially "switching off" conditioned analgesia (Wiertelak, Watkins, & Maier, 1992). The finding that (conditioned) safety signals produce acute anti-analgesic effects in animals is supportive of this view (Fanselow & Lester, 1988). Just as (conditioned) signals for danger elicit analgesia, (conditioned) signals for safety inhibit (conditioned) analgesia. Nociception, subsequently, evokes recuperative behavior.

The thalamus is the principal synaptic relay for information reaching the cortex (Kandel & Schwartz, 1991) and thus the gateway to awareness. All sensory information, except for olfaction, is routed through the thalamus to the cerebral cortex. The thalamus thus plays a major role in regulating arousal, the level of awareness, activity, and consciousness. The adaptive response at this stage, namely *functional sensory deafferentation* on the thalamic level, enables to turn or shut down vision, audition, and somatosensory and proprioceptive information. Changes in hearing, seeing, feeling occur. The thalamus has also been suggested to be involved in mediating the interaction between attention and arousal (Portas et al., 1998), both of which are relevant to the phenomenology of traumatic stress syndromes. Thalamic dysfunction in PTSD has previously been shown by Bremner et al. (1999) and Liberzon, Taylor, Fig, and Koeppe (1996/1997), and also in the laboratory of Lanius et al. (2001, 2003). High levels of arousal during traumatic experiences have been hypothesized to lead to altered thalamic sensory processing (Krystal, Bennett, Bremner, Southwick, & Charney, 1995), which in turn results in a disruption of transmission of sensory information to the cortex, cingulate gyrus, amygdala, and hippocampus. Hence, Krystal, Bremner, Southwick, and Charney (1998) have suggested that this mechanism may enable dissociative symptoms. It is interesting to note that in contrast to those with dissociative responses, persons who showed flashback/reliving/hyperarousal responses exhibited significantly less activation of the thalamus when confronted with trauma scripts (Lanius et al., 2003). Survivors of traumatic events who have experienced peritraumatic dissociative shut-down (e.g., skin contact with offender, presence of contaminating body fluids, and body penetration) often do not report immediate intrusive reexperiencing after the abuse; the emergence of involuntary sensory information about the events can be delayed for years or decades. In the study of Lanius et al. (2002) PTSD subjects who experienced dissociative responses to traumatic script-driven imagery reported that "I was looking down at myself from above," "I was detached from my body," "I was completely zoned out and floating," or "I was emotionless" during the script-driven imagery procedure. All PTSD patients included in this study had chronic histories of emotional, physical, and sexual abuse beginning in childhood, often continuing to the time of investigation. They reported that dissociation had been a defense they had used throughout their lives to escape overwhelming experiences. The lack of autonomic response often observed in PTSD patients during dissociative states is consistent with previous findings on depersonalization responses. Patients even showed a decrease in heart rate when they became depersonalized (Kelly & Walter, 1968; Lader, 1975; Lader & Wing, 1966; Sierra et al., 2002).

In addition, peritraumatically, during life-threat, the organism becomes insensitive to internal or external stimuli, that is, emotions (first anger, and only later fear) and pain. It is not just touch-insensitivity, but reduced nociception (analgesia) and numbing of feelings. A large majority of Albach's (1993) subjects who reported childhood sexual abuse experienced analgesia and kinesthetic anesthesia (insensitivity for touch). In fact, analgesia was the most commonly reported "hysterical" symptom. Laboratory studies with nociceptive stimulation found elevated pain thresholds in dissociative patients (Ludäscher et al., 2007; Schmahl et al., 2006) and demonstrated fear-induced hypoalgesia (Rhudy, Grimes, & Meagher, 2004). Reduced pain sensitivity under conditions of high stress can be central for adaptation and survival (Mayer & Fanselow, 2003; Millan, 2002). There is ample anecdotal evidence from soldiers or survivors of disasters that they could still run and take survival actions, although they were severely injured, bleeding, etc. Both pathways of pain processing seem to be progressively shut down along the defense cascade: the sensory-discriminative and the affective-motivational component (Schmahl et al., 2006). During life-threat victims do not feel pain and, probably most important, it does not matter to them. This rising cognitive, bodily, emotional indifference for the self, when being driven through the defense cascade, is the requirement to ensure survival. When the victim is about to be attacked, analgesia and numbing is functional: Perception of pain (nociception) or fear should not initiate recuperative behavior or draw attention and lead to defensive behavior.

Stage 4 = *Fright* (*Tonic Immobility – Unresponsive Immobility*) – Inhibition of Aggression Through Muscle Restraining When Being Overwhelmed by Threat

> "The frightened man stands like a statue motionless ... the heart beats quickly and violently, ... for the skin instantly becomes pale, as during incipient faintness. This paleness of the surface however, is probably in large part, or exclusively, due to the vasomotor centre being affected in such a manner as to cause the contraction of the small arteries of the skin ... and the superficial muscles shiver ... the breathing is hurried ... the mouth becomes dry ... one of the bestmarked symptoms is the trembling of all the muscles of the body ... " (Charles Darwin, *The Expression of the Emotions in Man and Animals*).

Fright can be understood as the turning point at which the change from the rising to the falling phase occurs, being essentially uninterrupted as it proceeds into the faint. The imminent stage is characterized by coactivation of the sympathetic and parasympathetic system (Löw, Lang, Smith, & Bradley, 2008; Ogden et al., 2006). The high dual autonomic tone is known as a risk for sudden cardiac death (Skinner, 1988, 1985).

The heightened muscle tonus, which enables better action performance, causes the muscles to be overly tense beyond a certain threshold, as well as rigid, and movements to become slow and difficult. At this stage overt behavioral actions are not an option; skeletal muscles tense to a stage of tonic immobility. "Playing dead" in the early ethological literature, or the technical term "fright," best captures the Kraepelinean concept of "*Schreck*" as in "*Schreckneurosen*" (1896). Tonic immobility has also been used to describe the paralysis, which often immobilizes animals such as rodents or birds and a similar state is known from invertebrates when they feel threatened by a predator. The immobility of the organism during the fright stage reminds the observer of spastic paralysis. It looks as if the organism is "frozen like ice" (temporary gross motor inhibition) because of the stiffness involved. This metaphor is used in much of the trauma literature referring to "freezing" as immobility of the body. (Note that the term "*freezing*" in this context should be avoided, as it is already reserved for the OR; see above). In tonic immobility, the organism is emotionally aroused and full of fear, yet unresponsive to even painful stimulation and the posture, which may be held for long periods of time, often appears bizarre (Gallup & Rager, 1996; Ratner, 1967). Memory functions are mainly intact since learning is not disrupted (Gallup, Boren, Suarez, Wallnau, & Gagliardi, 1980) at this stage. While the efferent pathways are already inhibited, the afferent pathways and central processing capabilities remain still intact until a later stage. Tonic immobility or "unresponsive immobility" has been defined by Marks (1987) as "the sudden onset of prolonged stillness and decreased responsivity in a previously active animal in the face of threatening stimulation" (p. 60). The organism appears dead or unresponsive to exteroceptive stimuli, internally the animal is highly alert (Marx, Forsyth, Gallup, Fusé, & Lexington, 2008). This unresponsive immobility is elicited most easily during intense fear and some form of physical restraint or perception of entrapment (Marx et al., 2008; Moskowitz, 2004). In human beings, tonic immobility can be understood as a defensive strategy, developed during an extended period of evolution in which human beings had to face predators in much the same way many animals do today, and designed to maximize the individual's chances of surviving a potentially lethal attack, for example a murderous killing. An immobile prey animal is less likely to be killed and eaten (Marx et al., 2008). Tonic immobility or "thanatosis" is a process by which mammals feign death in order to evade unwelcome attention (Miyatake et al., 2004; Pasteur, 1982). Such catatonia can be understood as an evolutionary-based fear response (Moskowitz, 2004), with features such as immobility, decreased vocalization, analgesia, "waxy flexibility," and evidence of alertness as well as the fixed eye gaze (Dixon, 1998), reducing visual input from the offender and thereby decreasing distress and arousal. At a later stage, a "waxy flexibility" is present.

Thus, the core catatonic symptoms of stupor, mutism, and immobility are directly linked to tonic immobility. In the past, this was for a long time seen as a consequence of "very severe physical or mental stress . . . [such as] a very terrifying experience" (Kahlbaum, 1874/1973, p. 31). The patient remains entirely motionless, without speaking, devoid of any will to move or react to any stimuli. The general impression conveyed by such patients is one of profound mental anguish or an immobility induced by severe mental shock. All in all, these patients give the impression of the deepest mental pain, of being paralyzed after a great fright. Finally, Krystal (1993) argued that catalepsy or catatanoid reactions seen in human beings under conditions of profound helplessness were akin to animal immobility, both of which he characterized as submissive responses in the face of unavoidable danger.

The lack of movement in unresponsive immobility has a fast on and off switch, but can last from a few seconds to many hours (Gallup & Maser, 1977) depending on the species and the situation. Marks (1987, pp. 68–69) conveys that during extreme fear, human beings may be "scared stiff" or "frozen with fear." A paralyzed conscious state with abrupt onset and termination is reported from survivors of attacks by wild animals, by shell-shocked soldiers, and by rape victims (Rocha-Rego et al., 2008; Suarez & Gallup, 1979). Rape-induced tonic immobility was first noted by Suarez and Gallup: inability to move, inability to call out or scream, no loss of consciousness/recall of details of the attack, apparent analgesia, that is, numbness and insensitivity to pain. The researchers noted as well a sensation of feeling cold and shivering. We assign the feeling of cold and trembling to the consequences of adrenaline and vasodilatation whereby body warmth is lost fast and leads to shivering (medical "shock"). Tonic immobility guarantees negative or quiescent behavior even in the presence of massive aversive stimulation (Foley, 1938), a stilled organism that makes no attempt to struggle for freedom or fight. Fear plus the physical prevention of flight seem to bring on the response named catatonic trance, action inhibition, or "death feigning," which appears suddenly (Moore & Amstey, 1962; Pavlov, 1923).

In the PTSD literature tonic immobility has been referred to as peritraumatic panic-like symptoms. The peritraumatic panic reaches its maximum in the fright response, which may enhance survival when there is no longer a perceived possibility of escaping or winning a fight or when there is direct physical contact with the perpetrator (Bracha, Williams, Ralston, Bracha, & Matsukawa, 2004). The clinical relevance of immobility as a survival response may best be illustrated in relation to the behavior of certain victims of violence or sexual assault who exhibit extreme passivity during the assault. Here again, an understanding of the genetically prepared nature of the response might help to ameliorate this dimension of the painful memories that plague some victims who wonder why they did not put up more of a fight. For a long time clinicians, researchers, and legal advocates wondered why only a minority of battered women who report childhood sexual and physical abuse actively resisted the perpetrator (Albach, 1993; Draijer, 1990). Barlow (Barlow, 2004; Burgess & Holmstrom, 1974, 1976) argues that immobility behavior had been overlooked since motor inhibition as evidenced in animals had not been thought to occur in human beings. But since the 1970s the parallel to animal immobility behavior became obvious. For example, Suarez and Gallup (1979) described similarities between tonic immobility and rape-induced paralysis as follows: Changes in body temperature, numbness, analgesia, suppressed vocal behavior, and vivid recall of details. In a later stage another form of immobility (flaccidity) will dominate (see below).

Since tonic immobility is elicited by extreme fear and helplessness in animals and human beings, younger and weaker organisms (i.e., children and women) will show this type of reaction with higher likelihood and frequency compared to adults or males. Tonic immobility is most useful when a slow-moving vulnerable organism (like the opossum) is confronted with a life-threatening situation involving mobile, large predators (Nesse, 1999). On the other hand, proximity of danger plays a critical role for the onset of immobility. In primates, man included, "fright" with tonic immobility is known to occur on seeing conspecifics that are being threatened, frightened, or mutilated, as a cue for live threat in the surroundings (Azevedo et al., 2005; Facchinetti, Imbiriba, Azevedo, Vargas, & Volchan, 2006; Hebb, 1946). We have many reports of child soldiers showing tonic immobility (not flaccid immobility) when witnessing man slaughter. As accurately expressed in Goethe's *Faust* however, "blood is a juice of very special kind." From our recent data we conclude that opposite to females it can act as a rewarding cue in male human hunters (Elbert & Weierstall, in press). In a fighter, fainting would be fatal or result in a drop in social hierarchy as key fitness indicator. In noncombatants, however, fainting in response to the sight or smell of blood may have evolved as an adaptive stress response that aided survival of victims during combat. For a noncombatant woman or preadolescent child, however, an approaching sharp object, experiencing skin penetration, or spilled fresh blood may be a crucial turning point from which onwards continued fight with its elevated sympathetic arousal may be an ineffective survival strategy, as opposed to fainting (Bienvenu & Eaton, 1998; Salazar, 2000). Epidemiological data support this view as syncopal response to blood, injection, and injury is significantly less common among adult men, with puberty as a turning point (Agras, Sylvester, & Oliveau, 1969; Costello, 1982; Trouern-Trend, Cable, Badon, Newman, & Popovsky, 1999). Tonic immobility is almost always displayed when the person is overwhelmed by threat and not allowed and not able to act aggressively against the threat. Thus immobility functions to supress anger in the victim and acts bidirectionally to inhibit aggression in a number of ways:

a) "Submission" after other strategies (like escaping, screaming, and fighting back) have failed in order to stop aggression (Marx et al., 2008): for example, a toddler shows a fright reaction as the adult displays rising aggression.
b) "Holding still" to reduce risk of tissue damage: for example, a penetrated rape victim or a victim having sharp objects touching the surface of the skin. When the skin is contacted by sharp objects (a knife, teeth) or penetrated at an orifice of the body, heavy movements, struggling, or pulling away with a sudden move will cause even more tissue damage and damage to mucous membranes, as well as deeper wounds. A more recent study showed that childhood sexual abuse involving attempted or completed penile/vaginal penetration was more likely to be associated with increased experiencing of tonic immobility, and reports of tonic immobility were associated with greater current psychological impairment (Heidt, Marx, & Forsyth, 2005).
c) "Eliminating cues" for predatory behavior: stiffening of the voluntary muscles can occur during direct physical contact with the carnivore or the human predator. Tonic immobility increases survival chances even when physical contact has been made, because movement cues are critical releasing stimuli for predatory behavior, and immobility eliminates these cues. Surviving through "motionless pretending to be dead" has its evolutionary roots as a defense mechanism against predators. Predation tests demonstrated that prey, which struggles or moves when attacked, is killed and eaten, but if prey remains immobile, feigning death, the predator loses interest and the prey survives (Miyatake et al., 2004).
d) "Escape preparedness" in case there is a chance to resume flight: captured prey that becomes tonically immobile rather than struggling and fighting may increase its chance of escaping when the predator temporarily loosens the grip under the assumption that its prey is indeed dead. In mammals, struggling prey is only held on to until resistance subsides. It is also a response that may be adaptive in human beings when there is no possibility to escape or win a fight (Perry, Pollard, Blakely, Baker, & Vigilante, 1995) and this behavior is in fact recommended by park authorities for encounters with a grizzly bear. An organism in tonic immobility is immobile but is markedly tachycardic, vasoconstricted, hyperalert, and prepared to flee in a moment of opportunity, a state that also characterizes human catatonia. It is often followed by assaultive behavior, at times directly out of a stuporous state (Fink & Taylor, 2003).

When the aggressor approaches rapidly and comes close, the organism can for a short time again dramatically change its behavior (Fanselow & Lester, 1988) in that it suddenly displays an explosive escape response (Hirsch & Bolles, 1980) in conjunction with aggressive behavior (Kalin, 1993). This fact demonstrates that high aggressive arousal (anger) is inhibited at that stage but present. If these explosive responses do not eliminate contact, immobility may return, reducing the likelihood of continued attack (Fanselow & Lester, 1988). This assaultiveness, well known in catatonia of human beings, is only present during catatonic states of immobility. Further on in the cascade, once the vagal tone has increased and tonic immobility has changed to flaccid immobility (see next chapter), the ability of acting out is no longer present.

A person's sensory processing (sight, hearing, smell, taste, and touch), of kinesthetic (perception of movement and muscular sense) and somesthetic (sensory data derived from skin, muscles, and body organs) stimuli normally continuously serves the perceiving self as evidence that it resides "in" the physical body: Somatic processing ordinarily is integrated with a sense of *self*. Some patients describe that they leave the body during the traumatic event. Out-of-body experiences (depersonalization) seem to be a dissociation between sensory processing of somatic events and the sense of self or identity. If all sensory and physiological information, emotions, and pain perceptions are shut down at a certain stage of the defense cascade and if there is no longer the usual continuous feedback, the self inevitably must interpret its own physical position as outside of the body.

There have been discussions about the question whether dissociation exists because biology has equipped us with the gift of a gracious death. However, "good dying" does not underlie selection pressure in evolution. Those who have the ability to die with ease do not pass on this attribute to their offspring through natural selection. On the contrary, the shut-down reaction is solely a matter of surviving and it is important to look at its survival indicators to come up with an evidence-based model for its treatment.

Stages 5 and 6 = *Flag* and *Faint*: Facing Contamination and Penetration/Invasion May Result in *Flaccid Immobility* (*Unresponsive Immobility*) or Even *Fainting*

Stage 5 of the defense armament encompasses forms of dissociation and is characterized by reduced sympathetic arousal and passivity or a "shut-down" peripherally dominated by vagal activity. The survival value of these massive threat-induced changes in CNS and ANS regulatory control as well as its evolutionary roots are still under debate. Some have argued that threat-induced flaccid immobility with its vasovagal shut-down may be a uniquely human response that only evolved during middle paleolithic conspecific violence (Bracha, 2004) while others note that it involves similar physiological mechanisms as in other vertebrates, pointing to a much earlier and common evolutionary root in mammals (Alboni et al., 2008), the "alarm bradycardia" as a decrease in heart rate during fear-induced immobility. Probably, both views hold parts of the truth: during a long history of violent intraspecific attacks and violence, evolution will have reshaped the pan-mammalian defense repertoire specifically in homo sapiens.

Threat-induced flaccid immobility up to fainting, a response also seen in blood-injection-injury phobia, could have evolved as a guard against the danger of cardiac failure during inescapable attacks. The inhibition of the sympathetic system in conjunction with a marked activation of the parasympathetic system will lead to vasodilation and an extraordinary drop in heart rate and blood pressure. A satisfactory theory for this vasovagal syncope, however, is still absent (Bizios & Sheldon, 2009; Van Dijk & Sheldon, 2008). A widely held misbelief regarding bloodletting-related fainting assumes that fainting increases the probability of survival through minimizing blood loss. This neglects the fact that the major loss of blood in survivors results from venous injury and is thus unaffected by pressure in the arteries. On the contrary, vasodilation will lead to a greater loss of blood in response to injury than during the Flight-Fight stages. Vasoconstriction and tachycardia rather than vasodilatation and bradycardia are the adaptive initial responses to blood loss (Bracha, Williams, Haynes, et al., 2004).

Vasovagal reactions are known to be caused by excess vagal tone and decreased sympathetic skeletal muscle response to central nervous system stimulation (for example, fear), with the outcome of a hypotensive-bradycardic reflex syndrome: Inadequate vasoconstriction with an abrupt drop in systolic blood pressure, followed shortly by profound bradycardia and a decrease in cardiac output (Marchiondo, 2010). Threat-induced flaccid immobility up to fainting, a response also seen in blood-injection-injury phobia, could therefore have evolved as a guard against the danger of cardiac failure during inescapable attacks to reduce myocardial oxygen consumption when cardiac strain is (expected to be) excessive ("heart defense hypothesis"; Alboni et al., 2008). In humans, hypotension and bradycardia are finally responsible for loss of consciousness as a result of global cerebral hypoperfusion (Brignole et al., 2004). A horizontal position secures blood supply to the brain.

Fainting seems to be mediated through disgust (Curtis & Biran, 2001), which enables emotional responses to potentially infectious or noxious material in advance of actual contact with such material, to avoid pathogens and their toxins or invasive procedures (Marchiondo, 2010). Across cultures, disgust is universally elicited by disease-salient contacts such as bodily secretions, viscous substances, vermin, and sick or dirty people (Curtis, Aunger, & Rabie, 2004). Experiencing, witnessing, or listening to situations perceived as "disgusting" (e.g., mucus/stool, suctioning, wounds, colostomies) can trigger vasovagal reactions (Marchiondo, 2010). Even chimpanzees avoid faeces and show disgust reactions (Goodall, 1976). Vasovagal syncopes as a consequence of strong emotional stimuli such as fear, pain, and disgust are a common problem in emergency aid and critical care (Dennin & Haupt, 2009). The finding that blood-injection-injury phobics as well as healthy people may faint in the presence of blood or injury (e.g., Kleinknecht, Thorndike, & Walls, 1996; Kroeger, Atkinson, Marcuse, & Pickering, 2006) also points to the possible involvement of disgust, as strong and unopposed (parasympathetic) disgust reactions may promote fainting. Indeed, vasovagal syncopes, triggered by "blood" as a cue, are controlled by the same pan-mammalian physiological mechanism that regulates disgust (Marks, 1988; Page, 1994). Sexual violence and forced penetration provoke an intense disgust reaction, as does the sight of blood (Berntson, Cacioppo, Quigley, & Fabro, 1994; Merckelbach, Muris, de Jong, & de Jongh, 1999). Disgust and the associated phenomena of nausea and vomiting are thought to have evolved to prevent physical contact with disgusting stimuli (Cisler, Olantunji, & Lohr, 2008) and protect omnivores from the risk of ingesting pathogen-laden food. Spontaneous vomiting is seen as an automatic reflex of involuntarily rejecting material that is disgusting to see, taste, smell, or feel around orifices of the body. Withdrawal and avoidance are likely to increase survival. Page (1994) noted that "when the (parasympathetic) processes underlying disgust combine with a homeostatic increase in parasympathetic activity (which counteracts the initial sympathetically mediated fight or flight response), the joint effect may produce a pattern of vascular and vagal responding responsible for fainting" (p. 452). People with blood-injection-injury phobia exhibit a unique biphasic response pattern of typical sympathetic followed by massive parasympathetic activation. This biphasic process may account for the fainting that is observed in up to 75% of people with this condition when they are exposed to phobic stimuli. Disgust has become implicated in the vasovagal syncope response because it is associated with parasympathetic activity and reductions in diastolic blood pressure leading to fainting sensations (Page, 2003). Although the disgust-fainting relationship in blood-injection-injury phobia has not been a consistent finding (Olatunji et al., 2006), there is consistent evidence that people with this phobia report more intense disgust than controls.

While a trauma reminder may produce strong post-traumatic anxiety and arousal in a patient who had responded with flight/fight during the traumatic stressor, a patient with flag conditioning would be highly unresponsive and disengaged. In contrast to tonic immobility, flaccid immobility has a slow onset and slow termination. Only over the course of several minutes dissociative reactions begin to dominate (an abrupt onset is observable only, once once the response is conditioned). The muscle stiffening changes to flaccidity, voluntary movements stop, so does speech. Even if there is effort from the survivor, language production fails; the mouth might open, but there is no vocal sound. The central skeletal muscles are flagging, so that the posture subsides. The patient reports that perception of internal or external stimuli becomes attenuated, sounds and voices become distant, visual stimuli fade or become unreal (derealization). Kinesthetic, somesthetic, nociceptive stimuli no longer seem to reach the central processing units, causing changes in body awareness and loss of control (depersonalization). Numbness prevails. During reactivation of flaccid immobility, there is often a more or less intense feeling of nausea present as well. Conscious processing of the events becomes limited, making meaning seems irrelevant. The crucial difference between flaccid and tonic immobility (or catatonic states) is, that in a more progressed flag state, emotional involvement fades away, that is, no action dispositions are assembled and memory consolidation becomes weak and later rehearsal more difficult. It may require minutes to hours for a patient to be oriented in reality.

Reenactment of the Defense Stages When the Fear Network Is Triggered Due to Reminders or During Exposure Therapy

Learning associations between cues in the environment gives organisms the ability to predict impending danger. The last few decades of research have established that these stimulus-danger or fear associations are formed in the amygdala (Schiller & Johansen, 2009). Repeated experience of traumatic stress forms a fear network (see Figure 2) that can become pathologically detached from contextual cues such as time and location of the danger, a condition, which manifests itself as PTSD (Brewin, 2001; Elbert & Schauer, 2002; Schauer et al., 2005). Thus, survivors of life-threatening events with PTSD become "stuck" in the trauma. Intrusions

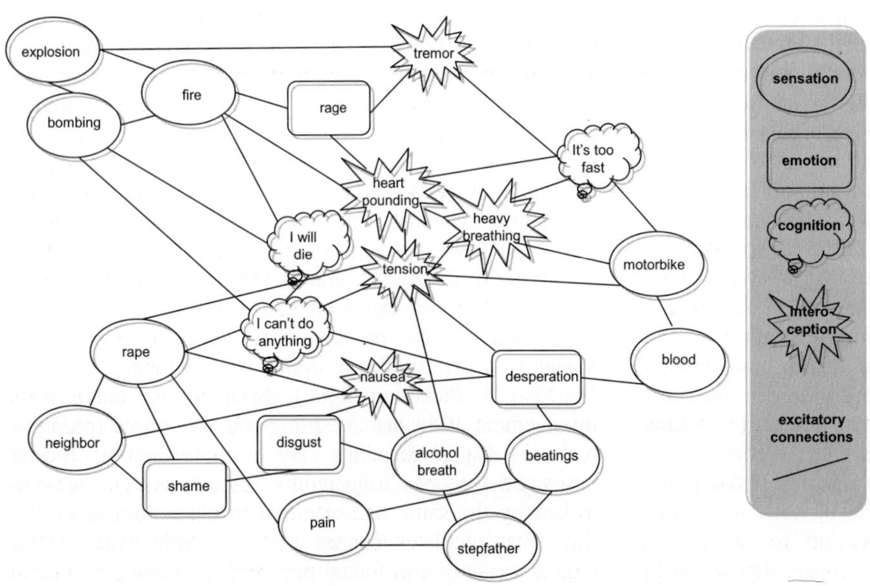

Figure 2. Illustration of a fear network in response to multiple traumatic stressors.

can therefore be understood as repetitive displays of parts/fragments of the events, which then elicit a corresponding response set that can be dominated by hyperarousal (Stages 2 and 3) or by dissociation (Stages 5 and 6), depending on the history of conditioning of physiological responses during the actual life-threatening experiences in the past.

Trauma-related emotional experiences are coded in memory as networks of mutually exciting chunks or information units. When one or several units are activated by cues, the activity spreads to adjacent units. Depending on the strength of activation, the entire structure may be engaged. The posttraumatic "fear network" may also be activated through narrative techniques, for example, when the survivor reports parts of his or her experiences. This will also activate the related support physiology of behavioral responses that have been engaged during the traumatic experience (Lang, 1979, 1984; Lang et al., 2000). Hence, we postulate that any activation of the trauma-related fear network will facilitate action replay of the defense behaviors the survivor has undergone peritraumatically. Repeated experience of traumatic stress may therefore produce at least two major subtypes of clinical symptom profiles, observable in the physiological responding during post-trauma exposure (Schauer & Elbert, 2008): Patients who experienced sympathetic activation (only) in response to the stressor show few signs of (shut-down) dissociation and passive avoidance during exposure treatment (Type 1), whereas those who went down the entire 6-F defense cascade, ending in parasympathetic dominance during the trauma, produce a corresponding replay of physiological responding when reminded by a cue (Type 2). The actual individual cascade of defense stages a survivor has gone through during the traumatic event will repeat itself every time the fear network – which has evolved peritraumatically – is activated again (i.e., through internal or external triggers or during exposure therapy). In relation to Figure 1, the two PTSD types may therefore be placed on the upstroke (uproar) (Type 1) or the downfall (shut-down) (Type 2) of the curve. A third type, positioned at the top, would manifest itself clinically among other symptoms in catatonia when the fear network is reactivated.

Dissociative responses are easily subject to conditioning (Bolles & Fanselow, 1980). In addition to classical conditioning, instrumental learning may reinforce the likelihood of dissociative responding. Survivors of trauma, who were rewarded with survival as a result of their "shut-down" during the offense, will also show a strong vasovagal dissociative response when confronted with trauma reminders, even decades later (Pitman, van der Kolk, Orr, & Greenberg, 1990; Van der Kolk, Pitman, & Orr, 1989).

In our recent studies we could confirm the two subtypes of responding. In survivors of organized violence, including sexual abuse and torture, we measured plasma and salivary cortisol levels and found that physical entrapment, body and mucosa contact with the offender and penetration by the perpetrator (especially rape vs. not being raped) during the traumatic event, modulated later cortisol responses to trauma reminders (Gola et al., 2010).

When survivors of severe human rights violations first speak about the trauma, for example, during a hearing or during exposure therapy, we can literally see that their hearts race, their hands become sweaty, and their breathing is heavy. Those who experienced multiple and extreme trauma, however, may soon stop to respond physiologically and report that they feel numb and unreal. This more clinical and anecdotal observation suggests that, just as the mind has a way of turning off strong emotions in overwhelming situations, the body can also turn off some of its stress responses, if feelings of terror and helplessness were strong. In another study (Ray et al., 2006) we observed that dissociative experiences are reflected in slow abnormal brainwaves, with generators residing in left ventro-lateral frontal cortex, an area that contributes to our ability to verbalize and to executive functioning, that is, the ability to plan, prepare, and be disposed for actions. In addition, these brain regions mirror and reflect the behavior of others and oneself (mirror neuron system). Focally generated slow waves as observed in this study often appear around structural or functional brain lesions. Correspondingly, we interpreted our findings of this left frontal brain activity as a sign of decoupling of these brain regions from both sensory experience and action – the only response that seems possible during the extreme helplessness induced by serious torture but that has devastating consequences later in life, as this brain reorganization is maintained even when the torture is over.

To summarize these findings we can conclude that those patients who merely underwent repeated sympathetic arousal during events show activation during exposure ("uproar-PTSD – Type 1"; typically called "simple trauma") and those who, at least once, reached the flag state will show dissociative shut-down reactions when reminded of the trauma ("shut-down-PTSD – Type 2"; typically called "complex trauma"). Therefore, a trauma-focused approach, which is necessary to overcome the trauma spectrum disorders, requires the management of dissociative stages (fright, flag, and faint) and this has obviously important treatment implications.

Self-Injury as a Means to Induce Vasovagal Shut-Down

Dissociative symptoms are common in borderline personality disorders (BPD) and the majority of patients meet the criteria for dissociative disorder diagnoses (e.g., Korzekwa, Dell, Links, Thabane, & Fougere, 2009). Characteristic for BPD is self-harming behavior including severe forms, such as cutting and burning. By self-injurious behavior patients may receive tension reduction and mood elevation from stress-induced aversive states or anxiety (Bohus et al., 2000; Klonsky, Oltmanns, & Turkheimer, 2003; Russ et al., 1992). Hence self-injurious behavior usually occurs in response to emotional stress or anxiety (Bierer et al., 2003; Yates, 2004). Self-injurious behavior appears to rapidly lower an escalating heart rate (Novak, 2003).

Based on the present model, we suggest that self-mutilating behavior facilitates tension relief through setting in motion the *flag* state. Self-mutilating behavior serves to initiate dissociation in the form of flaccid immobility. When mutilating the skin surface (i.e., cutting), a vasovagal reaction is launched. During this "shut-down" blood pressure and heart rate down, together with a fading emotional tension and a termination of ruminating thoughts, worries, and troubles, etc. The potentially reinforcing effects of self-injurious behavior may account for the failure of some treatment regimens. We conclude that borderline patients induce their own relaxing dissociative shut-down response (type 2) as a learned response.

Management of Dissociative *Fright, Flag,* and *Faint* Reactions During Trauma Treatment

Emotional engagement in traumatic memory is a necessary condition for successful processing of the event and resultant recovery (Breuer & Freud, 1895; Foa & Kozak, 1986; Horowitz, 1986; Jaycox et al., 1998). Fear activation during exposure therapy is usually positively related to treatment outcome (Borkovec & Sides, 1979; Foa & Kozak, 1986; Foa, Riggs, Massie, & Yarczower, 1995). In trauma survivors, however, exposure may reactivate the flag state or even result in fainting. When the survivor responded peritraumatically with vasovagal shut-down or has even fainted during the event, a replay of these responses and emotions during treatment will quickly result in therapeutic failure. The patient cannot properly hear and see the therapist any longer, is not capable to narrate and react, disabled to respond and move, and incompetent to reprocess emotion or cognition. During treatment, patients with the dissociative shut-down form of PTSD, so called "complex trauma" patients, need assistance to actively fight the replay risk of vasovagal dominance (i.e., loss of blood pressure, bradycardia, vasodilatation, and eventually fainting). Activation (active motoric engagement) may help to maintain arousal and prevent immobility. Relaxation techniques are at this point contraindicated since they would aggravate the cardiovascular problem and support fainting. During the first times when confronting such a fear network, recall of the trauma material should be paralleled with forced reality testing and therapist's active engagement in directive guidance the very moment sings of flagging or fainting appear (for specific intervention, please see Table 1).

In most of the trauma-focused techniques, information about the traumatic material is available before the beginning of the session, no matter whether the events are worked through in chronological biographical order (Narrative Exposure Therapy – NET, Schauer et al., 2005), or in hierarchical order (i.e., EMDR, prolonged exposure). Characteristics of events that may elicit dissociative fright, flag, or faint are:

a) imminence of threat/aggressor and total helplessness, for example, direct body contact with the perpetrator, fixation (constraint), skin contact, and danger of skin penetration (specially sharp objects, for example, teeth and knife);
b) rapid arousal peak, often with startle, due to unexpected and sudden proximity of threat or aggressor;
c) presence of fresh blood, mutilated bodies;
d) being contaminated, contact to infectious material such as mucosa and body fluids, including sperms, urine, and feces;
e) anal, vaginal, or oral penetration of the victim;[2] and
f) severe pain being inflicted on the victim.

How to Notice the Onset of Dissociative Shut-Down During Exposure?

"I have also noticed that under fear there is a strong tendency to yawn." (Charles Darwin, *The Expression of the Emotions in Man and Animals.*)

When confronted with traumatic material, there is – at least initially – a brief increase in sympathetic arousal, the "uproar" branch is activated even in survivors with "shutdown" PTSD types. During a period of agitation, heartbeat (palpitation) and blood pressure are rising, vasoconstriction (cold hands and pale face) and elevated emotional and physiological arousal can be observed. However, bodily numbing along with slight paralysis mainly in the legs are signs that dissociative shut-down stages will be entered soon. Sudden yawning in the middle of the arousing exposure or tinnitus may indicate that hypotension has already set in (yawning can support blood pressure and heartbeat frequency elevation (Platek, Mohamed, & Gallup, 2005)). The hands become warm and the skin may change slowly from pale to red. The patient reports dizziness, blurred vision, and weakness of the muscles. The three main areas of behavioral changes that characterize a shut-down reaction peritraumatically can also be observed later, when recalling the traumatic experiences:

1. Functional sensory deafferentation: incoming stimuli seem not to reach beyond the gates in spinal cord and thalamus, they are perceived as weak, distant, and unreal. During treatment, the patient may become unresponsive, with unfocused gaze.
2. Reversible palsy leads to a visible decrease of bodily movements and immobility, posturing and waxy flexibility also during treatment.
3. Inhibition or disconnection of areas responsible for language processing and production of speech (unclear/confused speech, fragmentation of sentences, inability to speak, and almost no or belated response to acoustic stimuli).

We assume that any of these areas can be instrumentally conditioned in isolation and that respective states, like functional blindness or palsy of a limb, may become tonic. Consequently, ICD-10 classifies conversion disorders as dissociative disorders.

[2] Fainting through penetration is not only associated with sexual penetration, it can also occur when instruments are inserted in the body. For instance, the aspiration of lungs in a newborn baby may cause reflexive bradycardia.

Table 1. Therapeutic intervention

	Therapeutic intervention when "uproar" is dominant during the exposure session	Therapeutic intervention when "shut-down" is dominant during the exposure session
	Activation of elements of the fear network in relation to their autobiographical context (space and time when event has happened).	*Activation of elements of the fear network in relation to their autobiographical context, supported and interrupted by continuous reality testing and* *- cardiovascular activation* *- sensory stimulation* *- encouragement of speech production* *until trauma material can be processed without shut-down.*
Sensory-afferent	Emphasize the exploration of sensory details of the *past* traumatic event, comparing/contrasting with sensations and emotions in the present during recall.	Emphasize the exploration of sensory details of the *past* traumatic event, comparing/contrasting with sensations and emotions in the present during recall. + stimulation of the senses in the *here and now*, for example: present positive fragrances (e.g., lemon) or tasting samples (peppermint oil or chili gum), switch on bright light, present tactile information (e.g., texture, ice-packs), lead attention to auditory stimuli in the here and now.
Motor-afferent		Emphasize activation of the skeletal muscles, enhance blood pressure and muscle tonus (above all, use applied tension, physical exercises, leg crossing, physical counter pressure maneuvers) and use body balancing tasks.
Language processing	Emphasize the narration of the *past* traumatic scene.	Emphasize the narration of the *past* traumatic scene, supported by the facilitation of continuous narrative engagement in the *here and now* (e.g., active communication; enhance speech production).
Emotional processing	Support the full emotional expression.	Support the full emotional expression, allowing and promoting specifically anger affect that has been inhibited peritraumatically.
Nutritional demands		Pay attention to adequate nutrition (caution for malnutrition/eating disorders); increase dietary salt and fluid intake in daily life; advise to drink water (approx. 500 ml, if tolerated) just before exposure to trauma material.
	Counteract and abstain from:	
	• Termination of exposure before contextualization and integration could take place (i.e., avoidance).	• Termination of exposure before contextualization and integration could take place. • Disengagement from the here and now. • Relaxation (instead of activation). • Sensory similarities between the trauma context and the therapeutic setting. • Stimuli that are associated with disgust or similar to body fluids and feces (i.e., ammoniac). • Threat cues in the here and now (instead: present safety signals). • Semi-darkness in the room and objects for hiding behind (e.g., large plants, furniture).

Measures to Counteract Dissociative Shut-Down During the Exposure Therapy Session

Before starting an exposure procedure with a "shut-down" prone, that is, dissociative patient, it is important that the blood sugar level is in the normal range, that is, that the patient has sufficient nutrition intake including salt and minerals. Shut-down reactions like fainting and bradycardia may also be aggravated by low fluid volume such as a lack of water, low sodium intake and dehydration (Kreipe & Birndorf, 2000; Pritts & Susman, 2003). On the other hand, vasovagal reactions could be shown to decrease when subjects drank water just before being exposed to sharp objects like needles or orthostatic testing (Newman et al., 2007; Claydon, Schroeder, Norcliffe, Jordan, & Hainsworth, 2006).

Following explicit education on the causes of "shut-down" reactions during recall, the therapeutic measures, which are likely to be applied during the exposure session, must be explained and consented to by the patient. At the first signs of a shut-down process, active mobilization and explicitly induced sensory contrasting of time and place contexts (past vs. presence) should be initiated by the therapist in parallel to the encouragement of recall of the traumatic event. Feared stimuli can be briefly presented, in the human being always interrupted by reality testing, so that a vasovagal syncope will not be elicited and a massed series of brief exposure trials can bring about fear extinction, as demonstrated in basic research (Grey, Rachman, & Sartory, 1981; Martasian, Smith, Neill, & Rieg, 1992; Renfrey & Spates, 1994). For survivors with shut-down PTSD we suggest continuous shifting of attention between trauma-related material and the present context by recalling reality, sensory stimulation in the here and now and motor activation (using applied muscle tension and physical counterpressure maneuvers). The therapist responds to prodromal fainting symptoms by engaging in context-contrasting and muscle tension techniques to counteract the incipient syncope. Active muscle tension appears as the new frontline treatment of reflex syncope inducing significant blood pressure increase due to clinical trials to avoid shut down (Krediet et al., 2002; France, France, & Patterson, 2006; European Society of Cardiology, 2009). Slowing the rhythm of the attentional shifts between the present and the past will allow the patient to process the trauma narrative unhindered by prior *Flag* or *Faint* responses and thus allow to inhibit the fear network via contextualization of the experience in the past. Moving in and out of the trauma scene according to the response of the client's ANS modulation needs active monitoring and fast intervention by the therapist. Practical examples to counter dissociation are presented in Table 1.

Outlook and Further Research

Dissociation is seen as a state of human beings who are engaged in response to acute threat. Dissociative behavior can be classically and instrumentally conditioned and thus appear when appropriately cued. Subsyndromes, like functional deafferentation or limited paralysis, may thus become tonic like in conversion disorders. Dissociative shut-down reactions following traumatic stress can be successfully treated when usual exposure techniques are complemented by methods that counteract flag and faint reactions. The etiological model can help to understand the survivor's psychophysiological state and provides guidelines for practical intervention techniques, depending on the particular stage in the cascade. The prevention of dissociative shut-down during exposure sessions not only facilitates the required processing of the traumatic events, it also results in a speedy decrease from dissociative responding in everyday life and hence a considerable relief for the patient. Certainly more empirical evidence is needed to further specify the model and to test its clinical utility for trauma-related psychopathology.

Acknowledgments

Research was supported by the Deutsche Forschungsgemeinschaft and the European Refugee Fund (EFF). We thank Dr. Elisabeth Schauer and Prof. Dr. Ulrich Schnyder for their valuable comments on an earlier version of this manuscript.

References

Adenauer, H., Catani, C., Keil, J., Aichinger, H., & Neuner, F. (2009). Is freezing an adaptive reaction to threat? Evidence from heart rate reactivity to emotional pictures in victims of war and torture. *Psychophysiology, 9999*, 1–8.

Agras, S., Sylvester, D., & Oliveau, D. (1969). The epidemiology of common fears and phobia. *Comprehensive Psychiatry, 10*, 151–156.

Albach, E. (1993). *Freud's seduction theory: Incest, trauma, and hysteria,*. Middelburg, The Netherlands: Stichting Petra.

Alboni, P., Alboni, M., & Bertorelle, G. (2008). The origin of vasovagal syncope: To protect the heart or to escape predation? *Clinical Autonomic Research, 18*, 170–178.

Allen, J. G. (2001). *Traumatic relationships and serious mental disorders*. New York, NY: Wiley.

Azevedo, T. M., Volchan, E., Imbiriba, L. A., Rodrigues, E. C., Oliveira, J. M., Oliveira, L. F., ... Vargas, C. D. (2005). A freezing-like posture to pictures of mutilation. *Psychophysiology, 42*, 255–260.

Barlow, D. H. (2004). *Anxiety and its disorders: The nature and treatment of anxiety and panic*. New York, NY: Guilford Press.

Bernstein, E. M., & Putnam, F. W. (1986). Development, reliability, and validity of a dissociation scale. *Journal of Nervous and Mental Disease, 174*, 727–735.

Berntson, G. G., Cacioppo, J. T., Quigley, K. S., & Fabro, V. T. (1994). Autonomic space and psychophysiological response. *Psychophysiology, 31*, 44–61.

Bienvenu, O. J., & Eaton, W. W. (1998). The epidemiology of blood-injection-injury phobia. *Psychological Medicine, 28*, 1129–1136.

Bierer, L. M., Yehuda, R., Schmeidler, J., Mitropoulou, V., New, A. S., Silverman, J. M., & Siever, L. J. (2003). Abuse and neglect in childhood: Relationship to personality disorder diagnoses. *CNS Spectrums, 8*, 737–754.

Birmes, P., Brunet, A., Carreras, D., Ducasse, J. L., Charlet, J. P., Lauque, D., ... Schmitt, L. (2003). The predictive power of peritraumatic dissociation and acute stress symptoms for posttraumatic stress symptoms: A three-month prospective study. *American Journal of Psychiatry, 160*, 1337–1339.

Bizios, A. S., & Sheldon, R. S. (2009). Vasovagal syncope: State or trait? *Current Opinion in Cardiology, 24*, 68–73.

Bohus, M., Limberger, M. F., Ebner, U. W., Glocker, F. X., Schwarz, B., Wernz, M., & Lieb, K. (2000). Pain perception during self-reported distress and calmness in patients with borderline personality disorder and self-mutilating behavior. *Psychiatry Research, 95*, 251–260.

Bolles, R. C., & Fanselow, M. S. (1980). A perceptual-defense-recuperative model of fear and pain. *Behavioral and Brain Sciences, 3*, 291–323.

Borkovec, T. D., & Sides, J. (1979). The contribution of relaxation and expectancy for fear reduction via graded imaginal exposure to feared stimuli. *Behaviour Research and Therapy, 17*, 529–540.

Bracha, H. S. (2004). Freeze, flight, fight, fright, faint: Adaptionist perspectives on the acute stress response spectrum. *CNS Spectrums, 9*, 679–685.

Bracha, H. S., Williams, A. E., Haynes, S. N., Kubany, E. S., Ralston, T. C., & Yamashita, J. M. (2004). The STRS (shortness of breath, tremulousness, racing heart, and sweating): A brief checklist for acute distress with panic-like autonomic indicators; development and factor structure. *Annals of General Hospital Psychiatry, 3*, 8.

Bracha, H. S., Williams, A. E., Ralston, T. C., Bracha, A. S., & Matsukawa, J. M. (2004). Does "fight or flight" need updating? *Psychosomatics, 45*, 448–449.

Bradley, M. M., Codispoti, M., Cuthbert, B. N., & Lang, P. J. (2001). Emotion and motivation I: Defensive and appetitive reactions in picture processing. *Emotion, 1*, 276–298.

Breh, D. C., & Seidler, G. H. (2007). Is peritraumatic dissociation a risk factor for PTSD? *Journal of Trauma and Dissociation, 8*, 53–69.

Bremner, J. D., Krystal, J. H., Putnam, F., Southwick, S. M., Marmar, C., Charney, D. S., & Mazure, C. M. (1998). Measurement of dissociative states with the Clinician Administered Dissociative States Scale (CADSS). *Journal of Traumatic Stress, 11*, 125–136.

Bremner, J. D., Staib, L., Kaloupek, D., Southwick, S. M., Soufer, R., & Charney, D. S. (1999). Neural correlates of exposure to traumatic pictures and sound in Vietnam combat veterans with and without posttraumatic stress disorder: A positron emission tomography study. *Biological Psychiatry, 45*, 806–816.

Breuer, J., & Freud, S. (1895). *Studien über Hysterie* [Studies on hysteria]. Leipzig, Germany: Franz Deuticke.

Brewin, C. R. (2001). A cognitive neuroscience account of posttraumatic stress disorder and its treatment. *Behaviour Research and Therapy, 39*, 373–393.

Brignole, M., Alboni, P., Benditt, D. G., Bergfeldt, L., Blanc, J. J., Bloch Thomsen, P. E., ... Wieling, W. (2004). Guidelines on management (diagnosis and treatment) of syncope – update 2004. *Europace, 6*, 467–537.

Brune, M. (2002). Toward an integration of interpersonal and biological processes: Evolutionary psychiatry as an empirically testable framework for psychiatric research. *Psychiatry – Interpersonal and Biological Processes, 65*, 48–57.

Bryant, R. A. (2007). Does dissociation further our understanding of PTSD? *Journal of Anxiety Disorders, 21*, 183–191.

Burgess, A. W., & Holmstrom, L. L. (1974). Rape trauma syndrome. *American Journal of Psychiatry, 131*, 981–986.

Burgess, A. W., & Holmstrom, L. L. (1976). Coping behavior of the rape victim. *American Journal of Psychiatry, 133*, 413–418.

Campbell, B. A., Wood, G., & McBride, T. (1997). Origins of orienting and defense responses: An evolutionary perspective. In P. J. Lang, R. F. Simmons & M. T. Balaban (Eds.), *Attention and orienting: Sensory and motivational processes* (pp. 41–67). Hillsdale, NJ: Erlbaum.

Cardena, E. (1994). The domain of dissociation. In S. J. Lynn & R. W. Rhue (Eds.), *Dissociation: Theoretical, clinical, and research perspectives* (pp. 15–31). New York, NY: Guilford.

Cisler, J. M., Olantunji, B. O., & Lohr, J. M. (2008). Disgust, fear and the anxiety disorders: A critical review. *Clinical Psychology Review, 29*, 34–46.

Claydon, V. E., Schroeder, C., Norcliffe, L. J., Jordan, J., & Hainsworth, R. (2006). Water drinking improves orthostatic tolerance in patients with posturally related syncope. *Clinical Science, 110*, 343–352.

Conway, M. A., & Pleydell-Pearce, C. W. (2000). The construction of autobiographical memories in the self-memory system. *Psychological Review, 107*, 261–288.

Costello, C. G. (1982). Fears and phobias in women: A community study. *Journal of Abnormal Psychology, 91*, 280–286.

Curtis, V., Aunger, R., & Rabie, T. (2004). Evidence that disgust evolved to protect from risk of disease. *Proceedings of the Royal Society of London. Series B, Biological Sciences, 271*, 131–133.

Curtis, V., & Biran, A. (2001). Dirt, disgust, and disease: Is hygiene in our genes? *Perspectives in Biology and Medicine, 44*, 17–31.

Darwin, C. (1998). *The Expression of the Emotions in Man and Animals*. New York, NY: Oxford University Press (Original work published 1872).

Dennin, M. A., & Haupt, W. F. (2009). *Syncope and vertigo from a neurologic point of view*. Berlin: Springer.

Dixon, A. K. (1998). Ethological strategies for defence in animals and humans: Their role in some psychiatric disorders. *British Journal of Medical Psychology, 71*, 417–445.

Draijer, N. (1990). *Sexual traumatization in childhood long-term consequences of sexual abuse by relatives*. Amsterdam, The Netherlands: SUA.

Dutra, L., Bureau, J.-F., Holmes, B., Lyubchik, A., & Lyons-Ruth, K. (2009). *Journal of Nervous and Mental Disease, 197*, 383–390.

Dyer, A., Priebe, K., Steil, R., Krüger, A., & Bohus, M. (2009). Dialektisch-Behaviorale Therapie zur Behandlung der Posttraumatischen Belastungsstörung mit schweren Störungen der Emotionsregulation [Dialectical behavioral theraphy in the treatment of PTSD with severe problems in emotion regulation]. *Verhaltenstherapie und Psychosoziale Praxis, 41*, 283–307.

Ebner-Priemer, U., Mauchnik, J., Kleindienst, N., Schmahl, C., Peper, M., Rosenthal, Z. M., ... Bohus, M. (2009). Emotional learning during dissociative states in borderline personality disorder. *Journal of Psychiatry & Neuroscience, 34*, 214–222.

Ehlers, A., & Clark, D. M. (2000). A cognitive model of posttraumatic stress disorder. *Behaviour Research and Therapy, 38*, 319–345.

Elbert, T., Rockstroh, B., Kolassa, I. T., Schauer, M., & Neuner, F. (2006). The influence of organized violence and terror on brain and mind – A co-constructive perspective. In P. Baltes, P. Reuter-Lorenz, & F. Rösler (Eds.), *Lifespan development and the brain: The perspective of biocultural co-constructivism* (pp. 326–349). Cambridge, UK: University Press.

Elbert, T., & Schauer, M. (2002). Psychological trauma: Burnt into memory. *Nature, 419*, 883.

Elbert, T., & Weierstall, R. (in press). Fascination violence – on mind and brain of man hunters. *European Archives of Psychiatry and Clinical Neuroscience*.

European Society of Cardiology. (2009). Guidelines for the diagnosis and management of syncope. *European Heart Journal, 30*, 2631–2671.

Facchinetti, L. D., Imbiriba, L. A., Azevedo, T. M., Vargas, C. D., & Volchan, E. (2006). Postural modulation induced by pictures depicting prosocial or dangerous contexts. *Neuroscience Letters, 410*, 52–56.

Fanselow, M. S., & Lester, L. S. (1988). A functional behavioristic approach to aversively motivated behavior: Predatory imminence as a determinant of the topography of defensive behavior. In R. C. Bolles & M. D. Beecher (Eds.), *Evolution and learning* (pp. 185–212). Hillsdale, NJ: Erlbaum.

Fink, M., & Taylor, M. A. (2003). *Catatonia: A clinician's guide to diagnosis and treatment*. Cambridge, UK: Cambridge University Press.

Fiszman, A., Mendlowicz, M. V., Marques-Portella, C., Volchan, E., Coutinho, E. S., Souza, W. F., ... Figueira, I. (2008). Peritraumatic tonic immobility predicts a poor response to pharmacological treatment in victims of urban violence with PTSD. *Journal of Affective Disorders, 107*, 193–197.

Foa, E. B., & Kozak, M. J. (1986). Emotional processing of fear: Exposure to corrective information. *Psychological Bulletin, 99*, 20–35.

Foa, E. B., Riggs, D. S., & Gershuny, B. S. (1995). Arousal, numbing, and intrusion: Symptom structure of PTSD following assault. *American Journal of Psychiatry, 152*, 116–122.

Foa, E. B., Riggs, D. S., Massie, E. D., & Yarczower, M. (1995). The impact of fear activation and anger on the efficacy of exposure treatment for posttraumatic stress disorder. *Behavior Therapy, 26*, 487–499.

Foley, J. P. (1938). Tonic immobility in the rhesus monkey (*Macaca mulatta*) induced by manipulation, immobilization and experimental inversion of the visual field. *Journal of Comparative Psychology, 26*, 515–526.

France, C. R., France, J. L., & Patterson, S. M. (2006). Blood pressure and cerebral oxygenation responses to skeletal muscle tension: A comparison of two physical maneuvers to prevent vasovagal reactions. *Clinical Physiology and Functional Imaging, 26*, 21–25.

Fusé, T., Forsyth, J. P., Marx, B., Gallup, G. G., & Weaver, S. (2007). Factor structure of the Tonic Immobility Scale in female sexual assault survivors: An exploratory and confirmatory factor analysis. *Journal of Anxiety Disorders, 21*, 265–283.

Gallup, G., Boren, J. L., Suarez, S. D., Wallnau, L. B., & Gagliardi, G. J. (1980). Evidence for the integrity of central processing during tonic immobility. *Physiology and Behavior, 25*, 189–194.

Gallup, G. G. Jr., & Maser, J. D. (1977). Tonic immobility: Evolutionary underpinnings of human catalepsy and catatonia. In M. E. P. Seligman (Ed.), *Psychopathology: Experimental models* (pp. 334–357). New York, NY: W. H. Freeman.

Gallup, G. G. Jr., & Rager, D. R. (1996). Tonic immobility as a model of extreme stress of behavioral inhibition: Issues of methodology and measurement. In M. Kavaliers (Ed.), *Motor activity and movement disorders* (pp. 57–80). Totowa, NJ: Humana Press.

Gola, H., Engler, H., Schauer, M., Adenauer, H., Elbert, T., & Kolassa, I.-T. (2010). Differential cortisol responses in patients with severe PTSD who were raped versus not raped. *Journal of Psychiatric Research*.

Goodall, J. (1976). *Tool using*. National Geographic Society. Educational Series Catalog No. 50331 (film), 5122776 (video).

Graham, F. K. (1979). Distinguishing among orienting, defense, and startle reflexes. In H. D. Kimmel, E. H. van Olst, & J. F. Orlebeke (Eds.), *The orienting reflex in humans* (pp. 137–167). Hillsdale, NJ: Erlbaum.

Gray, J. A. (1987). *The psychology of fear and stress*. Cambridge, UK: Cambridge University Press.

Grey, S. J., Rachman, S., & Sartory, G. (1981). Return of fear: The role of inhibition. *Behaviour Research and Therapy, 19*, 135–143.

Hebb, D. O. (1946). On the nature of fear. *Psychological Revue, 53*, 250–275.

Heidt, J. M., Marx, B. P., & Forsyth, J. P. (2005). Tonic immobility and childhood sexual abuse: A preliminary report evaluating the sequela of rape-induced paralysis. *Behaviour Research and Therapy, 43*, 1157–1171.

Hirsch, S. M., & Bolles, R. C. (1980). On the ability of prey to recognize predators. *Zeitschrift für Tierpsychologie, 54*, 71–84.

Holmes, E. A., Brown, R. J., Mansell, W., Fearon, R. P., Hunter, E. C. M., Frasquilho, F., & Oakley, D. A. (2005). Are there two qualitatively distinct forms of dissociation? A review and some clinical implications. *Clinical Psychology Review, 25*, 1–23.

Horowitz, M. J. (1986). Stress-response syndromes: A review of posttraumatic and adjustment disorders. *Hospital and Community Psychiatry, 37*, 241–249.

Hunter, E. C. M., Baker, D., Phillips, M. L., Sierra, M., & David, A. S. (2005). Cognitive-behaviour therapy for depersonalisation disorder: An open study. *Behaviour Research and Therapy, 43*, 1121–1130.

Janet, P. (1889). *L'automatisme psychologique* [Mental automatism]. Paris, France: Nouvelle Édition.

Jaycox, L. H., Foa, E. B., & Morral, A. R. (1998). Influence of emotional engagement and habituation on exposure therapy for PTSD. *Journal of Consulting and Clinical Psychology, 66*, 185–192.

Jones, I., & Blackshaw, J. K. (2000). An evolutionary approach to psychiatry. *Australian & New Zealand Journal of Psychiatry, 34*, 8–13.

Kahlbaum, K. L. (1973). Pridan T. (1973). *Catatonia*. Baltimore, MA: Johns Hopkins University Press. (Original work published 1874).

Kalin, N. H. (1993). The neurobiology of fear. *Scientific American, 268*, 94–101.

Kalin, N. H., & Shelton, S. E. (1989). Defensive behaviors in infant rhesus monkeys: Environmental cues and neurochemical regulation. *Science, 243*, 1718–1721.

Kandel, E. R., & Schwartz, J. H. (Eds.). (1991). *Principles of neural science*. New York, NY: Elsevier.

Keane, T. M., Zimering, R. T., & Caddell, J. M. (1985). A behavioural formulation of posttraumatic stress disorder in combat veterans. *Behaviour Therapist, 8*, 9–12.

Kelly, D. H. W., & Walter, C. J. S. (1968). The relationship between clinical diagnosis and anxiety, assessed by forearm blood flow and other measurements. *British Journal of Psychiatry, 114*, 611–626.

Kleinknecht, R. A., Thorndike, R. M., & Walls, M. M. (1996). Factorial dimensions and correlates of blood, injection, and related medical fear: Cross validation of the medical fear survey. *Behaviour Research and Therapy, 34*, 323–331.

Klonsky, E. D., Oltmanns, T. F., & Turkheimer, E. (2003). Deliberate self-harm in a nonclinical population: Prevalence and psychological correlates. *The American Journal of Psychiatry, 160*, 1501–1508.

Kolassa, I. T., & Elbert, T. (2007). Structural and functional neuroplasticity in relation to traumatic stress. *Current Directions in Psychological Science, 16*, 326–329.

Kolassa, I. T., Wienbruch, C., Neuner, F., Schauer, M., Ruf, M., Odenwald, M., & Elbert, T. (2007). Altered oscillatory brain dynamics after repeated traumatic stress. *BMC Psychiatry, 7*, 56.

Korzekwa, M. I., Dell, P. F., Links, P. S., Thabane, L., & Fougere, P. (2009). Dissociation in borderline personality disorder: A detailed look. *Journal of Trauma and Dissociation, 10*, 346–367.

Kraepelin, E. (1896). Die Schreckneurosen [The fright neuroses]. In J. A. Barth (Ed.), *Ein Lehrbuch für Studierende und Ärzte* (Vol. II) Leipzig, Germany: Barth.

Krediet, T., Paul, B. S., van Dijk, N., Linzer, M., van Lieshout, J. J., & Wieling, W. (2002). Management of vasovagal syncope: Controlling or aborting faints by leg crossing and muscle tensing. *Circulation, 106*, 1684–1689.

Kreipe, R. E., & Birndorf, S. A. (2000). Eating disorders in adolescents and young adults. *The Medical Clinics of North America, 84*, 1027–1049.

Kroeger, A. T., Atkinson, W. L., Marcuse, E. K., & Pickering, L. (2006). General recommendations on immunization: Recommendations of the Advisory Committee on Immunization Practices (ACIP). *Morbidity and Mortality Weekly Report. Recommendations and Reports, 55*, 1–48.

Krystal, H. (1993). *Integration and self healing: Affect trauma, alexithymia*. Hillsdale, NJ: Analytic Press.

Krystal, J. H., Bennett, A. L., Bremner, J. D., Southwick, S. M., & Charney, D. S. (1995). Toward a cognitive neuroscience of dissociation and altered memory functions in post-traumatic stress disorder. Neurobiological and clinical consequences of stress. In M. J. Friedmen, D. S. Charney, & A. Y. Deutsch (Eds.), *Normal adaptions to PTSD* (pp. 239–268). New York, NY: Raven Press. [chap. 14].

Krystal, J. H., Bremner, J. D., Southwick, S. M., & Charney, D. S. (1998). The emerging neurobiology of dissociation: Implications for the treatment of posttraumatic stress disorder. In J. D. Bremner & C. R. Marmer (Eds.), *Trauma, memory, and dissociation* (pp. 321–363). Washington, DC: American Psychiatric Press.

Lader, M. H. (1975). *The psychophysiology of mental illness*. London, UK: Routledge and Kegan Paul.

Lader, M. H., & Wing, L. (1966). Physiological measures, sedative drugs and morbid anxiety. In *Maudsley Monographs, No. 14*. London, UK: Oxford University Press.

Lang, P. (1979). A bio-informational theory of emotional imagery. *Psychophysiology, 16*, 495–512.

Lang, P. (1984). Dead souls: Or why the neurobehavioral science of emotion should pay attention to cognitive science. In T. Elbert, B. Rockstroh, T. Lutzenberger, & N. Birbaumer (Eds.), *Self-regulation of the brain and behavior* (pp. 255–272). Berlin, Germany: Springer.

Lang, P., Bradley, M. M., & Cuthbert, B. N. (1998). Emotion, motivation, and anxiety: Brain mechanisms and psychophysiology. *Biological Psychiatry, 44*, 1248–1263.

Lang, P. J., Davis, M., & Öhman, A. (2000). Fear and anxiety: Animal models and human cognitive psychophysiology. *Journal of Affective Disorders, 61*, 137–159.

Lanius, R. A., Bluhm, R., Lanius, U., & Pain, C. (2006). A review of neuroimaging studies in PTSD: Heterogeneity of response to symptom provocation. *Journal of Psychiatric Research, 40*, 709–729.

Lanius, R. A., Williamson, P. C., Boksman, K., Densmore, M., Gupta, M., Neufeld, R. W. J., ... Menon, R. S. (2002). Brain activation during script-driven imagery induced dissociative responses in PTSD: A functional MRI investigation. *Biological Psychiatry, 52*, 305–311.

Lanius, R. A., Williamson, P. C., Densmore, M., Boksman, K., Gupta, M. A., Neufeld, R. W., ... Menon, R. S. (2001). Neural correlates of traumatic memories in posttraumatic stress disorder: A functional MRI investigation. *American Journal of Psychiatry, 158*, 1920–1922.

Lanius, R. A., Williamson, P. C., Hopper, J., Densmore, M., Boksman, K., Gupta, M. A., ... Menon, R. S. (2003). Recall of emotional states in posttraumatic stress disorder: An fMRI investigation. *Biological Psychiatry, 53*, 204–210.

Liberzon, I., Taylor, S. F., Fig, L. M., & Koeppe, R. A. (1996/1997). Alterations of corticothalamic perfusion ratios during a PTSD flashback. *Depression and Anxiety, 4*, 146–150.

Linehan, M. (1993). *Cognitive-behavioral treatment of borderline personality disorder*. New York, NY: Guilford.

Löw, A., Lang, P. J., Smith, J. C., & Bradley, M. M. (2008). Both predator and prey: Emotional arousal in threat and reward. *Psychological Science, 19*, 865–873.

Ludäscher, P., Bohus, M., Lieb, K., Philipsen, A., Jochims, A., & Schmahl, C. G. (2007). Elevated pain thresholds correlate with dissociation and aversive arousal in patients with borderline personality disorder. *Psychiatry Research, 149*, 291–296.

Marchiondo, K. J. (2010). Recognizing and treating vasovagal syncope. *American Journal of Nursing, 110*, 50–53.

Marks, I. M. (1987). *Fears, phobias, and rituals: Panic, anxiety, and their disorders*. New York, NY: Oxford University Press.

Marks, I. (1988). Blood-injury phobia: A review. *The American Journal of Psychiatry, 45*, 1207–1213.

Marmar, C. R., Weiss, D. S., & Metzler, T. J. (1998). Peritraumatic dissociation and posttraumatic stress disorder. In J. D. Bremner & C. R. Marmar (Eds.), *Trauma, memory, and dissociation* (pp. 229–252). Washington, DC: American Psychiatric Press.

Martasian, P. J., Smith, N. F., Neill, S. A., & Rieg, T. S. (1992). Retention of massed vs. distributed response prevention treatments in rats and a revised training procedure. *Psychological Reports, 70*, 339–355.

Marx, B. P., Forsyth, J. P., Gallup, G. G., Fusé, T., & Lexington, J. M. (2008). Tonic immobility as an evolved predator defense: Implications for sexual assault survivors. *Clinical Psychology: Science and Practice, 15*, 74–90.

Mayer, E. A., & Fanselow, M. S. (2003). Dissecting the components of the central response to stress. *Nature Neuroscience, 6*, 1011–1012.

Merckelbach, H., Muris, P., de Jong, P. J., & de Jongh, A. (1999). Disgust sensitivity, blood-injection-injury fear, and dental anxiety. *Clinical Psychology and Psychotherapy, 6*, 279–285.

Millan, M. J. (2002). Descending control of pain. *Progress in Neurobiology, 66*, 355–474.

Miyatake, T., Katayama, K., Takeda, Y., Nakashima, A., Sugita, A., & Mizumoto, M. (2004). Is death feigning adaptive? Heritable variation in fitness difference of death-feigning behaviour. *Proceedings of the Royal Society of London. Series B, Biological Sciences, 271*, 2293–2296.

Moore, A. U., & Amstey, M. S. (1962). Tonic immobility: Differences in susceptibility of experimental and normal sheep and goats. *Science, 135*, 729–730.

Moskowitz, A. (2004). "Scared stiff": Catatonia as an evolutionary-based fear response. *Psychological Review, 111*, 984–1002.

Nesse, R. M. (1999). Proximate and evolutionary studies of anxiety, stress and depression: Synergy at the interface. *Neuroscience and Biobehavioral Reviews, 23*, 895–903.

Newman, B., Tommolino, E., Andreozzi, C., Joychan, S., Pocedic, J., & Heringhausen, J. (2007). The effect of a 473-ml (16-oz) water drink on vasovagal donor reaction rates in high-school students. *Transfusion, 47*, 1524–1533.

Nijenhuis, E. R. S., Spinhoven, P., Vanderlinden, J., Van Dyck, R., & Van der Hart, O. (1998). Somatoform dissociative symptoms as related to animal defensive reactions to predatory imminence and injury. *Journal of Abnormal Psychology, 107*, 63–73.

Nijenhuis, E. R. S., Van Engen, A., Kusters, I., & Van der Hart, O. (2001). Peritraumatic somatoform and psychological dissociation in relation to recall of childhood sexual abuse. *Journal of Trauma and Dissociation, 2*, 49–68.

Novak, M. A. (2003). Self-injurious behavior in rhesus monkeys: New insights into its etiology, physiology, and treatment. *American Journal of Primatology, 59*, 3–19.

Ogden, P., Minton, K., & Pain, C. (2006). *Trauma and the body: A sensorimotor approach to psychotherapy*, New York, NY: W.W. Norton.

Olatunji, B. O., Williams, N. L., Sawchuk, C. N., & Lohr, J. M. (2006). Disgust, anxiety, and fainting symptoms in blood-injection-injury fears: A structural model. *Journal of Anxiety Disorders, 20*, 23–24.

Page, A. C. (1994). Blood-injury phobia. *Clinical Psychology Review, 14*, 443–461.

Page, A. C. (2003). The role of disgust in faintness elicited by blood and injection stimuli. *Journal of Anxiety Disorders, 17*, 45–58.

Pasteur, G. (1982). A classification review of mimicry systems. *Annual Review of Ecology and Systematics, 13*, 169–199.

Pavlov, I. P. (1923). The identity of inhibition with sleep and hypnosis. *Scientific Monthly, 17*, 603–608.

Pavlov, I. P. (1927). *Conditioned Reflexes: An Investigation of the Physiological Activity of the Cerebral Cortex*. London, UK: Oxford University Press.

Perry, B. D., Pollard, R. A., Blakely, T. L., Baker, W. L., & Vigilante, D (1995). Childhood trauma, the neurobiology of adaptation, and "use-dependent" development of the brain. How "states" become "traits". *Infant Mental Health Journal, 16*, 271–291.

Pitman, R. K., Van der Kolk, B. A., Orr, S. P., & Greenberg, M. S. (1990). Naloxone reversible stress induced analgesia in post traumatic stress disorder. *Archives of General Psychiatry, 47*, 541–547.

Platek, S. M., Mohamed, F. B., & Gallup, G. G. (2005). Contagious yawning and the brain. *Cognitive Brain Research, 23*, 448–452.

Pole, N. (2007). The psychophysiology of posttraumatic stress disorder: A meta-analysis. *Psychological Bulletin, 133*, 725–746.

Porges, S. W. (1995). Orienting in a defensive world: Mammalian modifications of our evolutionary heritage: A polyvagal theory. *Psychophysiology, 32*, 301–318.

Portas, C. M., Rees, G., Howseman, A. M., Josephs, O., Turner, R., & Frith, C. D. (1998). A specific role for the thalamus in mediating the interaction of attention and arousal in humans. *Journal of Neuroscience, 18*, 8979–8989.

Pritts, S. D., & Susman, J. (2003). Diagnosis of Eating Disorders in Primary Care. *American Family Physician, 67*, 311–312.

Putnam, F. W. (1989). Pierre Janet and modern views of dissociation. *Journal of Traumatic Stress, 4*, 413–429.

Ratner, S. C. (1967). Comparative aspects of hypnosis. In J. E. Gordon (Ed.), *Handbook of clinical and experimental hypnosis* (pp. 550–587). New York, NY: Macmillan.

Rauch, S. L., Whalen, P. J., Shin, L. M., McInerney, S. C., Macklin, M. L., Lasko, N. B., ... Pitman, R. K. (2000). Exaggerated amygdala response to masked facial stimuli in posttraumatic stress disorder: A functional MRI study. *Biological Psychiatry, 47*, 769–776.

Ray, W. J., Odenwald, M., Neuner, F., Schauer, M., Ruf, M., Wienbruch, C., ... Elbert, T. (2006). Decoupling neural networks from reality: Dissociative experiences in torture victims are reflected in abnormal brain waves in left frontal cortex. *Psychological Science, 17*, 825–829.

Renfrey, G., & Spates, C. R. (1994). Eye movement desensitization: A partial dismantling study. *Journal of Behavior Therapy and Experimental Psychiatry, 25*, 231–239.

Rhudy, J. L., Grimes, J. S., & Meagher, M. W. (2004). Fear-induced hypoalgesia in humans: Effects on low intensity thermal stimulation and finger temperature. *The Journal of Pain, 5*, 458–468.

Rocha-Rego, V., Fiszman, A., Portugal, L. C., Pereira, M. G., de Oliveira, L., Mendlowicz, M. V., ... Volchan, E. (2008). Is tonic immobility the core sign among conventional peritraumatic signs and symptoms listed for PTSD? *Journal of Affective Disorders, 115*, 269–273.

Rockstroh, B., Johnen, M., Elbert, T., Lutzenberger, W., Birbaumer, N., Rudolph, K., ... Schnitzler, H. U. (1987). The pattern and habituation of the orienting response in man and rats. *The International Journal of Neuroscience, 37*, 169–182.

Russ, M. J., Roth, S. D., Lerman, A., Kakuma, T., Harrison, K., Shindledecker, R. D., ... Mattis, S. (1992). Pain perception in self-injurious patients with borderline personality disorder. *Biological Psychiatry, 32*, 501–511.

Salazar, C. F. (2000). *The treatment of war wounds in Graeco-Roman antiquity (studies in ancient medicine)*. Boston, MA: Brill Academic.

Schauer, M., & Elbert, T. (2008). *Psychophysiology of the defence cascade – Implications for the treatment of post-traumatic stress disorder (PTSD) and dissociative disorders*, Invited Lecture. Society for Applied Neuroscience, Biennial SAN Conference, Seville, 2008; http://www.applied-neuroscience.org/.

Schauer, M., Neuner, F., & Elbert, T. (2005). *Narrative exposure therapy (NET). A short-term intervention for traumatic stress disorders after war, terror, or torture*. Cambridge, MA: Hogrefe & Huber.

Schiller, D., & Johansen, J. (2009). Prelimbic prefrontal neurons drive fear expression: A clue for extinction-reconsolidation interactions. *Journal of Neuroscience, 29*, 13432–13434.

Schmahl, C., Bohus, M., Esposito, F., Treede, R. D., Di Salle, F., Greffrath, W., ... Seifritz, E. (2006). Neural correlates of antinociception in borderline personality disorder. *Archives of General Psychiatry, 63*, 659–667.

Siegfried, B., Frischknecht, H. R., & Nunez de Souza, R. (1990). An ethological model for the study of activation and interaction of pain, memory, and defensive systems in the attacked mouse: Role of endogenous opioids. *Neuroscience and Biobehavioral Reviews, 14*, 481–490.

Sierra, M., Senior, C., Dalton, J., McDonough, M., Bond, A., Phillips, M. L., ... David, A. S. (2002). Autonomic response in depersonalization disorder. *Archives of General Psychiatry, 59*, 833–838.

Simeon, D., Guralnik, O., Knutelska, M., Yehuda, R., & Schmeidler, J. (2003). Basal norepinephrine in depersonalization disorder. *Psychiatry Research, 121*, 93–97.

Skinner, J. (1985). Regulation of cardiac vulnerability by the cerebral defense system. *Journal of the American College of Cardiology, 5/6 (Suppl.)*, 88–94.

Skinner, J. E. (1988). Brain involvement in cardiovascular disorders. In T. Elbert, W. Langosch, A. Steptoe & D. Vaitl (Eds.), *Behavioral medicine in cardiovascular disorders* (pp. 229–253). Chichester, UK: Wiley.

Sokolov, Y. N. (1963). Waydenfeld S. W. (1963). *Perception and the conditioned reflex*. New York, NY: Macmillan Original work published 1958.

Spitzer, C., Barnow, S., Freyberger, H. J., & Grabe, H. J. (2006). Recent developments in the theory of dissociation. *World Psychiatry, 5*, 82–86.

Spitzer, C., Barnow, S., Freyberger, H. J., & Grabe, H. J. (2007). Pathologische Dissoziation – ein sinnvolles Konzept [Pathological dissociation – A useful concept?]. *Trauma & Gewalt, 1*, 34–44.

Suarez, S. D., & Gallup, G. G. (1979). Tonic immobility as a response to rape in humans: A theoretical note. *Psychological Record, 29*, 315–320.

Trouern-Trend, J. J., Cable, R. G., Badon, S. J., Newman, B. H., & Popovsky, M. A. (1999). A case-controlled multicenter study of vasovagal reactions in blood donors: influence of sex, age, donation status weight, blood pressure, and pulse. *Transfusion, 39*, 316–320.

Van der Hart, O., Nijenhuis, E., Steele, K., & Brown, D. (2004). Trauma-related dissociation: Conceptual clarity lost and found. *Australian and New Zealand Journal of Psychiatry, 38*, 906–914.

Van der Kolk, B. A. (1994). The body keeps the score: Memory and the evolving psychobiology of posttraumatic stress. *Harvard Review of Psychiatry, 1*, 253–265.

Van der Kolk, B. A., McFarlane, A. C., & Weisaeth, L. (Eds.). (1996). *Traumatic stress: The effects of overwhelming experience on mind body, and society.* New York, NY: The Guilford Press.

Van der Kolk, B. A., Pitman, R. K., & Orr, M. S. (1989). Endogenous opiods, stress-induced analgesia and post-traumatic stress disorder. *Psychopharmacology Bulletin, 25*, 108–112.

Van Dijk, J. D., & Sheldon, R. (2008). Is there any point to vasovagal syncope? *Clinical Autonomic Research, 18*, 167–169.

Vila, J., Guerraa, P., Muñoz, M. A., Vico, C., Viedma-del Jesús, M. I., Delgado, L. C., ... Rodríguez, S. (2007). Cardiac defense: From attention to action. *International Journal of Psychophysiology, 66*, 169–182.

Wakefield, J. C. (1992). The concept of mental disorder: On the boundary between biological facts and social values. *American Psychologist, 47*, 373–388.

Wakefield, J. C. (1999). Evolutionary versus prototype analyses of the concept of disorder. *Journal of Abnormal Psychology, 108*, 374–399.

Wiertelak, E. P., Watkins, L. R., & Maier, S. F. (1992). Conditioned inhibition of analgesia. *Animal Learning and Behavior, 20*, 339–349.

Yates, T. M. (2004). The developmental psychopathology of self-injurious behavior: Compensatory regulation in posttraumatic adaptation. *Clinical Psychology Review, 24*, 35–74.

Maggie Schauer

Department of Psychology
University of Konstanz & vivo International
at the Center for Psychiatry Reichenau
Feuersteinstr. 55
D-78479 Reichenau-Lindenbühl
Germany
Tel. +49 7531 88 4623 3151
Fax +49 7531 88 4601
E-mail margarete.schauer@uni-konstanz.de

Pilot Neuroimaging Study in Civilian Trauma Survivors

Episodic Recognition Memory, Hippocampal Volume, and Posttraumatic Stress Disorder Symptom Severity

Denise Dörfel,[1,2] Annett Werner,[3] Michael Schaefer,[4] and Anke Karl[5]

[1]Department of Psychology, Biopsychology Group, University of Technology, Dresden, Germany, [2]Department of Child and Adolescent Psychiatry, University Hospital Carl Gustav Carus, University of Technology, Dresden, Germany, [3]Department of Neuroradiology, University Hospitals Carl Gustav Carus, University of Technology, Dresden, Germany, [4]Department of Neurology, Otto-von-Guericke University Magdeburg, Germany, [5]School of Psychology, University of Exeter, UK

Abstract. Despite its hypothesized role in the etiology of posttraumatic stress disorder (PTSD), little research has investigated neural correlates of episodic memory impairment in trauma survivors. This pilot study utilized a correlational design to investigate the association between PTSD symptom severity, hippocampal volume, episodic memory, and brain activation during the Remember-Know task. Eleven non-medicated, right-handed survivors of civilian trauma participated in the study. Significant positive correlations were found between PTSD symptom severity and the activation of brain areas implicated in the episodic recognition network such as hippocampus, precuneus, and occipital gyrus. Higher PTSD symptoms were also significantly negatively correlated with brain activations in areas associated with episodic memory but also visuospatial attention such as the superior parietal lobule and the supramarginal gyrus. The pattern of results indicates specific alterations in the recruitment of the episodic memory network, possibly with a focus on internal mental imagery at the cost of integration between internal processes and external visuospatial online monitoring.

Keywords: recognition memory, fMRI, PTSD, hippocampus

Neuroscientific models describe posttraumatic stress disorder (PTSD) as a disorder of memory with vivid intrusive recollections (flashbacks) and fragmented episodic verbal memory of the event (Brewin, 2001). A large body of research studied intrusions using symptom provocation techniques and revealed increased amygdala and lower frontal cortical activation as the basic neural substrates (Lanius, Bluhm, Lanius, & Pain, 2006). Remarkably less experimental research has been done on the neural correlates of verbal or non-trauma-related memory deficits though recent meta-analyses of neuropsychological studies suggest particular impairment in this domain (Brewin, Kleiner, Vasterling, & Field, 2007; Johnsen & Asbjornsen, 2008). It can be hypothesized that verbal contextual memory functioning is a fundamental part of the ability to successfully integrate the traumatic memory in one's own past.

Only three neuroimaging studies have investigated non-trauma-related, explicit memory functioning (Bremner et al., 2003; Shin et al., 2004; Whalley, Rugg, Smith, Dolan, & Brewin, 2009). Only Whalley et al. (2009) found poorer memory performance in PTSD patients. Whereas Bremner et al. (2003) revealed no group differences for brain activity during neutral recall, Shin et al. (2004) found lower hippocampal activation for recall of deeply encoded items in the PTSD group. Within the PTSD group, however, they found a positive correlation between hippocampal activation across stimuli and PTSD symptom severity. In PTSD patients, as compared to controls, memory for emotional items resulted in different brain activations such as lower frontal and higher occipital (Bremner et al., 2003) or higher precuneus (Whalley et al., 2009) activation. For the hippocampus the two studies found opposite effects. These partially inconclusive results might be due to methodological differences and the fact that tasks did not always systematically differentiate between semantic and episodic memory during recall/recognition. In light of the specific clinical presentations of disintegrated trauma memory it is conceivable that semantic memory (familiarity and know) but not episodic memory (recollection and remember) may be intact.

Animal and human research points to partially different neural substrates (e.g., Aggleton & Brown, 1999; Skinner & Fernandes, 2007) of these two distinct recognition memory systems (i.e., dual-process signal-detection model) (Gardiner, Ramponi, & Richardson-Klavehn, 2002; Yonelinas, 2002). Among the key brain areas for episodic recognition is the hippocampus, which has also been widely implicated in episodic, spatial, and relational memory (Eichenbaum & Fortin, 2005; Konkel & Cohen, 2009;

DOI: 10.1027/0044-3409/a000019

Maguire, 1997) and which has been shown to be structurally and functionally altered in PTSD (for reviews see Karl et al., 2006; Karl & Werner, 2010; Rauch, Shin, & Phelps, 2006). Using psychophysiological interaction analyses of functional magnetic resonance imaging (fMRI) data, our group found recently that episodic recognition as measured by the Remember-Know (R/K) task was characterized by higher functional coupling between the hippocampus and the left precuneus than semantic recognition (Dörfel, Werner, Schaefer, von Kummer, & Karl, 2009). The precuneus has been associated with mental imagery during episodic memory (Cavanna & Trimble, 2006). Additionally, this structure was associated with recognition of emotionally encoded neutral visual objects in PTSD patients (Whalley et al., 2009).

The aim of this pilot study was to explore if PTSD symptom severity is associated with reduced verbal episodic memory, reduced brain activation in the episodic recognition memory network, and smaller hippocampal size. For this, non-medicated survivors of civilian trauma were invited to complete an fMRI-adapted R/K task (Eldridge, Knowlton, Furmanski, Bookheimer, & Engel, 2000), a neuropsychological screening and diagnostic interviews. Memory performance, level of psychopathology, brain activation (BOLD response) during episodic and semantic recognition, and hippocampal size were determined.

Methods

Participants

Initially, 14 trauma survivors were screened; one had to be excluded due to current substance abuse and two left the study at their own request before completing fMRI and neuropsychological testing. A total of 11 non-medicated, right-handed trauma survivors completed the diagnostic interview and either the fMRI task or neuropsychological screening or both. Ten had survived severe traffic accidents (car or motorbike accidents, two had an accident as pedestrians), one had experienced the suicide of a significant other. The mean age of the sample was 41.7 (±16.0; range 18–64) years. Seven (64%) females participated in the study. Table 1 shows the individuals' demographic and clinical characteristics. All participants gave written informed consent and the study protocol was approved by the ethics committee of the German Psychological Association.

Assessment of Psychopathology

Participants were invited for a diagnostic interview to establish symptom status. The Clinician Administered PTSD Scale (Blake et al., 1995; German: Schnyder & Moergeli, 2002) was used to determine categorical diagnosis of current PTSD as well as severity scores for PTSD and its symptom cluster as defined in the Diagnostic and Statistical Manual of Mental Disorders (DSM-IV; American Psychiatric Association, 1994). In addition, using the Structured Clinical Interview for the DSM-IV (First, Spitzer, Gibbon, & Williams, 1996; German: Wittchen, Wunderlich, Gruschwitz, & Zaudig, 1997) we evaluated the presence of concurrent and lifetime DSM-IV Axis I disorders such as depression. Participants also answered the Beck Depression Inventory (BDI) (Beck & Steer, 1987; German: Hautzinger, Bailer, Worall, & Keller, 1994) to assess severity of depressive symptoms and the State-Trait Anxiety Inventory (Spielberger, Gorsuch, & Lushene, 1970; German: Laux, Glanzmann, Schaffner, & Spielberger, 1981).

Neuropsychological Screening Assessment

Participants were also assessed for neuropsychological functioning, specifically general intellectual functioning and memory. The revised Wechsler Memory Scale (WMS) (Härting et al., 2000) assesses memory abilities in different domains: verbal memory, visual memory, attention, delayed recall, and general memory. Furthermore, general premorbid (crystalline) level of intellectual functioning was screened using a multiple choice vocabulary test (Mehrfachwahl-Wortschatz-Intelligenztest) (Lehrl, 1977). In order to screen visual-spatial (fluid) intelligence, a logical reasoning test, the subtest 3, recognizing irregularities in geometrical figures, of the Intellectual Performance Test (Leistungs-Pruef-System, LPS) (Horn, 1983) was administered.

R/K Task

The R/K task was adapted from Eldridge et al. (2000) and is similar to that described in Dörfel et al. (2009). The stimuli consisted of 177 nonemotional and non-arousing nouns from a standardized wordlist (Hager & Hasselhorn, 1994). In the study phase, 30 min prior to scanning, subjects had to learn a list of 150 nouns within 7 min. In the recognition phase during fMRI, the subjects were shown 108 old words and 27 new words. In each 5-s trial, subjects first saw the word for 3 s and within that time period had to decide whether or not they recognized it (first response). Subsequently, for recognized items, they were prompted to decide whether they remembered or knew the item within 2 s (second response). Responses were recorded via button presses. Between trials, subjects maintained fixation for 15 s. The classification of the answers into different recognition types [correct Remember (corrRem), correct Know (corrKnow), false Remember (falseRem), false Know (false-Know), correct Rejection (corrRej), and missed responses (Miss)] was obtained using the second responses.

MRI Data Acquisition

Images were acquired using a 1.5-T whole-body scanner (Sonata, running under Syngo VA25A, Siemens, Erlangen, Germany) equipped with an 8-array head coil. Participants wore earplugs for noise protection and lay on a padded

Table 1. Demographic and clinical information about the sample

Participant	Gender	Age	Time since trauma (weeks)	PTSD diagnosis (CAPS)	PTSD severity (CAPS)	CAPS Intrusion	CAPS Avoid	CAPS Avoid2	CAPS Numb	CAPS Hyper	SCID Depr	BDI	Trait STAI
1	Female	34	124	No PTSD	0	0	0	0	0	0	–	9	47
2	Male	38	62	No PTSD	7	0	7	3	4	0	Current	–	44
3	Female	21	45	No PTSD	12	8	0	0	0	4	No	0	40
4	Female	18	42	No PTSD	17	3	5	0	5	9	No	6	36
5	Male	44	1,015	No PTSD	28	2	9	0	9	17	No	14	43
6	Female	64	78	Sub-PTSD	15	3	1	1	0	11	Current	8	50
7	Female	29	651	Sub-PTSD	16	3	2	2	0	11	Current	6	37
8	Male	57	40	Sub-PTSD	24	9	3	3	0	12	No	9	45
9	Female	42	320	Sub-PTSD	33	6	5	0	5	22	No	20	46
10	Female	64	459	PTSD	38	17	13	7	6	8	No	14	53
11	Male	49	81	PTSD	87	21	34	9	25	32	Lifetime	39	48

Note. Splitting the Avoidance/Numbing cluster has been performed based on empirical work showing that these two dimensions diverge as differentiable dimensions (Asmundson et al., 2000).
CAPS = Clinician Administered PTSD Scale, CAPS Avoid2 = sum of items C1 and C2, CAPS Numb = sum of items C3–C7, SCID = Structured Clinical Interview for the DSM-IV, BDI = Beck Depression Inventory, STAI = State-Trait Anxiety Inventory.

Table 1. Continued

Participant	LPS	MWT	WMS gen	WMS verbal	WMS visual	WMS delayed	corrRem	corrKnow	Left hippocampus	Right hippocampus
1	–	–	–	–	–	–	0.263	0.354	2.33	2.35
2	119	93	90	81	112	84	0.326	0.236	–	–
3	105	90	85	72	123	86	–	–	2.64	2.24
4	117	80	101	103	97	107	0.375	0.239	–	–
5	127	115	102	96	114	101	0.090	0.340	1.90	1.85
6	100	121	90	83	104	97	–	–	1.71	1.96
7	135	125	129	125	121	130	0.432	0.242	2.41	2.27
8	–	–	77	65	102	79	–	–	–	–
9	90	121	113	106	121	107	0.129	0.435	2.29	2.32
10	113	112	102	88	124	112	0.481	0.306	2.17	2.19
11	93	112	85	76	105	94	0.483	0.000	2.37	2.46

LPS = logical reasoning score (fluid intelligence screening), MWT = multiple choice vocabulary test (crystalline intelligence screening), WMS = Wechsler Memory Scale, corrRem = Remember (episodic recognition), corrKnow = Know (semantic recognition).

scanner table in a dimly lit room. Foam padding minimized head movement. Stimuli were generated by Presentation (version 0.71, Neurobehavioral Systems, Albany, CA, USA) and were projected with a video projector onto a transparent plastic screen installed in front of the scanner. Participants viewed the stimuli through an angled mirror positioned immediately in front of their eyes. One structural scan was recorded before the functional scans using a three-dimensional T1 sequence (104 slices; TR, 6 ms; TE, 2.92 ms; matrix 512 · 512; orientation, sagittal; slice thickness, 2 mm; bandwidth, 240 Hz/Pix). Functional data were acquired using a T2*-weighted EPI sequence (30 slices; TR, 3,000 ms; TE, 45 ms; FOV, 230 mm; matrix, 64 · 64; orientation, axial; slice thickness, 3 mm; bandwidth, 750 Hz/Pix) to measure the blood oxygen level-dependent contrast. Functional data were collected in nine runs, each run containing 104 volumes (scans) covering the whole brain.

Magnetic Resonance Imaging Data Analysis

Functional data analysis: For the preprocessing and statistical analyses, the Statistical Parametric Mapping software package (SPM2, Wellcome Department of Imaging Neuroscience, Institute of Neurology, London) implemented in Matlab 6.5 (Release 13, Mathworks, Inc., Natick, MA, USA) was used. The functional data were realigned to correct for movement artifacts and coregistered to the mean image of the realigned functional scans. Next, parameters for spatial normalization of the coregistered T1 to the standard space of the Montreal Neurological Institute brain were determined. The normalization parameters were then applied to both the structural T1 and the functional EPI images (4th degree B-Spline interpolation). Smoothing was executed with a three-dimensional Gaussian filter with a full width at half maximum of 6 mm. We classified the subjects' responses as "correct Remember" (corrRem, old word correctly recognized and remembered, hence episodic memory) and "correct Know" (corrKnow, old word correctly recognized and known, hence semantic memory) to model the regressors of events within the general linear model framework by the canonical hemodynamic response function (hrf). The beginning of the word prompt paralleled the beginning of the hrf. Voxel-wise statistical parametric maps (SPM) were calculated for Recollection versus Familiarity (contrast: corrRem vs. corrKnow). The results of these *t*-contrast from each subject were then entered into a random-effects analysis at the group level. Then it was analyzed which brain regions, that are more activated during correct Remember as compared to correct Know, were significantly correlated with PTSD severity (total CAPS-score). Regions were labeled with the SPM toolbox Automatic Anatomical Labeling (Tzourio-Mazoyer et al., 2002). To obtain correlation coefficients, the contrast estimates of the contrast corrRem versus Know for each significant correlated region were extracted and additional correlation analyses with the CAPS-score were conducted using SPSS 17 for Windows (SPSS Inc., Chicago, IL, USA).

Determination of hippocampal volume: Hippocampus volumetry was conducted using Amira 3.1.1 (Department for Scientific Visualization, Konrad-Zuse-Zentrum für Informationstechnik Berlin, ZIB, Germany) by two trained independent raters. The raters used a standard protocol recommended by Pruessner et al. (2000).

Results

Memory Performance, Neuropsychology, and Symptom Severity

Significant correlations were found between PTSD avoidance symptoms and both semantic ($r = -.73$, $p = .04$) and episodic ($r = .74$, $p = .03$) recognition. No further correlations between symptom severity and recognition performance became significant. There were also no significant correlations between symptom severity and neuropsychological measures. However, medium effect size (ES) negative correlations (see Section Post Hoc Consideration of Statistical Power for further information) were observed between visual-spatial logical reasoning score (LPS) and PTSD (total, intrusion, and hyperarousal, *r*s ranging from $-.48$ to $-.49$, n.s.), trait anxiety ($r = -.52$, n.s.) and depression ($r = -.50$, n.s.).

BOLD Response in Episodic Memory Network and Symptom Severity

For the right hippocampus, the precuneus and the occipital gyrus (all central in the episodic memory network; Skinner & Fernandes, 2007) increased activity was highly significantly positively associated with PTSD symptom severity ($T > 5.89$, $p < .001$; total symptom severity and intrusion with correlations ranging from $r = .78$, $p = .04$ to $r = .98$, $p < .001$, see Figure 1). Significant negative correlations were found between PTSD severity (total and intrusion) and areas involved in episodic buffering but also semantic processing and visuospatial orientation such as right supramarginal gyrus and right superior parietal lobule (Culham & Valyear, 2006; Vilberg & Rugg, 2008) ($T > 5.89$, $p < .001$; with *r*s ranging from $r = -.81$, $p = 03$ to $r = -.97$, $p < .001$, see Figure 1).

Hippocampal Volume and Symptom Severity

There was no significant correlation between right hippocampal volume and symptom severity or memory performance. However, we found a number of nonsignificant medium ES correlations (see also Section Post Hoc Consideration of Statistical Power) between right hippocampal volume and PTSD intrusion, avoidance and BDI (*r*s ranging from $r = .40$ to $.44$, all n.s.) and episodic ($r = .44$, n.s.) and semantic ($r = -.50$, n.s.) recognition. Furthermore, there was a medium ES negative correlation for right hippocampal volume and visuospatial logical reasoning score (LPS) ($r = -.42$, n.s.). For left hippocampal volume, there was only one significant negative association with age of the participants ($r = -.75$, $p = .03$). In addition, nonsignificant medium ES positive hippocampal volume correlations were observed for episodic recognition and WMS visual (*r*s between $r = .55$ and $.56$).

BOLD Response in Episodic Memory Network, Memory and Neuropsychological Performance

There were no significant associations between episodic memory network activation and memory respective neuropsychological functioning. However, nonsignificant positive medium ES correlations were found between activation of right hippocampus during episodic recognition and visual WMS ($r = .69$, n.s.). A similar association was observed between occipital gyrus activation and visual WMS ($r = .68$, n.s.). Nonsignificant negative medium ES correlations were revealed between supramarginal gyrus activation and visual WMS ($r = -.72$, n.s.). Visuospatial logical reasoning (LPS) tended to be negatively associated with hippocampus and precuneus activation (*r*s from $-.50$ to $-.68$, n.s.) during episodic recognition and it was positively associated with supramarginal gyrus and superior parietal lobe activation (*r*s from = .58 to .81, n.s.).

Post Hoc Consideration of Statistical Power

Due to the small sample size we were only able to detect statistical significances when large ES occurred. This resulted in only a few statistically significant effects. However, we obtained a number of correlation coefficients indicating

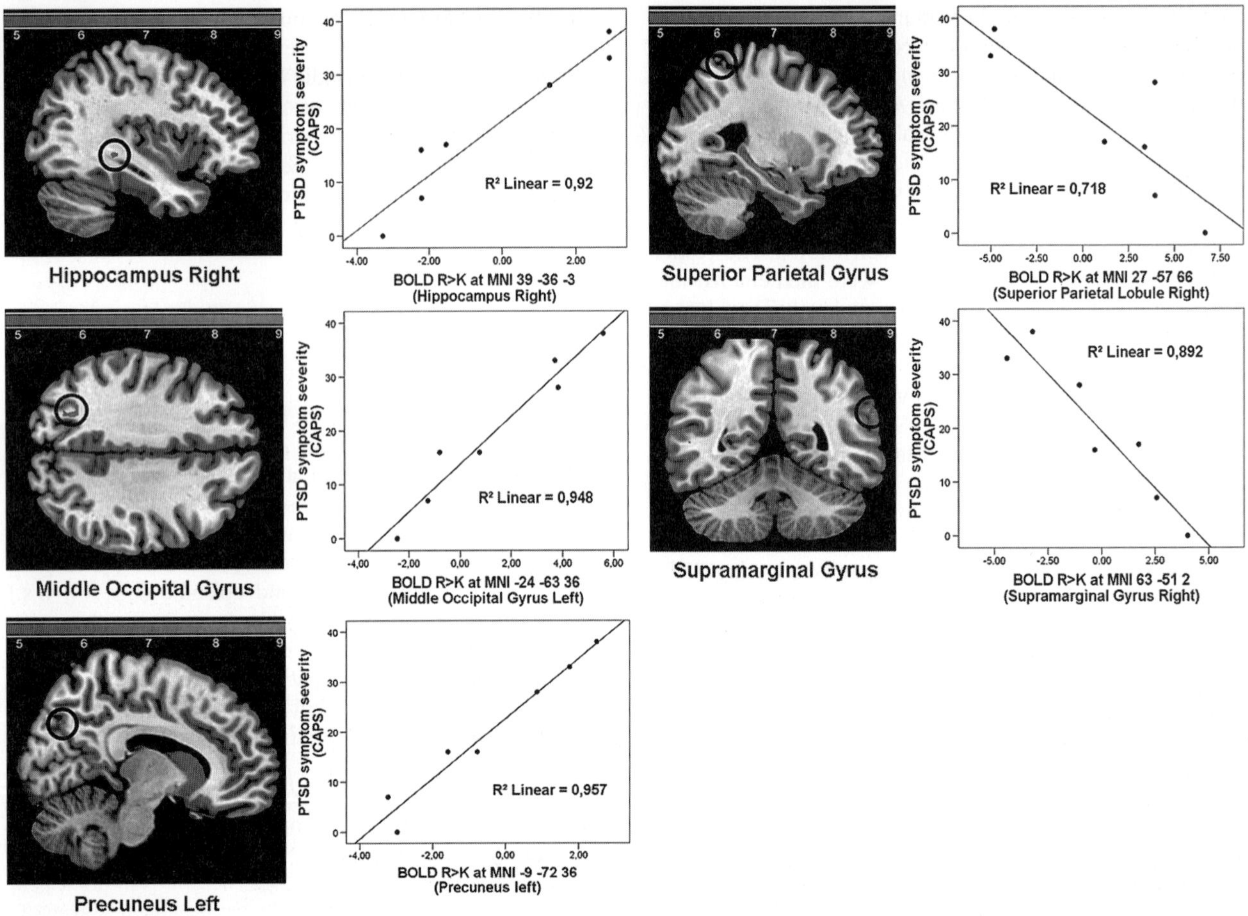

Figure 1. Correlations between PTSD symptom severity (CAPS total score) and BOLD response during Remember (episodic recognition) in different brain areas. The left panel shows positive associations between symptom severity and brain response; the right shows negative associations.

medium ES. Therefore, post hoc power calculations for bivariate correlations were performed using G*Power 3.0 (Faul, Erdfelder, Lang, & Buchner, 2007). It was revealed that in order to detect significant correlations between these associations at a statistical power of .8 and alpha of .05, a sample size of between 22 and 44 participants would have been required.

Discussion

This study aimed to investigate the relationship between PTSD symptom severity, memory performance, and brain activation during episodic recognition in trauma survivors. Whereas PTSD symptoms were not significantly associated with memory performance and neuropsychological measures, memory performance was found to be highly significantly associated with activations in brain structures previously associated with episodic memory recognition when participants performed the R/K task for previously studied items in the fMRI. In contrast to our hypothesis, higher PTSD symptom severity was associated with higher activation in the right hippocampus, the left precuneus, and the left occipital gyrus, whereas PTSD symptom severity was associated with deactivation in regions relevant for episodic memory but also for semantic, language, and spatial orientation such as the supramarginal gyrus and the superior parietal lobule. That increased right hippocampal activation during episodic recognition was associated with higher PTSD symptom severity may be counterintuitive but is in line with findings by Shin et al. (2004) and in line with previous research from our group showing increased right-hemisphere brain activation to be associated with higher PTSD severity and its treatment-related reduction (Rabe, Beauducel, Zollner, Maercker, & Karl, 2006; Rabe, Zoellner, Beauducel, Maercker, & Karl, 2008). Increased hippocampal activity in the light of lower functionality (e.g., lower memory performance, and smaller volume) might also be interpreted as a compensatory mechanism. Increased occipital (Bremner et al., 2003) and precuneus (Whalley et al., 2009) activation during explicit memory in PTSD is also in line with previous research. Of interest is that activation in some areas of the episodic recognition network was negatively associated with PTSD symptom severity. These areas have been hypothesized to function as an episodic buffer, that is, they contribute to the generation and maintenance of an integrated representation of retrieved information and interface between episodic memory and executive systems (Vilberg & Rugg, 2008). In addition, they are involved in the control of visuospatial attention and visuoconstruction (Culham & Valyear, 2006).

In order to explore potential underlying structural changes, hippocampal volumes were determined. No significant associations were revealed between volume, symptom severity, or memory performance, whereas age was negatively associated with left but not right hippocampal volume. Of interest for future research might be that some correlation coefficients indicating associations between hippocampal size, symptom severity, episodic recognition and visual memory performance and visuospatial logical reasoning did not reach significance due to the small sample size.

Taken together these findings suggest that in the presence of increased PTSD symptoms, episodic recognition relies on altered recruitment of its neural network with increases in areas relevant for visual mental imagery (e.g., precuneus and occipital cortex) and decreases in areas involved in the orientation toward the environment or keeping the balance between internal and external process monitoring (e.g., supramarginal gyrus). The pattern of brain activations and associations with memory and neuropsychological performance may also point to the role of visuospatial impairment in PTSD such as recently revealed by Gilbertson et al. (2007) who hypothesize that a dysfunction in this domain may contribute to less efficient extinction of the learned fear response. In addition, in a clinical sample we recently revealed visuospatial impairment using the Rey Osterrieth Complex Figure Test (Newell, Lee, Garner, Baldwin, & Karl, 2010) which incorporates a visuoconstructive component impaired in patients with right supramarginal gyrus lesions.

The interpretation of these pilot results warrants some caution. First, due to the small sample size we were only able to detect large effects. A post hoc power consideration revealed that a number of medium size correlations might have reached significance in a larger sample of approximately 20 or more participants. Most previous studies find only medium ESs for their relationships between symptoms, brain, and behavior (see, e.g., meta-analysis by Karl et al., 2006). Second, the sample was heterogenous with respect to age and gender, trauma types and levels of psychopathology. This required a correlational approach and precluded group analyses as the small sample size did not allow differentiating those with and without formal DSM-IV diagnosis. The requirement of including non-medicated subjects may also have resulted in a recruitment bias toward less impaired individuals. In line with previous studies there was also a high correlation between PTSD and depressive symptoms ($r = .92$, $p < .001$). We also have no healthy control group included. Thus, no unequivocal disorder-specific conclusions can be drawn from the obtained associations.

In summary, these pilot results point to altered recruitment of structures of the episodic memory network when trauma survivors show higher PTSD symptoms. Further research is needed to confirm the results in a larger sample and explore the mechanisms behind this.

References

Aggleton, J. P., & Brown, M. W. (1999) Episodic memory, amnesia, and the hippocampal-anterior thalamic axis. *Behavior and Brain Sciences, 22*, 425–444, discussion 444–489.

American Psychiatric Association. (1994). *Diagnostic and statistical manual of mental disorders*, (4th ed.). Washington, DC: DSM–IV.

Asmundson, G. J., Frombach, I., McQuaid, J., Pedrelli, P., Lenox, R., & Stein, M. B. (2000). Dimensionality of posttraumatic stress symptoms: A confirmatory factor analysis of DSM-IV symptom clusters and other symptom models. *Behaviour Research and Therapy, 38*, 203–214.

Beck, A. T., & Steer, R. A. (1987). *Beck depression inventory.* San Antonio, TX: The Psychological Cooperation.

Blake, D. D., Weathers, F. W., Nagy, L. M., Kaloupek, D. G., Charney, D. S., & Keane, T. M. (1995). *Clinician-Administered PTSD Scale for DSM-IV (CAPS-DX)*. Boston, MA: National Center for Posttraumatic Stress Disorder, Behavioral Science Division, Boston VA Medical Center.

Bremner, J. D., Vythilingam, M., Vermetten, E., Southwick, S. M., McGlashan, T., Staib, L. H., et al. (2003). Neural correlates of declarative memory for emotionally valenced words in women with posttraumatic stress disorder related to early childhood sexual abuse. *Biological Psychiatry, 53*, 879–889.

Brewin, C. R. (2001). A cognitive neuroscience account of posttraumatic stress disorder and its treatment. *Behaviour Research and Therapy, 39*, 373–393.

Brewin, C. R., Kleiner, J. S., Vasterling, J. J., & Field, A. P. (2007). Memory for emotionally neutral information in posttraumatic stress disorder: A meta-analytic investigation. *Journal of Abnormal Psychology, 116*, 448–463.

Cavanna, A. E., & Trimble, M. R. (2006). The precuneus: A review of its functional anatomy and behavioural correlates. *Brain, 129*, 564–583.

Culham, J. C., & Valyear, K. F. (2006). Human parietal cortex in action. *Current Opinion in Neurobiology, 16*, 205–212.

Dörfel, D., Werner, A., Schaefer, M., von Kummer, R., & Karl, A. (2009). Distinct brain networks in recognition memory share a defined region in the precuneus. *European Journal of Neuroscience, 30*, 1947–1959.

Eichenbaum, H., & Fortin, N. J. (2005). Bridging the gap between brain and behavior: Cognitive and neural mechanisms of episodic memory. *Journal of Experimental Analysis of Behavior, 84*, 619–629.

Eldridge, L. L., Knowlton, B. J., Furmanski, C. S., Bookheimer, S. Y., & Engel, S. A. (2000). Remembering episodes: A selective role for the hippocampus during retrieval. *Nature Neuroscience, 3*, 1149–1152.

Faul, F., Erdfelder, E., Lang, A. G., & Buchner, A. (2007). G*Power 3: A flexible statistical power analysis program for the social, behavioral, and biomedical sciences. *Behavior Research Methods, 39*, 175–191.

First, M. B., Spitzer, R. L., Gibbon, M., & Williams, J. B. (1996). *Structured clinical interview for DSM-IV axis I disorders*. New York: Biometrics Research Department, New York State Psychiatric Institute.

Gardiner, J. M., Ramponi, C., & Richardson-Klavehn, A. (2002). Recognition memory and decision processes: A meta-analysis of remember, know, and guess responses. *Memory, 10*, 83–98.

Gilbertson, M. W., Williston, S. K., Paulus, L. A., Lasko, N. B., Gurvits, T. V., Shenton, M. E., et al. (2007). Configural cue performance in identical twins discordant for posttraumatic stress disorder: Theoretical implications for the role of hippocampal function. *Biological Psychiatry, 62*, 513–520.

Hager, W., & Hasselhorn, M. (1994). *Handbuch deutschsprachiger Wortnormen* [Handbook of German Word Norms]. Göttingen: Hogrefe.
Härting, C., Markowitsch, H. J., Neufeld, H., Calabrese, P., Deisinger, K., & Kessler, J. (2000). *Wechsler Gedächtnistest – revidierte Fassung (WMS-R)*. Göttingen: Huber [Revised Wechsler Memory Scale].
Hautzinger, M., Bailer, M., Worall, H., & Keller, F. (1994). *Beck-Depressions-Inventar (BDI)*. Bern, Göttingen, Toronto, Seattle: Huber.
Horn, W. (1983). *L-P-S Leistungsprüfsystem* [LPS Intellectual Performance Test]. Göttingen: Hogrefe.
Johnsen, G. E., & Asbjornsen, A. E. (2008). Consistent impaired verbal memory in PTSD: A meta-analysis. *Journal of Affective Disorders, 111*, 74–82.
Karl, A., Schaefer, M., Malta, L. S., Dörfel, D., Rohleder, N., & Werner, A. (2006). A meta-analysis of structural brain abnormalities in PTSD. *Neuroscience and Biobehavioural Review, 30*, 1004–1031.
Karl, A., & Werner, A. (2010). The use of proton magnetic resonance spectroscopy in PTSD research – meta-analyses of findings and methodological review. *Neuroscience and Biobehavioural Review, 34*, 7–22.
Konkel, A., & Cohen, N. J. (2009). Relational memory and the hippocampus: Representations and methods. *Frontiers in Neuroscience, 3*, 166–174.
Lanius, R. A., Bluhm, R., Lanius, U., & Pain, C. (2006). A review of neuroimaging studies in PTSD: Heterogeneity of response to symptom provocation. *Journal of Psychiatry Research, 40*, 709–729.
Laux, L., Glanzmann, P., Schaffner, P., & Spielberger, C. D. (1981). *Das State-Trait-Angstinventar* [The State Trait Anxiety Inventory]. Weinheim: Beltz-Test.
Lehrl, S. (1977). *Mehrfachwahlwortschatztest MWT-A* [Multiple Choice Vocabulary Test]. Erlangen, Germany: Straube.
Maguire, E. A. (1997). Hippocampal involvement in human topographical memory: Evidence from functional imaging. *Philosophical Transactions of the Royal Society London B Biological Sciences, 352*, 1475–1480.
Newell, T., Lee, V., Garner, M., Baldwin, D., & Karl, A. (2010). *Impaired visual spatial recall in post-traumatic stress disorder*, Manuscript in preparation.
Pruessner, J. C., Li, L. M., Serles, W., Pruessner, M., Collins, D. L., Kabani, N., et al. (2000). Volumetry of hippocampus and amygdala with high-resolution MRI and three-dimensional analysis software: Minimizing the discrepancies between laboratories. *Cerebral Cortex, 10*, 433–442.
Rabe, S., Beauducel, A., Zollner, T., Maercker, A., & Karl, A. (2006). Regional brain electrical activity in posttraumatic stress disorder after motor vehicle accident. *Journal of Abnormal Psychology, 115*, 687–698.
Rabe, S., Zoellner, T., Beauducel, A., Maercker, A., & Karl, A. (2008). Changes in brain electrical activity after cognitive behavioral therapy for posttraumatic stress disorder in patients injured in motor vehicle accidents. *Psychosomatic Medicine, 70*, 13–19.
Rauch, S. L., Shin, L. M., & Phelps, E. A. (2006). Neurocircuitry models of posttraumatic stress disorder and extinction: Human neuroimaging research – past, present, and future. *Biological Psychiatry, 60*, 376–382.
Schnyder, U., & Moergeli, H. (2002). German version of Clinician-Administered PTSD Scale. *Journal of Traumatic Stress, 15*, 487–492.
Shin, L. M., Shin, P. S., Heckers, S., Krangel, T. S., Macklin, M. L., Orr, S. P., et al. (2004). Hippocampal function in posttraumatic stress disorder. *Hippocampus, 14*, 292–300.
Skinner, E. I., & Fernandes, M. A. (2007). Neural correlates of recollection and familiarity: A review of neuroimaging and patient data. *Neuropsychologia, 45*, 2163–2179.
Spielberger, C. D., Gorsuch, R. L., & Lushene, R. E. (1970). *STAI Manual for the State-Trait Anxiety Inventory.* Palo Alto, CA: Consulting Psychologists Press.
Tzourio-Mazoyer, N., Landeau, B., Papathanassiou, D., Crivello, F., Etard, O., Delcroix, N., et al. (2002). Automated anatomical labeling of activations in SPM using a macroscopic anatomical parcellation of the MNI MRI single-subject brain. *Neuroimage, 15*, 273–289.
Vilberg, K. L., & Rugg, M. D. (2008). Memory retrieval and the parietal cortex: A review of evidence from a dual-process perspective. *Neuropsychologia, 46*, 1787–1799.
Whalley, M. G., Rugg, M. D., Smith, A. P., Dolan, R. J., & Brewin, C. R. (2009). Incidental retrieval of emotional contexts in post-traumatic stress disorder and depression: An fMRI study. *Brain and Cognition, 69*, 98–107.
Wittchen, H.-U., Wunderlich, U., Gruschwitz, S., & Zaudig, M. (1997). *SKID. Strukturiertes Klinisches Interview für DSM-IV. Achse I.* Göttingen: Hogrefe.
Yonelinas, A. P. (2002). The nature of recollection and familiarity: A review of 30 years of research. *Journal of Memory and Language, 469*, 441–517.

Anke Karl

School of Psychology
University of Exeter
Washington Singer Laboratories
Perry Road
Exeter EX4 4QG
UK
Tel. +44 1392 725271
Fax +44 1392 724623
E-mail a.karl@exeter.ac.uk

Learning and Consolidation of Verbal Declarative Memory in Patients with Posttraumatic Stress Disorder

Slawomira J. Diener, Herta Flor, and Michèle Wessa

Department of Cognitive and Clinical Neuroscience, Central Institute of Mental Health, University of Heidelberg, Mannheim, Germany

Abstract. Impairments in declarative memory have been reported in posttraumatic stress disorder (PTSD). Fragmentation of explicit trauma-related memory has been assumed to impede the formation of a coherent memorization of the traumatic event and the integration into autobiographic memory. Together with a strong non-declarative memory that connects trauma reminders with a fear response the impairment in declarative memory is thought to be involved in the maintenance of PTSD symptoms. Fourteen PTSD patients, 14 traumatized subjects without PTSD, and 13 non-traumatized healthy controls (HC) were tested with the California Verbal Learning Test (CVLT) to assess verbal declarative memory. PTSD symptoms were assessed with the Clinician Administered PTSD Scale and depression with the Center of Epidemiological Studies Depression Scale. Several indices of the CVLT pointed to an impairment in declarative memory performance in PTSD, but not in traumatized persons without PTSD or HC. No group differences were observed if recall of memory after a time delay was set in relation to initial learning performance. In the PTSD group verbal memory performance correlated significantly with hyperarousal symptoms, after concentration difficulties were accounted for. The present study confirmed previous reports of declarative verbal memory deficits in PTSD. Extending previous results, we propose that learning rather than memory consolidation is impaired in PTSD patients. Furthermore, arousal symptoms may interfere with successful memory formation in PTSD.

Keywords: declarative memory, Posttraumatic Stress Disorder, trauma, explicit memory, California Verbal Learning Test

Impairments in declarative memory have often been reported in posttraumatic stress disorder (PTSD) (for an overview see Brewin, Kleiner, Vasterling, & Field, 2007). Two recent meta-analyses found small to medium effects of memory impairment in PTSD patients when they were compared to either a trauma-exposed or a never trauma-exposed control group (Brewin et al., 2007; Johnsen & Asbjornsen, 2008). The effect was larger and more consistent for declarative verbal memory while effects for declarative visual memory were mixed (Brewin et al., 2007). The authors interpret this result as supportive of the dual representation theory of PTSD that assumes a dissociation of verbally and situationally accessible memory in PTSD (Brewin, Dalgleish, & Joseph, 1996). More precisely, the theory suggests one conscious, declarative memory representation of the traumatic event, which is verbally accessible and deliberately editable and one unconscious, non-declarative memory representation that cannot be deliberately accessed but can be triggered by perceptual cues (Brewin et al., 1996). In line with this theory, Ehlers and Clark (2000) proposed two processing streams for autobiographical memory formation. One is labeled conceptual processing and refers to the storage of data within the context of other information, such as time, place, and meaning. This conception is analogous to declarative memory formation. The other is labeled data-driven processing, implying the storage of sensory, physiological, and motor aspects of the event and thus referring to non-declarative memory formation. Conceptual data processing is supposed to be hippocampus-dependent and requires large processing capacities (Metcalfe & Mischel, 1999). In PTSD patients, these capacities might be limited due to high levels of stress during the traumatic situation, which hamper the formation of episodic memories and thereby create a highly selective and fragmented traumatic memory (Brewin et al., 1996). In contrast, high arousal during the traumatic event accentuates the formation of affect-laden memories and leads to an extensive network of perceptual cues that facilitate high emotional reactivity to trauma reminders in PTSD patients. In sum, the introduced theories assume disorganized and fragmented declarative trauma memories in PTSD patients together with high emotional responsivity to trauma cues. A number of neuroimaging studies are in support of the dual representation memory theory. In these studies, PTSD patients show a right-hemispheric activation pattern during flashbacks and trauma-related imagery (Lanius et al., 2004) as well as greater right-hemispheric electroencephalography asymmetry during emotional processing (Curtis & Cicchetti, 2007). A pattern of increased right-sided activation during exposure to a trauma-related picture was also observed in a recent study in PTSD and sub-syndromal PTSD after severe motor vehicle accidents

(Rabe, Zoellner, Beauducel, Maercker, & Karl, 2008). Interestingly, right-hemispheric brain activation has been associated with affect-laden autobiographical memories that are stored in a nonverbal representational system (Paivio, 1986). In contrast, in the above-mentioned studies healthy controls activated mainly left-sided brain regions that are associated with verbal autobiographical memories (Maguire, 2001). However, the empirical evidence for disturbances in autobiographical memory concerning the traumatic event or another unpleasant but non-traumatic events in trauma-exposed individuals remains inconclusive. While some studies reported impairments in the recall of traumatic events in PTSD patients (Harvey, Bryant, & Dang, 1998; Jones, Harvey, & Brewin, 2007), other studies failed to find a difference between PTSD patients and traumatized controls (Merckelbach, Dekkers, Wessel, & Roefs, 2003; Wessa, Jatzko, & Flor, 2006). It seems that the disorganization of trauma memories is a more stable finding than a difference in the remembered quantity (Jelinek, Randjbar, Seifert, Kellner, & Moritz, 2009). Moreover, whether the theoretical assumptions of dual representation theory can be transferred to non-autobiographical neutral contents has not been investigated yet. Based on the dual coding approach (Brewin et al., 2007; Paivio, 1986) it might be argued that the two memory representations might also develop when non-autobiographical material is learned and recalled and that this could explain the differences in verbal and visual memory performance in PTSD patients. However, the underlying mechanisms for the proposed analogy between a dual memory representation for autobiographical, traumatic events and the formation of these two types of memory (declarative and non-declarative) for non-autobiographical information are not clear to date. One explanation could be a general deficit in verbal memory that exists already before the traumatic experience in PTSD patients and might then facilitate the development of the disorder by amplifying the formation of situationally accessible memory (Bustamante, Mellman, David, & Fins, 2001; Jelinek et al., 2009). Alternatively, the amount of intrinsic arousal during memory formation might interfere with declarative learning and consolidation of information. Indeed, Sandi and Pinelo-Nava (2007) propose that intrinsic stress increases the acquisition of non-declarative learning and memory (e.g., fear-conditioning) but decreases the acquisition of declarative memories at very low and very high levels of stress. In PTSD increased and sustained hyperarousal, which constitutes a core symptom of the disorder, may therefore act as intrinsic stressor that leads to impairments in declarative memory formation. Considering the suggestion of Sandi and Pinelo-Nava (2007), such impairments should then be present during acquisition (encoding) rather than consolidation of declarative memories (long-term memory formation) (Sandi & Pinelo-Nava, 2007). In accordance with these assumptions, Johnsen and Asbjornsen (2009) reported an impairment in encoding strategies in the learning phase, particularly deficits in serial clustering in PTSD patients as compared to trauma-exposed persons without PTSD. The authors suggested that these impairments might be responsible for the deficits in non-autobiographical declarative verbal memory in PTSD.

The goal of the present study was an investigation of declarative, non-autobiographical verbal memory by the analysis of learning progress as well as of long-term memory formation in PTSD patients and traumatized and non-traumatized controls. In addition, PTSD symptom clusters were correlated with memory performance. We expected to replicate impaired verbal declarative memory findings in PTSD patients with regard to the acquisition but not the consolidation of verbal material. Furthermore, the deficits in learning were expected to correlate with hyperarousal symptoms in the PTSD group.

Methods

Participants

In this study 14 PTSD patients, 14 traumatized persons without PTSD (NPTSD), and 13 non-traumatized healthy subjects (HC) were investigated. The participants did not significantly differ with regard to sex, age, and education (see Table 1). Subjects were recruited by public announcements and from earlier studies at the Department of Clinical and Cognitive Neuroscience at the Central Institute of Mental Health (Mannheim, Germany). All NPTSD met the A-criterion for PTSD of the Diagnostic and Statistical Manual of Mental Disorders IVth edition with Text Revision (DSM-IV-TR; American Psychiatric Association, 1994). The PTSD patients met DSM IV-TR criteria for chronic PTSD. Furthermore, two PTSD patients reported a current major depressive episode. For all study participants, exclusion criteria were comorbid mental disorder such as current and lifetime substance dependence, borderline personality disorder or schizophrenia, but also cardiovascular or neurological disorders, brain injury, continuous pain medication, and pregnancy. All participants were unmedicated. Participants received a reimbursement of €80. The study was approved by the Ethics Committee of the Medical Faculty Mannheim, University of Heidelberg, Germany. The participants gave written informed consent after detailed description of the complete study.

Instruments and Design

All subjects were interviewed by a trained clinical psychologist using structured clinical interviews (SCID I and II) for DSM IV Axes I and II (First, Gibbon, Spitzer, Williams, & Benjamin, 1997; First, Spitzer, Gibbon, & Williams, 1997; German versions: Fydrich, Renneberg, Schmitz, & Wittchen, 1997; Wittchen, Wunderlich, Gruschwitz, & Zaudig, 1997) as well as the Clinician Administered PTSD Scale (CAPS) (Blake et al., 1995; German version: Wessa et al., 2010). They also completed the Center for Epidemiologic Studies Depression Scale (CES-D) (Radloff, 1977; German version: Hautzinger & Bailer, 1993). Furthermore, the California Verbal Learning Test (CVLT; Delis, Kramer, & Kaplan, 1987; German version: Niemann, Sturm, Thöne-Otto, & Willmes, 2008), a verbal learning and mem-

Table 1. Demographic and psychometric data for the PTSD patients, the NPTSD persons, and the HC

	PTSD $N = 14$	NPTSD $N - 14$	HC $N - 13$	Group statistics
Gender, no. m/f	9/5	8/6	7/6	$\chi^2(2) = .32, p = .85$
Age in years, mean (*SD*)	41.29 (14.28)	39.64 (13.26)	42.46 (13.69)	$F(2, 38) = .14, p = .87$
Intelligence quotient				
MWT-B[a] mean (*SD*)	113.71 (11.87)	119.29 (14.20)	122.00 (14.04)	$F(2, 38) = 1.35, p = .27$
CFT-20[b] mean (*SD*)	111.79 (11.23)	123.43 (17.43)	123.23 (12.92)	$F(2, 38) = 3.08, p = .06$
CAPS				
Reexperiencing items 1–5, mean (*SD*)	1.6 (0.91)	0.1 (0.16)	–	$t(25) = -5.55, p < .001$
Avoidance items 6–12, mean (*SD*)	1.59 (0.91)	0.05 (0.15)	–	$t(25) = -6.01, p < .001$
Hyperarousal items 13–17, mean (*SD*)	1.89 (0.79)	0.14 (0.28)	–	$t(25) = -7.46, p < .001$
CES-D, mean (*SD*)	23.07 (11.56)	6.14 (6.00)	6.77 (6.43)	$F(2, 38) = 17.95, p < .001$

[a]Multiple Choice Word Fluency Test (MWT-B).
[b]Culture-Fair Intelligence Test (CFT-20).

ory test, was administered. In the CVLT a list containing 16 words (List A) from four categories is read to the participant for five times and the number of words that can be recalled after each trial is noted. After that an interference list (List B) is read once and immediately recalled, followed by a free recall of the previously learned List A (short delay free recall) and a cued recall where each of the four categories the words belong is given as a cue for the recall of the words. After a 20-min break, in which the participants underwent a nonverbal intelligence test (see below), List A had to be recalled again with and without the category cues (long delay free recall and long delay cued recall). Finally, a list of 44 words that contained words from Lists A and B is read to the participant who has to recognize the words from List A and negate all other words. For the CVLT the following indices were calculated: Number of words remembered after the first and the fifth trial, representing immediate retentiveness and learning progress. Furthermore number of words remembered after short delay free recall, long delay free and cued recall was analyzed, all representing active recall of consolidated memory. Additionally discrimination accuracy, meaning the percentage of hits minus percentage of false positives in the recognition test, was calculated which is a measure of passive recognition of consolidated memory. Finally the differences of recalled words between the fifth trial and the long delay free recall and between the fifth trial and the long delay cued recall were computed. These last two values constitute measures of memory consolidation, which is assumed to be hippocampus-dependent (Golomb et al., 1994).

In addition to the CVLT, a test for premorbid intelligence (Multiple Choice Word Fluency Test, MWT-B; Lehrl, 2005) and a nonverbal intelligence test (CFT-20-R, Culture-Fair Intelligence Test – Scale 2; Weiß, 2006) were administered to all study participants (see Table 1).

Statistical Analysis

Unpaired samples *t* tests were conducted for the comparison of PTSD symptoms in the traumatized subjects with and without PTSD. For the CVLT data, analyses of variance (ANOVAs) were conducted with group (PTSD, NPTSD, and HC) as between-factor and the CLVT indices as dependent variables. ANOVAs were also calculated for the intelligence tests and the depression questionnaire. Post hoc group comparisons were conducted using Bonferroni corrections. In order to explore the relationship between PTSD symptoms, depression, and memory deficits, correlations between the memory performance and the CAPS subscales as well as CES-D sum scores were calculated in the PTSD group.

Results

For declarative memory significant group differences were found on almost all indices of the CVLT (see Table 2), with the exception of the differences between the two memory consolidation indices (fifth learning trial minus the long delay free recall and fifth learning trial minus the long delay cued recall). Post hoc comparisons revealed that the significant group differences were always between the PTSD and the two control groups, except for discrimination accuracy where the comparison between PTSD and HC failed to reach significance ($p = .076$). To control for the influence of intelligence all ANOVAs were recalculated with the CFT-20 included as covariate. The CFT-20 was chosen as indicator of intelligence, as this test yielded almost significant group differences in contrast to the MWT-B (see Table 1). Inclusion of the CFT-20 only changed the significant group difference in long delay cued recall into a trend ($p = .09$) and the same was true for recognition accuracy ($p = .06$). Correlation analyses in the PTSD group revealed significant negative correlations between hyperarousal symptom severity and performance in the short and long delay free recall ($r = -.77$, $p = .001$ and $r = -.67$, $p = .009$) as well as long delay cued recall ($r = -.66, p = .01$) and recognition performance ($r = -.67$, $p = .009$). All correlations indicated worse memory performance along with higher hyperarousal. These correlations also remained significant when analyzed without the CAPS

Table 2. Results of the CVLT and the picture-memory test of the PTSD patients, the NPTSD persons, and the HC

	PTSD $N = 14$ mean (*SD*)	NPTSD $N = 14$ mean (*SD*)	HC $N = 13$ mean (*SD*)	Group statistics
CVLT				
Trial 1	6.21 (1.48)	8.79 (1.89)	8.15 (2.23)	$F(2, 38) = 7.08, p = .002$
Trial 5	11.57 (2.90)	15.14 (1.23)	14.08 (1.32)	$F(2, 38) = 11.89, p < .001$
Short delay	9.50 (3.55)	13.64 (2.95)	13.54 (1.51)	$F(2, 38) = 9.66, p < .001$
Long delay	10.21 (3.36)	14.45 (2.73)	13.82 (1.60)	$F(2, 33) = 8.95, p = .001$
Long delay cued	11.21 (2.94)	14.36 (2.41)	13.77 (1.64)	$F(2, 38) = 6.72, p = .003$
CVLT recognition list				
Discrimination accuracy	85.40 (18.05)	97.90 (3.55)	95.40 (5.19)	$F(2, 38) = 4.90, p = .013$
CVLT memory consolidation				
Trial 5 – long delay free recall	1.36 (2.98)	0.64 (2.01)	0.00 (0.78)	$F(2, 33) = 1.17, p = .32$
Trial 5 – long delay cued recall	0.36 (2.37)	0.79 (1.97)	0.31 (0.95)	$F(2, 38) = .27, p = .77$

Table 3. Correlation coefficients between the CVLT indices, the CES-D, memory performance in the picture-memory test, and PTSD symptom severity in PTSD patients assessed with the CAPS

	Reexperiencing (CAPS)	Avoidance (CAPS)	Hyperarousal (CAPS)	Hyperarousal without concentration	CES-D
CVLT					
Trial 1	−.36	−.43	−.22	−.26	−.19
Trial 5	−.43	.00	−.41	−.34	−.41
Short delay	−.37	−.15	−.77**	−.72**	−.66*
Long delay	−.45	−.37	−.67**	−.62*	−.73**
Long delay cued	−.45	−.19	−.66**	−.60*	−.65*
CVLT recognition list					
Discrimination accuracy	−.56*	−.49	−.67**	−.71*	−.70**
CVLT memory consolidation					
Trial 5 – long delay free recall	.09	.42	.35	.37	.42
Trial 5 – long delay cued recall	.03	.24	.32	.33	.30

Note. $^{*}p < .05$, $^{**}p < .01$.

hyperarousal item that is directly related to concentration [short and long delay free recall ($r = -.72$, $p = .004$ and $r = -.62$, $p = .017$) and recognition performance ($r = -.60$, $p = .023$) Table 3]. Furthermore, reexperiencing symptoms were significantly correlated with recognition performance ($r = -.56$, $p = .036$), indicating more false positive answers in the recognition test when more reexperiencing was reported (Table 3). Finally, depression scores (CES-D) were found to correlate significantly with the performance in the short and long delay free recall, long delay cued recall, and the discrimination accuracy (Table 3). Due to an overlap between hyperarousal and CES-D items, the correlation analysis for the CES-D sum score and CVLT variables was repeated, now controlling for hyperarousal. By adjusting for the effect of hyperarousal no significant correlation between CVLT and the CES-D was left (short delay free recall $r = -.11$, $p = .73$; long delay free recall $r = -.44$, $p = .14$; long delay cued recall $r = -.26$, $p = .39$; and discrimination accuracy $r = -.37$, $p = .21$).

Discussion

The results of the present study indicate impairments in learning and short-term storage of verbal material in PTSD patients compared to traumatized and non-traumatized control subjects. The results are in line with recent meta-analyses that reported medium effect sizes for impairments in verbal declarative memory in PTSD patients (Brewin et al., 2007; Johnsen & Asbjornsen, 2008). However, no significant group differences were found if delayed recall of learned material was set in relation to the initial learning progress suggesting deficits in learning but intact memory consolidation in PTSD. The decreased number of recalled words after the short and long delay in the PTSD patients was thus mainly dependent on a lower learning rate after the first five trials of the CVLT. Similarly, Golier, Harvey, Legge, and Yehuda (2006) and also Johnsen, Kanagaratnam, and Asbjornsen (2008) found no significant differences in verbal memory retention in PTSD, if delayed recall performance was controlled for the amount learned before. It might thus be that the often reported verbal memory deficits in PTSD are in fact the result of encoding and acquisition difficulties in the beginning of a memory task and not of impairments in memory consolidation. This result is in line with recent findings of altered encoding strategies with less serial clustering, more intrusive errors, and an enhanced recency effect in PTSD compared to traumatized controls without PTSD (Johnsen & Asbjornsen, 2009). In some tests the differentiation between acquisition and recall is not possible as the assessment of learning curves is not included (e.g., the Narrative Memory Test; Jelinek et al., 2009). In the meta-analysis of Brewin et al. (2007) studies that analyzed both immediate and delayed recall were excluded, so that no conclusions can be drawn about the change in memory performance when immediate learning outcome is taken into account. However, Brewin et al. (2007) analyzed immediate versus delayed recall as moderator variable but found no significant effects on the calculated effect sizes of verbal memory impairment in PTSD. This result indicates worse memory performance in PTSD patients independent of a time delay, which again can be interpreted as a sign of intact memory consolidation but impaired short-term storage. In our study, short and long delay recall correlated significantly with the severity of hyperarousal symptoms in PTSD patients. It seems that increased hyperarousal interferes with the amount of recalled words, even after adjustment for self-reported concentration deficits in the PTSD group. High intrinsic arousal was indeed shown to decrease explicit memory formation but not memory consolidation (Sandi & Pinelo-Nava, 2007). High stress levels are also supposed to hinder formation of a so-called cool memory system, which corresponds to the verbally accessible memory system in the dual memory representation theory (Brewin et al., 1996) and which is specialized for complex spatiotemporal and episodic representation and is liable to self-control (Metcalfe & Mischel, 1999). In PTSD patients, intrinsic arousal might thus interfere with the successful formation of a cool memory, here of the CVLT word lists. On the biological level numerous findings suggest stress-dependent alterations in hippocampus morphology (Sandi & Pinelo-Nava, 2007) that might be responsible for the deficits in explicit learning in PTSD. In a positron emission tomography study Bremner et al. (2003) found indeed smaller hippocampi together with decreased hippocampal activation during a declarative verbal memory task in PTSD patients, suggesting a neuronal basis for the observed behavioral differences. Taken together, it appears that PTSD is associated with impaired learning and short-term storage of verbal information with additional deficits in delayed recall in those patients, who report exceedingly high hyperarousal symptoms.

Significant group differences between traumatized persons with and without PTSD were also observed in recognition accuracy, which assesses the ability of passive recognition in relation to inhibition of false positive answers. Furthermore, recognition accuracy was found to correlate with both hyperarousal and reexperiencing in PTSD patients. In PTSD patients, more severe reexperiencing symptoms might hamper the ability to differentiate between relevant (here familiar items) and irrelevant (here distractor items) information. Indeed, a previous study (Johnsen & Asbjornsen, 2009) found an increased number of intrusive responses during recall in PTSD patients, which was interpreted as a general pattern of impaired inhibition and cognitive control by the authors.

Limitations

First, the sample size of the present study was rather small. However, in contrast to the majority of studies, investigating declarative memory function, we included trauma-exposed individuals with and without PTSD as well as never trauma-exposed HC, allowing to disentangle effects of mere trauma exposure and psychopathology.

Second, depression scores were quite high in our sample and the effect of depression rather than PTSD symptoms on verbal memory cannot be ruled out (see also Johnsen et al., 2008).

Conclusions

In sum, the present study confirmed previous reports of verbal memory deficits in PTSD. However, extending previous results, we showed that learning rather than memory consolidation is impaired in PTSD patients, a differentiation that has not been made previously.

Acknowledgments

This research was supported by a grant of the Deutsche Forschungsgemeinschaft to Herta Flor (SFB 636/ C1).

References

American Psychiatric Association. (1994). *Diagnostic and statistical manual of mental disorders* (4th ed., DSM-IV). Washington DC: American Psychiatric Association.

Blake, D. D., Weathers, F. W., Nagy, L. M., Kaloupek, D. G., Gusman, F. D., Charney, D. S., et al. (1995). The development of a Clinician-Administered PTSD Scale. *Journal of Traumatic Stress, 8*, 75–90.

Bremner, J. D., Vythilingam, M., Vermetten, E., Southwick, S. M., McGlashan, T., Nazeer, A., et al. (2003). MRI and PET study of deficits in hippocampal structure and function in women with childhood sexual abuse and posttraumatic stress disorder. *The American Journal of Psychiatry, 160*, 924–932.

Brewin, C. R., Dalgleish, T., & Joseph, S. (1996). A dual representation theory of posttraumatic stress disorder. *Psychological Review, 103*, 670–686.

Brewin, C. R., Kleiner, J. S., Vasterling, J. J., & Field, A. P. (2007). Memory for emotionally neutral information in posttraumatic stress disorder: A meta-analytic investigation. *Journal of Abnormal Psychology, 116*, 448–463.

Bustamante, V., Mellman, T. A., David, D., & Fins, A. I. (2001). Cognitive functioning and the early development of PTSD. *Journal of Traumatic Stress, 14*, 791–797.

Curtis, W. J., & Cicchetti, D. (2007). Emotion and resilience: A multilevel investigation of hemispheric electroencephalogram asymmetry and emotion regulation in maltreated and nonmaltreated children. *Development and Psychopathology, 19*, 811–840.

Delis, D. C., Kramer, J., & Kaplan, E. (1987). *California verbal learning test (CVLT) research edition – Adult version*. New York: Psychological Corporation.

Ehlers, A., & Clark, D. M. (2000). A cognitive model of posttraumatic stress disorder. *Behaviour Research and Therapy, 38*, 319–345.

First, M., Gibbon, M., Spitzer, R., Williams, J., & Benjamin, L. (1997). *User's guide for the structured clinical interview for DSM-IV axis II personality disorders (SCID-II)*. Washington DC: American Psychiatric Press.

First, M., Spitzer, R., Gibbon, M., & Williams, J. (1997). *User's guide for the structured clinical interview for DSM-IV axis I disorders (SCID-I)-clinical version*. Washington DC: American Psychiatric Press.

Fydrich, T., Renneberg, B., Schmitz, B., & Wittchen, H.-U. (1997). *Strukturiertes Klinisches Interview für DSM-IV. Achse II: Persönlichkeitsstörungen* [User's guide for the structured clinical interview for DSM-IV axis II personality disorders (SCID-II)]. Göttingen: Hogrefe.

Golier, J. A., Harvey, P. D., Legge, J., & Yehuda, R. (2006). Memory performance in older trauma survivors: Implications for the longitudinal course of PTSD. *Annals of the New York Academy of Sciences, 1071*, 54–66.

Golomb, J., Kluger, A., de Leon, M. J., Ferris, S. H., Convit, A., Mittelman, M. S., et al. (1994). Hippocampal formation size in normal human aging: A correlate of delayed secondary memory performance. *Learning & Memory, 1*, 45–54.

Harvey, A. G., Bryant, R. A., & Dang, S. T. (1998). Autobiographical memory in acute stress disorder. *Journal of Consulting and Clinical Psychology, 66*, 500–506.

Hautzinger, M., & Bailer, M. (1993). *Allgemeine Depressions Skala (ADS)* [General depression scale]. Weinheim, Germany: Beltz Test.

Jelinek, L., Randjbar, S., Seifert, D., Kellner, M., & Moritz, S. (2009). The organization of autobiographical and nonautobiographical memory in posttraumatic stress disorder (PTSD). *Journal of Abnormal Psychology, 118*, 288–298.

Johnsen, G. E., & Asbjornsen, A. E. (2008). Consistent impaired verbal memory in PTSD: A meta-analysis. *Journal of Affective Disorders, 111*, 74–82.

Johnsen, G. E., & Asbjornsen, A. E. (2009). Verbal learning and memory impairments in posttraumatic stress disorder: The role of encoding strategies. *Psychiatry Research, 165*, 68–77.

Johnsen, G. E., Kanagaratnam, P., & Asbjornsen, A. E. (2008). Memory impairments in posttraumatic stress disorder are related to depression. *Journal of Anxiety Disorders, 22*, 464–474.

Jones, C., Harvey, A. G., & Brewin, C. R. (2007). The organisation and content of trauma memories in survivors of road traffic accidents. *Behaviour Research and Therapy, 45*, 151–162.

Lanius, R. A., Williamson, P. C., Densmore, M., Boksman, K., Neufeld, R. W., Gati, J. S., et al. (2004). The nature of traumatic memories: A 4-T FMRI functional connectivity analysis. *The American Journal of Psychiatry, 161*, 36–44.

Lehrl, S. (2005). *Mehrfachwahl-Wortschatz-Intelligenztest MWT-B* (5th ed.) [Multiple choice vocabulary test MWT]. Balingen, Germany: Spitta Verlag GmbH.

Merckelbach, H., Dekkers, T., Wessel, I., & Roefs, A. (2003). Amnesia, flashbacks, nightmares, and dissociation in aging concentration camp survivors. *Behaviour Research and Therapy, 41*, 351–360.

Metcalfe, J., & Mischel, W. (1999). A hot/cool-system analysis of delay of gratification: Dynamics of willpower. *Psychological Review, 106*, 3–19.

Niemann, H., Sturm, W., Thöne-Otto, A., & Willmes, K. (2008). *CVLT – California verbal learning test – Deutsche adaptation*. Frankfurt: Pearson.

Paivio, A. (1986). *Mental representations: A dual coding approach*. New York: Oxford University Press.

Rabe, S., Zoellner, T., Beauducel, A., Maercker, A., & Karl, A. (2008). Changes in brain electrical activity after cognitive behavioral therapy for posttraumatic stress disorder in patients injured in motor vehicle accidents. *Psychosomatic Medicine, 70*, 13–19.

Radloff, L. S. (1977). The CES-D scale: A self-report depression scale for research in the general population. *Applied Psychological Measurement, 1*, 385–401.

Sandi, C., & Pinelo-Nava, M. T. (2007). Stress and memory: Behavioral effects and neurobiological mechanisms. *Neural Plasticity, 2007*, 78970.

Weiß, R. (2006). *Grundintelligenztest Skala 2 – Revision – (CFT 20-R)* [Culture fair intelligence test]. Göttingen: Hogrefe.

Wessa, , M., Griesel, D., Rabe, S., Dörfel, D., Flor, H., & Karl, A. (2010). *Reliability, validity and factor structure of the Clinician-Administered PTSD Scale in a heterogeneous trauma sample.* Submitted for publication.

Wessa, M., Jatzko, A., & Flor, H. (2006). Retrieval and emotional processing of traumatic memories in posttraumatic stress disorder: Peripheral and central correlates. *Neuropsychologia, 44*, 1683–1696.

Wittchen, H.-U., Wunderlich, U., Gruschwitz, S., & Zaudig, M. (1997). *Strukturiertes Klinisches Interview für DSM-IV. Achse I: Psychische Störungen* [User's guide for the structured clinical interview for DSM-IV axis I disorders (SCID-I) – clinical version]. Göttingen: Hogrefe.

Herta Flor

Department of Cognitive Clinical and Neuroscience
Central Institute of Mental Health
University of Heidelberg
J 5
68159 Mannheim
Germany
Tel. +49 621 1703-6302
Fax +49 621 1703-6305
E-mail herta.flor@zi-mannheim.de

Opinion

Understanding and Treating Unwanted Trauma Memories in Posttraumatic Stress Disorder

Anke Ehlers

Department of Psychology, Institute of Psychiatry, King's College London, UK

Distressing and intrusive reexperiencing of the trauma is a hallmark symptom of posttraumatic stress disorder (PTSD; American Psychiatric Association, 1994). However, unwanted memories of trauma are not a sign of pathology per se. In the initial weeks after a traumatic experience, intrusive memories are common. For most trauma survivors, intrusions become less frequent and distressing over time. A central question for understanding and treating patients with PTSD is therefore what *maintains* distressing intrusive reexperiencing in these people. Three factors appear to be important: (1) memory processes responsible for the easy triggering of intrusive memories, (2) the individuals' interpretations of their trauma memories, and (3) their cognitive and behavioral responses to trauma memories.

Characteristics of Reexperiencing in PTSD

Clues about the memory processes underlying reexperiencing symptoms in PTSD can be drawn from their phenomenological characteristics. Note that unlike the convention in DSM-IV (American Psychiatric Association, 1994), which classifies ruminative thoughts about the trauma such as "Why did it happen to me" or "If only I had . . ." as a part of reexperiencing, the author distinguishes between intrusive memories and rumination about the trauma (Ehlers & Clark, 2000; Ehlers & Steil, 1995). Evidence is accumulating that these cognitions are phenomenologically and functionally distinct (e.g., Evans, Ehlers, Mezey, & Clark, 2007b; Speckens, Ehlers, Hackmann, Ruths, & Clark, 2007).

Systematic comparisons of *intrusive trauma memories* in people with and without PTSD pointed to many important similarities. The intrusions most commonly take the form of relatively brief, vivid sensory impressions such as images, sounds, body sensations, tastes, or smells (e.g., Ehlers et al., 2002; Michael, Ehlers, & Halligan, 2005a). Yet, there are also a number of differences between the intrusions in people with and without PTSD. These have been shown to predict chronic PTSD, over and above what can be predicted from the frequency of early intrusions, and shown to change with successful therapy (Hackmann, Ehlers, Speckens, & Clark, 2004; Michael, Ehlers, Halligan, & Clark, 2005b; Speckens, Ehlers, Hackmann, & Clark, 2006).

(1) *Nowness*: Trauma survivors with PTSD describe to a greater extent that their intrusive memories appear to happen in the *here and now* than those without PTSD (Michael et al., 2005b). Most dramatically, in a posttraumatic flashback people lose all contact with current reality and respond as if the trauma was happening at that moment (see, e.g., Ehlers, Hackmann, & Michael, 2004). To a lesser degree, this sense of nowness is also characteristic of other intrusive trauma memories in PTSD (Michael et al., 2005b). Furthermore, people with PTSD may also show *affect without recollection* (Ehlers & Clark, 2000), that is, emotions and behavior from the trauma *without* having a conscious memory of the trauma (e.g., collapsing in a fetal position when seeing someone who resembles the assailant). Thus, some of the reexperiencing symptoms lack the autonoetic awareness which is a defining feature of episodic memories (Tulving, 2002).

(2) *Lack of context*: Intrusive memories in PTSD lack contextual information and appear *disjointed* from other relevant autobiographical information (Ehlers et al., 2004; Michael et al., 2005b). People with PTSD keep reexperiencing moments of the trauma and the corresponding emotions (e.g., when they believed they would never see their children again), even if they know the predicted outcome did not occur. Thus, during intrusive trauma memories, people with PTSD have difficulties retrieving other information that corrected their original impressions and predictions during these moments or their meanings.

(3) *Ease of triggering by matching cues*: In PTSD, a wide range of situations can trigger intrusive memories, including those that do not have an obvious meaningful connection with the trauma and those that the individual does not recognize as triggers. This has the effect that intrusions may appear to come "out of the blue." Closer analysis of these situations shows that triggers often have *sensory* similarities with stimuli present shortly before or during the trauma (e.g., similar color, shape, smell, or body sensation; Ehlers et al., 2002).

(4) *Distress*: Trauma survivors with PTSD describe their intrusive memories as more distressing than those without PTSD (e.g., Michael et al., 2005b).

Zeitschrift für Psychologie / Journal of Psychology 2010; Vol. 218(2):141–145
DOI: 10.1027/0044-3409/a000021

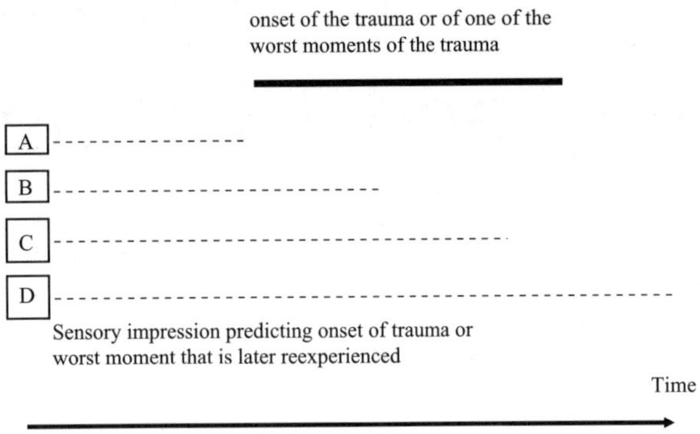

Figure 1. Warning signal hypothesis of intrusive memories (Ehlers et al., 2002). Possible temporal relationships between content of intrusion and worst moments of the trauma.

What Is Reexperienced?

Many things happen during a traumatic event. What determines what is later reexperienced? Patients with PTSD reported in systematic interviews that they reexperienced brief moments from the trauma such as "hearing footsteps behind me" or "seeing the perpetrator stand before me with a knife" (Ehlers et al., 2002). Further analysis of these intrusions indicated that they represented sensory impressions that signaled the onset of the trauma or the onset of its worst moments. Ehlers et al. (2002) therefore suggested that the intrusions had functional significance in that they represented stimuli that predicted the worst moments of trauma and had thus acquired the status of warning signals, consistent with modern associative learning models that highlight the information value of conditioned stimuli (CS) in predicting the unconditioned stimuli (UCS) (Rescorla, 1988). Thus, in Pavlovian conditioning terms, it appears that people with PTSD reexperience the CS rather than the UCS after trauma. Evidence for this hypothesis comes from studies of PTSD patients and violent offenders who had intrusive memories of their crime (Evans, Ehlers, Mezey, & Clark, 2007a; Hackmann et al., 2004).

Ehlers et al.'s (2002) emphasis that the sensory impressions that are later reexperienced *preceded* the trauma or its worst moments has been interpreted by some authors (e.g., Berntsen & Rubin, 2008) as meaning that they needed to be *finished* before trauma onset (Possibility A in Figure 1). However, consistent with what is known about CS in Pavlovian conditioning (Rescorla, 1988), the hypothesis concerns sensory impressions that *started* just before the worst moment and thus had *predictive* information value. They may well have still been present during the worst moment (this includes possibilities B to D in Figure 1). Furthermore, it is important to note that the worst moments of the trauma are defined *subjectively* in Ehlers et al. (2002), from the perspective of the individual with PTSD, not from the perspective of what other people may find most distressing. Furthermore, it is important to note that in prolonged trauma, there are usually several moments when the meaning of the event changed for the worse, and each of them may be represented in reexperiencing.

Hypothesized Memory Mechanisms Underlying Reexperiencing

Ehlers and Clark (2000) suggested that reexperiencing and the ease with which it is triggered in PTSD can be explained by a combination of three memory processes, namely strong perceptual priming, strong associative learning, and poor memory elaboration (binding with other information in autobiographical memory). Experimental evidence for the role of each of these processes in reexperiencing is emerging (e.g., priming: Ehlers, Michael, Chen, Payne, & Shan, 2006; Michael & Ehlers, 2007; Michael et al., 2005a; associative learning: Sündermann, Ehlers, Böllinghaus, Gamer, & Glucksman, 2010; Wessa & Flor, 2007; poor binding with other autobiographical information: Kleim, Wallott, & Ehlers, 2008).

The description of phenomenological characteristics of reexperiencing and intentional trauma recall in PTSD by Ehlers and Clark (2000) has been interpreted by some theorists (Berntsen, 2009) as an argument for *special mechanisms* that are unique to trauma memories. This is incorrect. The Ehlers and Clark (2000) model proposes that the phenomenology of reexperiencing can be explained by the above three basic memory processes. One important difference between the Ehlers and Clark (2000) model and other approaches that aim to explain involuntary memories of trauma by general memory mechanisms (Berntsen, 2009; Rubin, Boals, & Berntsen, 2008) is the range of memory phenomena under consideration. Whereas Ehlers and Clark's (2000) model was developed to explain the full range of intrusive reexperiencing in PTSD, including those that lack autonoetic awareness, Berntsen (2009) and Rubin et al. (2008) only include the involuntary retrieval of memory content that is recognized by the individual as a trauma memory. Berntsen (2009) explicitly excludes involuntary auditory and visual imagery that is not deemed autobiographical and "phenomena in which the involuntary mental contents overrule reality more or less completely" (p. 15). Thus, many of the phenomena that the Ehlers and Clark (2000) theory aims to explain (such as flashbacks where patients lose all contact with current reality, other intrusions that are not recognized by the individual as a memory, reexperiencing strong emotions, physiological reactions, or behavior from the trauma without recollection of the trauma), are excluded from consideration. However, these phenomena are important for understanding PTSD and for developing effective treatments. The wider range of reexperiencing symptoms under consideration explains why the Ehlers and Clark (2000) model emphasizes memory processes that facilitate cue-driven reexperiencing, namely priming and associative learning.

Are There Deficits in the Intentional Recall of Trauma Memories?

Several theorists suggest that compromised cognitive processing during the trauma leads to *deficits in intentional recall* of the trauma. Different hypotheses about the nature of this deficit have been suggested in the literature, for example, a deficit in memory representations that facilitate intentional recall (Brewin, Dalgleish, & Joseph, 1996) or highly fragmented memories (e.g., Foa & Rothbaum, 1998; van der Kolk & Fisler, 1995). Building on the work on transfer-appropriate processing (for a review see Roediger, 1990), Ehlers and Clark (2000) suggested that data-driven processing during trauma (i.e., the predominant processing the sensory impressions) will facilitate strong perceptual priming for accompanying stimuli and (in combination with a lack of self-referent processing) will lead to relatively weaker intentional recall of the worst moments of the trauma.

Other theorists (Berntsen, 2009; Rubin et al., 2008) predict the opposite and hypothesize that trauma memories are highly accessible so that intentional and unintentional retrieval is enhanced. Empirical tests of these hypotheses in clinical populations are sparse (for reviews see Ehlers et al., 2004; McNally, 2003). There is very little evidence for complete psychogenic amnesia (Evans et al., 2009; McNally, 2003, but also see Markowitsch et al., 1998). Unless there are organic causes for poor memory (e.g., head injury or drugs), trauma survivors usually remember most of what happened. There is evidence, however, for more subtle problems with intentional recall. People with PTSD may be confused about the order of events, have small gaps in memory, or may fail to remember details that are important for the meaning of especially distressing parts of the event (e.g., a rape survivor who blamed herself for not fighting the perpetrator did not remember that he had threatened her with a knife beforehand). Trauma survivors with PTSD give more disorganized narratives of traumatic events than those without PTSD (e.g., Halligan, Michael, Clark, & Ehlers, 2003; Harvey & Bryant, 1999).

In the author's view, the controversy about deficient versus enhanced intentional recall of trauma in PTSD can be resolved by considering the trauma as a series of events rather than one event (Ehlers et al., 2004). Earlier work defines the traumatic event from an external point of view and refers to the memory for this externally defined event as "the trauma memory." The author believes that this is misleading. From the trauma survivors' perspective, the traumatic experience may have several distinct parts that are not necessarily remembered as one integrated event. For example, Ehlers and Clark (2000) described a patient with PTSD who had intrusive memories that contradicted each other and stemmed from different parts of the (prolonged) traumatic event. Furthermore, it is important to bear in mind that only some moments from the traumatic event are later reexperienced. Thus, the proposed problems in intentional retrieval may mainly apply to the memory for these moments. In line with this argument, Evans et al. (2007a) found that narratives of the moments that were reexperienced were more disorganized than other segments of the trauma narrative that were not; furthermore in 23% of the cases these moments were not included in the narrative at all.

Further clarity is needed about the exact nature of the problems in voluntary recall of parts of the trauma memory in PTSD and the pathways by which they contribute to the persistence of PTSD. Ehlers et al. (2004) suggested that the *disjointedness* of the memories of the worst moments during the trauma from other relevant autobiographical information is particularly relevant in PTSD. Kleim et al. (2008) found experimental support for this hypothesis. Disjointedness has the effect that when the individual remembers the worst moments, they have difficulty accessing other information that puts the meaning of these moments into perspective. This maintains a sense of current threat (Ehlers & Clark, 2000). Furthermore, poor memory elaboration is thought to contribute to reexperiencing as it leads to poor inhibition of cue-driven retrieval. Note that this would only be expected to lead to distressing reexperiencing symptoms if there is also strong priming for potential triggers and strong associations between the triggers and emotional responses as (Ehlers & Clark, 2000; Ehlers et al., 2004).

Nontrauma Autobiographical Memories in PTSD

People with and without PTSD also differ in how they remember other events in their lives. Like people with depression, those with PTSD have difficulty remembering specific autobiographical events (see Moore & Zoellner, 2007, for a review). This effect is not due to differences in verbal intelligence (Schönfeld & Ehlers, 2006). Low autobiographical memory specificity at 2 weeks after trauma predicts chronic PTSD (Kleim & Ehlers, 2008).

Relationship Between Memory and Appraisals in PTSD

An important predictor of chronic PTSD is how people *interpret* their memories of the trauma. Ehlers and Steil (1995) suggested that people with PTSD show negative idiosyncratic interpretations of intrusive trauma memories such as "I am going crazy," which lead to a sense of ongoing threat and distress, and motivate dysfunctional control strategies such as rumination, memory suppression, and excessive safety-seeking behaviors that maintain PTSD. Prospective longitudinal studies of trauma survivors supported this suggestion (e.g., Dunmore, Clark, & Ehlers, 2001; Ehlers, Mayou, & Bryant, 1998; Ehring, Ehlers, & Glucksman, 2008; Halligan, Michael, Clark, & Ehlers, 2003; Michael, Halligan, Clark, & Ehlers, 2007; Murray, Ehlers, & Mayou, 2002; Steil & Ehlers, 2000).

Similarly, Ehlers and Clark (2000) suggested that negative interpretations of problems in intentional recall such as memory gaps or difficulties in remembering the exact order of events (e.g., "I must have a brain damage" and "Something even worse and unbearable must have happened") contribute to the maintenance of PTSD. Studies by Dunmore et al. (2001) and Halligan et al. (2003) supported this suggestion.

Furthermore, what is remembered can contribute to problematic appraisals of the trauma. Problems in remembering the order of events can contribute to self-blame for the event (Ehlers & Clark, 2000). Low autobiographical memory specificity contributes to appraisals of being permanently changed (Schönfeld, Ehlers, Böllinghaus, & Rief, 2007).

Clinical Implications

The above analysis of memory processes in PTSD and their link with problematic appraisals and behaviors that maintain PTSD has led to the development of specific theory-guided treatment procedures for this condition (Ehlers & Clark, 2000; Ehlers, Clark, Hackmann, McManus, & Fennell, 2005).

The *Updating Trauma Memories* procedure addresses the *disjointedness* of memories of the worst moments of the trauma from information that gives them a less threatening meaning. This procedure includes (1) identifying the moments during the trauma that create the greatest distress and sense of "nowness" ("hotspots") through imaginal reliving or writing a narrative, and identification of the patient's intrusive memories, (2) identifying the personal meanings of these moments, and (3) identifying "updating" information that puts the impressions the patient had at the time or the problematic meanings into perspective. This information can be either relevant details from the course, circumstances, and outcome of the trauma or the result of cognitive restructuring of the highly idiosyncratic meanings of the trauma, and (4) actively linking the updating information to the hotspots in memory, for example, by bringing the hotspot vividly to mind and simultaneously using verbal reminders, images, incompatible actions, or incompatible sensations to remind the patient of the new meanings.

Stimulus discrimination training addresses the *easy triggering* of intrusive memories by matching sensory cues. Patients learn to identify the subtle sensory triggers of reexperiencing and learn to realize that they are responding to a memory. They learn to pay close attention to the differences between the harmless trigger and its present context ("now") and the stimulus configuration that occurred in the context of trauma ("then").

Reclaiming your life homework assignments address appraisals of permanent change and problems in retrieving specific memories of the patient's life before the trauma. These assignments involve doing things that the patient has given up since the trauma, for example, resuming social contacts, sports, or other leisure activities. These activities provide retrieval cues for specific memories of themselves before the trauma.

Negative interpretations of intrusive memories and problems in intentional recall are addressed through information, cognitive restructuring, and behavioral experiments. The patient is encouraged to experiment with dropping dysfunctional behaviors such as rumination, hypervigilance, and excessive precautions.

The treatment program (*Cognitive Therapy for PTSD*) has been shown to be highly effective and acceptable to patients with PTSD after a range of traumas in randomized controlled trials and effectiveness studies (Duffy, Gillespie, & Clark, 2007; Ehlers et al., 2003, 2005; Gillespie, Duffy, Hackmann, & Clark, 2002; Smith et al., 2007).

Acknowledgments

The work described here was funded by the Wellcome Trust (069777).

References

American Psychiatric Association. (Ed.). (1994). *Diagnostic and statistical manual of mental disorders* (4th ed.). Washington, DC: American Psychiatric Association.

Berntsen, D. (2009). *Involuntary autobiographical memories*. Cambridge, UK: Cambridge University Press.

Berntsen, D., & Rubin, D.C. (2008). The reappearance hypothesis revisited: Recurrent involuntary memories after traumatic events and in everyday life. *Memory & Cognition, 36*, 449–460.

Brewin, C.R., Dalgleish, T., & Joseph, S. (1996). A dual representation theory of posttraumatic stress disorder. *Psychological Review, 103*, 670–686.

Duffy, M., Gillespie, K., & Clark, D. M. (2007). Post-traumatic stress disorder in the context of terrorism and other civil conflict in Northern Ireland: Randomised controlled trial. *British Medical Journal, 334*, 1147–1150.

Dunmore, E., Clark, D. M., & Ehlers, A. (2001). A prospective study of the role of cognitive factors in persistent posttraumatic stress disorder after physical or sexual assault. *Behaviour Research and Therapy, 39*, 1063–1084.

Ehlers, A., & Clark, D. M. (2000). A cognitive model of posttraumatic stress disorder. *Behaviour Research and Therapy, 38*, 319–345.

Ehlers, A., Clark, D. M., Hackmann, A., McManus, F., & Fennell, M. (2005). Cognitive therapy for PTSD: Development and evaluation. *Behaviour Research and Therapy, 43*, 413–431.

Ehlers, A., Clark, D. M., Hackmann, A., McManus, F., Fennell, M., Herbert, C., et al. (2003). A randomized controlled trial of cognitive therapy, self-help booklet, and repeated assessment as early interventions for PTSD. *Archives of General Psychiatry, 60*, 1024–1032.

Ehlers, A., Hackmann, A., & Michael, T. (2004). Intrusive reexperiencing in posttraumatic stress disorder: Phenomenology, theory, and therapy. *Memory, 12*, 403–415.

Ehlers, A., Hackmann, A., Steil, R., Clohessy, S., Wenninger, K., & Winter, H. (2002). The nature of intrusive memories after trauma: The warning signal hypothesis. *Behaviour Research and Therapy, 40*, 1021–1028.

Ehlers, A., Mayou, R. A., & Bryant, B. (1998). Psychological predictors of chronic PTSD after motor vehicle accidents. *Journal of Abnormal Psychology, 107*, 508–519.

Ehlers, A., Michael, T., Chen, Y. P., Payne, E., & Shan, S. (2006). Enhanced perceptual priming for neutral stimuli in a traumatic context: A pathway to intrusive memories? *Memory, 14*, 345–358.

Ehlers, A., & Steil, R. (1995). Maintenance of intrusive memories in posttraumatic stress disorder: A cognitive approach. *Behavioural and Cognitive Psychotherapy, 23*, 217–249.

Ehring, T., Ehlers, A., & Glucksman, E. (2008). Do cognitive models help in predicting the severity of posttraumatic stress disorder, phobia and depression after motor vehicle accidents? A prospective longitudinal study. *Journal of Consulting and Clinical Psychology, 76*, 219–230.

Evans, C., Ehlers, A., Mezey, G., & Clark, D. M. (2007a). Intrusive memories in perpetrators of violent crime: Emotions and cognitions. *Journal of Consulting and Clinical Psychology, 75*, 134–144.

Evans, C., Ehlers, A., Mezey, G., & Clark, D. M. (2007b). Intrusive memories and ruminations related to violent crime among young offenders: Phenomenological characteristics. *Journal of Traumatic Stress, 20*, 183–196.

Evans, C., Mezey, G., & Ehlers, A. (2009). Amnesia for violent crime. *The Journal of Forensic Psychiatry and Psychology, 20*, 85–106.

Foa, E. B., & Rothbaum, B. O. (1998). *Treating the trauma of rape. Cognitive-behavior therapy for PTSD*. New York: Guilford.

Gillespie, K., Duffy, M., Hackmann, A., & Clark, D. M. (2002). Community based cognitive therapy in the treatment of posttraumatic stress disorder following the Omagh bomb. *Behaviour Research and Therapy, 40*, 345–357.

Hackmann, A., Ehlers, A., Speckens, A., & Clark, D. M. (2004). Characteristics and content of intrusive memories in PTSD and their changes with treatment. *Journal of Traumatic Stress, 17*, 231–240.

Halligan, S. L., Michael, T., Clark, D.M., & Ehlers, A. (2003). Posttraumatic stress disorder following assault: The role of cognitive processing, trauma memory, and appraisals. *Journal of Consulting and Clinical Psychology, 71*, 419–431.

Harvey, A. G., & Bryant, R. A. (1999). A qualitative investigation of the organization of traumatic memories. *British Journal of Clinical Psychology, 38*, 401–405.

Kleim, B., & Ehlers, A. (2008). Reduced autobiographical memory specificity predicts depression and posttraumatic stress disorder after recent trauma. *Journal of Consulting and Clinical Psychology, 76*, 231–242.

Kleim, B., Wallott, F., & Ehlers, A. (2008). Are trauma memories disjointed from other autobiographical memories in PTSD? An experimental investigation. *Behavioural and Cognitive Psychotherapy, 36*, 221–234.

Markowitsch, H. J., Kessler, J., Van der Ven, C., Weber-Luxemburger, G., Albers, M., & Heiss, W. D. (1998). Psychic trauma causing grossly reduced brain metabolism and cognitive deterioration. *Neuropsychologia, 36*, 77–82.

McNally, R. J. (2003). *Remembering trauma*. Cambridge, MA: The Belknap Press/Harvard University Press.

Michael, T., & Ehlers, A. (2007). Enhanced perceptual priming for neutral stimuli occurring in a traumatic context: Two experimental investigations. *Behaviour Research and Therapy, 45*, 341–358.

Michael, T., Ehlers, A., & Halligan, S. L. (2005a). Perceptual priming for trauma-related material in posttraumatic stress disorder. *Emotion, 5*, 103–112.

Michael, T., Ehlers, A., Halligan, S., & Clark, D.M. (2005b). Unwanted memories of assault: What intrusion characteristics predict PTSD? *Behaviour Research and Therapy, 43*, 613–628.

Michael, T., Halligan, S., Clark, D. M., & Ehlers, A. (2007). Rumination in posttraumatic stress disorder. *Depression and Anxiety, 24*, 307–317.

Moore, S. A., & Zoellner, L. A. (2007). Overgeneral autobiographical memory and traumatic events: An evaluative review. *Psychological Bulletin, 133*, 419–437.

Murray, J., Ehlers, A., & Mayou, R. A. (2002). Dissociation and posttraumatic stress disorder: Two prospective studies of road traffic accident victims. *British Journal of Psychiatry, 180*, 363–368.

Rescorla, R. A. (1988). Pavlovian conditioning. It's not what you think it is. *American Psychologist, 43*, 151–160.

Roediger, H. L. (1990). Implicit memory: Retention without remembering. *American Psychologist, 45*, 1043–1056.

Rubin, D. C., Boals, A., & Berntsen, D. (2008). Memory on posttraumatic stress disorder: Properties of voluntary and involuntary, traumatic and nontraumatic autobiographical memories in people with and without posttraumatic stress disorder symptoms. *Journal of Experimental Psychology: General, 137*, 591–614.

Schönfeld, S., & Ehlers, A. (2006). Overgeneral memory extends to pictorial retrieval cues and correlates with cognitive features in posttraumatic stress disorder. *Emotion, 6*, 611–622.

Schönfeld, S., Ehlers, A., Böllinghaus, I., & Rief, W. (2007). Overgeneral memory and suppression of trauma memories in posttraumatic stress disorder. *Memory, 15*, 339–352.

Smith, P., Yule, W., Perrin, S., Tranah, T., Dalgleish, T., & Clark, D. M. (2007). Cognitive-behavioral therapy for PTSD in children and adolescents: A preliminary randomized controlled trial. *Journal of the American Academy of Child and Adolescent Psychiatry, 46*, 1051–1061.

Speckens, A. E. M., Ehlers, A., Hackmann, A., & Clark, D. M. (2006). Changes in intrusive memories associated with imaginal reliving in posttraumatic stress disorder. *Journal of Anxiety Disorders, 20*, 328–341.

Speckens, A., Ehlers, A., Hackmann, A., Ruths, F., & Clark, D. M. (2007). Intrusions and rumination in patients with posttraumatic stress disorder: A phenomenological study. *Memory, 15*, 249–257.

Steil, R., & Ehlers, A. (2000). Dysfunctional meaning of posttraumatic intrusions in chronic PTSD. *Behaviour Research and Therapy, 38*, 537–558.

Sündermann, O., Ehlers, A., Böllinghaus, I., Gamer, M., & Glucksman, E. (2010). Early heart rate responses to standardized trauma-related pictures predict posttraumatic stress disorder – a prospective longitudinal study. *Psychosomatic Medicine, 72*, 302–310.

Tulving, E. (2002). Episodic memory. *Annual Review of Psychology, 53*, 1–25.

van der Kolk, B. A., & Fisler, R. (1995). Dissociation and the fragmentary nature of traumatic memories: Overview and exploratory study. *Journal of Traumatic Stress, 8*, 505–525.

Wessa, M., & Flor, H. (2007). Failure of extinction of fear responses in posttraumatic stress disorder: Evidence from second-order conditioning. *American Journal of Psychiatry, 164*, 1684–1692.

Anke Ehlers

Department of Psychology (PO77)
King's College London
Institute of Psychiatry
De Crespigny Park
London SE5 8AF
UK
Tel. +44 20 7848 5033
Fax +44 20 7848 0591
E-mail anke.ehlers@kcl.ac.uk

Overgeneralization of Conditioned Fear in the Anxiety Disorders

Putative Memorial Mechanisms

Shmuel Lissek and Christian Grillon

National Institute of Mental Health, Mood and Anxiety Disorders Program, Bethesda, MD, USA

According to many conditioning accounts of clinical anxiety, the central pathogen can be found in aberrant acquisition or extinction of learned fear to neutral stimuli (i.e., conditioned stimuli [CS]) paired with an aversive unconditioned stimulus (US). While overresponding to the CS is an important candidate source of anxiety pathology, both clinical observation and mounting experimental data implicate generalization of fear to stimuli resembling the CS as an equally promising candidate (e.g., Grillon & Morgan, 1999; Lissek et al., 2005; Lissek et al., 2010; Mineka & Zinbarg, 1996). Important to the current issue on "Trauma and Memory," generalization of fear to stimuli resembling those present during a traumatic event is a core feature of the posttraumatic stress response (American Psychiatric Association, 2000) and is likely influenced by conditioning-dependent modifications to the neural representation of the CS stored in memory. The current paper (1) summarizes the connection between conditioned-fear generalization and pathologic anxiety including a recent empirical example demonstrating the link and (2) explores memorial substrates of conditioned generalization and the ways they are related to overgeneralization of the kind seen in anxiety pathology.

Conditioned Generalization and Clinical Anxiety

Evidence linking pathologic anxiety to conditioned generalization dates back to Watson and Rayner (1920) who famously demonstrated generalization of conditioned fear to all things fury in a toddler ("Little Albert") following acquisition of fear-conditioning to a white rat. Since then, fear generalization has been adopted as a core feature of anxiety pathology by clinical practitioners and theorists (e.g., Mineka & Zinbarg, 1996) but has received little empirical attention. Indeed, few analyses of conditioning data in clinical anxiety have looked specifically at the generalization process (Grillon & Morgan, 1999; Kopp, Schlimm, & Hermann, 2005; Lissek et al., 2005; Lissek et al., 2009), and systematic psychobiological assessments of conditioned generalization with the aim of understanding anxiety pathology have been conducted only very recently (Lissek et al., 2008; Lissek et al., 2010). The weight of the data from this small experimental literature implicates overgeneralization of conditioned fear as a robust marker of clinical anxiety generally, and posttraumatic stress disorder (PTSD) and panic disorder (PD) specifically. While the US in PTSD (trauma) is distinct from that in PD (panic attack), both USs are thought to confer anxiogenic valence to CSs occurring coincident with the US and, by way of generalization, to stimuli resembling the CS (e.g., Bouton, Mineka, & Barlow, 2001; Foa, Steketee, & Olasov-Rothbaum, 1989). This latter generalization process results in the proliferation of trauma/panic cues in the individual's environment that then serve to sustain anxiety related to the disorder.

Figure 1 displays the results of a recent study using rings of varying sizes as conditioned and generalization stimuli to demonstrate overgeneralization in panic patients (Lissek et al., 2010). In this study, anxious reactivity was assessed to a conditioned danger cue (CS+); a conditioned safety cue (CS−); and four generalization stimuli (GS_1, GS_2, GS_3, and GS_4) forming a continuum-of-similarity between the CS+ and CS−. The central finding is represented by data-points highlighted in green, reflecting classes of stimuli eliciting anxious arousal relative to the CS−. Whereas healthy controls displayed anxious reactivity to the CS+ that generalized to GSs with only one degree of differentiation from the CS+ (i.e., GS_4), panic patients displayed anxiety responses to the CS+ that generalized to GSs with up to three degrees of differentiation (GS_4, GS_3, and GS_2). This finding clinically validates the paradigm as a tool with which to explore neural and psychological substrates of overgeneralization, including the putative contribution of memorial mechanisms to which our attention will now turn.

Memorial Substrates of Conditioned Generalization

During mammalian fear-conditioning, the amygdala activates the nucleus basalis of Meynert (Kapp, Whalen, Supple, & Pascoe, 1992) which then projects to the visual, auditory,

Zeitschrift für Psychologie / Journal of Psychology 2010; Vol. 218(2):146–148
DOI: 10.1027/0044-3409/a000022

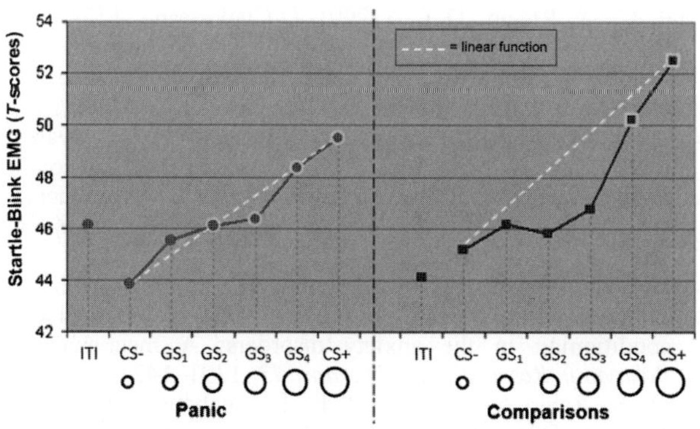

Figure 1. Overgeneralization of conditioned fear in panic patients as indexed by *fear-potentiated startle*: the reliable, amygdala-mediated, enhancement of the startle reflex by fear states (Davis & Astrachan, 1978; Grillon et al., 1991). Data reflect average, standardized startle-blink electromyogram (EMG) magnitudes across patients and healthy comparisons during presentation of conditioned stimuli paired (CS+) and unpaired (CS−) with electric shock; classes of generalization stimuli (GS_1, GS_2, GS_3, and GS_4); and inter-trial-intervals (ITI). White dotted lines reflect linear decreases in startle from CS+ to CS− with which to visualize the deviation of generalization gradients from linearity. Such deviations reflect a Group × Stimulus quadratic trend (p = .03) driven by a significant quadratic component (i.e., departure from linearity) in the gradient of healthy comparisons (p = .001) but not panic patients (p = .62). The green outlined data-points signify stimulus classes for which startle is potentiated relative to the CS− (at the $p \leq .05$ level). Such results indicate greater generalization in PD as reflected by: (1) less steep declines in responding as the presented stimulus diverges from the CS+ among patients and (2) the transfer of anxious arousal to stimuli with up to three units of CS+ differentiation (GS_4, GS_3, and GS_2) in patients, as compared to one unit of differentiation (GS_4) in healthy comparisons.

and somatosensory cortices – providing acetylcholine to the representation of the CS+ in sensory cortex (Weinberger, 2007). This influx of acetylcholine has been shown to retune receptive fields in sensory cortex toward CS+ attributes, such that an increased number of sensory neurons become responsive to the CS+ (for a review, see Weinberger, 2007). Importantly, neurons that retune to the CS+ following conditioning have also been shown to retune to stimuli resembling the CS+ (Scheich, Simonis, Ohl, Thomas, & Tillein, 1992) with decreasing levels of retuning as the stimulus becomes less similar to the CS+ (Weinberger, 2007). Thus the memorial representation of the post-acquisition CS+ includes an enlarged population of cortical neurons that extends beyond those engaged by the pre-acquisition CS+ to neurons comprising the cortical representation of sensory stimuli similar to the CS+. This conditioning-induced neural overlap between the CS+ representation and its approximations increases the likelihood that post-acquisition exposure to stimuli similar to the CS+ will activate the CS+ representation, culminating in the neural and behavioral constituents of the fear response (i.e., fear generalization to the CS+ approximate).

As mentioned previously, the nucleus-basalis-mediated cholinergic influx into sensory cortex during aversive conditioning follows from fear-related amygdala excitation of the nucleus basalis (Kapp et al., 1992). Given findings of increased amygdala activity during fear-conditioning in clinical anxiety (Bremner et al., 2005), it logically follows that anxiety patients undergoing fear-conditioning may incur greater influx of acetylcholine into sensory cortex, increased neural overlap between the memorial representations of the CS+ and its approximations, and a heightened likelihood of activating the CS+ representation – and the associatively linked fear circuitry – upon exposure to stimuli resembling the CS+. Such a mechanism by which anxiety patients may develop overgeneralization of conditioned fear derives logically from animal findings but awaits empirical testing in human beings. We are currently pursuing this line of work with an fMRI version of our paradigm using retinotopic mapping annuli (rings) as CSs/GSs. Each CS/GS is represented by an annulus of distinct eccentricity (i.e., size) that provides a unique neural signature in the calcarine sulcus (Engel, Glover, & Wandell, 1997). Use of these retinotopic stimuli allows for assessment of the conditioning-induced overlap in calcarine representations of the CS+ and its approximations, as well as the contribution of this overlap toward generalization.

A second neural mechanism with promise for understanding the memorial contributions to conditioned generalization is the NMDA-dependent rise in intracellular Ca^{2+} in lateral amygdala neurons, thought essential for the formation of associative links between the CS and US (Rodrigues, Schafe, & LeDoux, 2004). Consistent with this idea, the partial NMDA agonist D-cycloserine (DCS) has been found to enhance acquisition (e.g., Monahan, Handelmann, Hood, & Cordi, 1989) and retention (e.g., Land & Riccio, 1999) of conditioned fear – a learning critically reliant on the CS-US connection. Such results support the potential efficacy of (partial) NMDA agonists, such as DCS, for reducing generalization of conditioned fear by strengthening the accuracy of the conditioning memory and thereby reducing the frequency of "generalization errors." This possibility receives support from animal findings demonstrating that DCS dose-dependently improves acquisition of conditioning and results in less generalization to stimuli resembling the CS+ (Thompson & Disterhoft, 1997). Such findings support the potential utility of DCS for reversing overgeneralization associated with clinical anxiety by increasing the strength and accuracy of the encoded conditioning memory – an effect apt for testing given the favorable neurotoxicity profile of DCS in human beings.

Concluding Thoughts

The long known connection between generalization of conditioned fear and anxiety pathology is only now becoming the focus of empirical testing. Such recent efforts have provided a psychophysiologically validated, conditioned-generalization paradigm with which to interrogate the neural, pharmacologic, and genetic basis of this central, yet understudied conditioning marker of clinical anxiety. One promising area of interrogation, informed by conditioning findings in animals, is the way neural substrates of memory contribute to conditioned generalization. Because memory is the mechanism by which psychopathological consequences of aversive events are retained over time, it is not surprising that generalization – an associative consequence of aversive conditioning that retains post-conditioning fear-reactivity – derives in part from memorial processes.

Acknowledgment

This work was supported by the Intramural Research Program of the National Institute of Mental Health.

References

American Psychiatric Association. (2000). *Diagnostic and statistical manual of mental disorders 4th ed., text revision (DSM-IV-TR)*. Washington, DC: American Psychiatric Association.

Bouton, M. E., Mineka, S., & Barlow, D. H. (2001). A modern learning theory perspective on the etiology of panic disorder. *Psychological Review, 108*, 4–32.

Bremner, J. D., Vermetten, E., Schmahl, C., Vaccarino, V., Vythilingam, M., Afzal, N., et al. (2005). Positron emission tomographic imaging of neural correlates of a fear acquisition and extinction paradigm in women with childhood sexual-abuse-related post-traumatic stress disorder. *Psychological Medicine, 35*, 791–806.

Davis, M., & Astrachan, D. I. (1978). Conditioned fear and startle magnitude: Effects of different footshock or backshock intensities used during training. *Journal of Experimental Psychology: Animal Behavior Processes, 4*, 95–103.

Engel, S. A., Glover, G. H., & Wandell, B. A. (1997). Retinotopic organization in human visual cortex and the spatial precision of functional MRI. *Cerebral Cortex, 7*, 181–192.

Foa, E. B., Steketee, G., & Olasov-Rothbaum, B. O. (1989). Behavioral/cognitive conceptualizations of post-traumatic stress disorder. *Behavior Therapy, 20*, 155–176.

Grillon, C., Ameli, R., Woods, S. W., Merikangas, K., & Davis, M. (1991). Fear-potentiated startle in humans: Effects of anticipatory anxiety on the acoustic blink reflex. *Psychophysiology, 28*, 588–595.

Grillon, C., & Morgan, C. A. (1999). Fear-potentiated startle conditioning to explicit and contextual cues in Gulf war veterans with posttraumatic stress disorder. *Journal of Abnormal Psychology, 108*, 134–142.

Kapp, B. S., Whalen, P. J., Supple, W. F., & Pascoe, J. P. (1992). Amygdaloid contributions to conditioned arousal and sensory information processing. In J. Aggleton (Ed.), *The amygdala: Neurobiological aspects of emotion, memory, and mental dysfunction* (pp. 229–254). New York: Wiley-Liss.

Kopp, B., Schlimm, M., & Hermann, C. (2005). Memory-emotional interactions as revealed by fear generalization in animal-fearful individuals. *Journal of Behavior Therapy and Experimental Psychiatry, 36*, 145–166.

Land, C., & Riccio, D. C. (1999). D-Cycloserine: Effects on long-term retention of a conditioned response and on memory for contextual attributes. *Neurobiology of Learning and Memory, 72*, 158–168.

Lissek, S., Biggs, A. L., Rabin, S. J., Cornwell, B. R., Alvarez, R. P., Pine, D. S., et al. (2008). Generalization of conditioned fear-potentiated startle in humans: Experimental validation and clinical relevance. *Behaviour Research and Therapy, 46*, 678–687.

Lissek, S., Powers, A. S., McClure, E. B., Phelps, E. A., Woldehawariat, G., Grillon, C., et al. (2005). Classical fear conditioning in the anxiety disorders: A meta-analysis. *Behaviour Research and Therapy, 43*, 1391–1424.

Lissek, S., Rabin, S. J., Heller, R. E., Luckenbaugh, D., Geraci, M., Pine, D. S., & Grillon, C. (2010). Overgeneralization of conditioned fear as a pathogenic marker of panic disorder. *American Journal of Psychiatry, 167*, 47–55.

Lissek, S., Rabin, S. J., McDowell, D. J., Dvir, S., Bradford, D. E., Geraci, M., et al. (2009). Impaired discriminative fear-conditioning resulting from elevated fear responding to learned safety cues among individuals with panic disorder. *Behaviour Research and Therapy, 47*, 111–118.

Mineka, S., & Zinbarg, R. (1996). Conditioning and ethological models of anxiety disorders: Stress-in-dynamic-context anxiety models. In D. A. Hope (Ed.), *Perspective on anxiety, panic, & fear* (Vol. 43, pp. 135–210). Lincoln and London: University of Nebraska Press.

Monahan, J. B., Handelmann, G. E., Hood, W. F., & Cordi, A. A. (1989). D-cycloserine, a positive modulator of the N-methyl-D-aspartate receptor, enhances performance of learning tasks in rats. *Pharmacology, Biochemistry, and Behavior, 34*, 649–653.

Rodrigues, S. M., Schafe, G. E., & LeDoux, J. E. (2004). Molecular mechanisms underlying emotional learning and memory in the lateral amygdala. *Neuron, 44*, 75–91.

Scheich, H., Simonis, C., Ohl, F., Thomas, H., & Tillein, J. (1992). *Learning related plasticity of gerbil auditory cortex: Feature maps versus meaning maps*. London: Kluwer Academic Publishers.

Thompson, L. T., & Disterhoft, J. F. (1997). Age- and dose-dependent facilitation of associative eyeblink conditioning by D-cycloserine in rabbits. *Behavioral Neuroscience, 111*, 1303–1312.

Watson, J. B., & Rayner, R. (1920). Conditioned emotional reactions. *Journal of Experimental Psychology, 3*, 1–14.

Weinberger, N. M. (2007). Associative representational plasticity in the auditory cortex: A synthesis of two disciplines. *Learning & Memory, 14*, 1–16.

Dr. Shmuel Lissek

National Institute of Mental Health
Mood and Anxiety Disorders Program
15K North Drive
Bldg 15k
MSC 2670
Bethesda, MD 20892-2670
USA
Tel. +1 301 402 7219
Fax +1 301 402 6353
E-mail lisseks@intra.nimh.nih.gov

Opinion

Facilitation of Fear Extinction and Psychotherapy by D-Cycloserine

Michael Davis

Emory University, Yerkes National Primate Center, and the Center for Behavioral Neuroscience, Atlanta, GA, USA

I can't get the memories out of my mind! The images come flooding back in vivid detail, triggered by the most inconsequential things, like a door slamming or the smell of stir-fried pork. Last night, I went to bed, was having a good sleep for a change. Then in the early morning a storm front passed through and there was a bolt of crackling thunder. I awoke instantly, frozen in fear. I am right back in Viet Nam, in the middle of the monsoon season at my guard post. I am sure I'll get hit in the next volley and convinced I will die. My hands are freezing, yet sweat pours from my entire body. I feel each hair on the back of my neck standing on end. I can't catch my breath and my heart is pounding. I smell a damp sulfur smell. Suddenly I see what's left of my buddy Troy, his head on a bamboo platter, sent back to our camp by the Viet Cong. Propaganda messages are stuffed between his clenched teeth. The next bolt of lightning and clap of thunder makes me jump so much that I fall to the floor.

Perhaps there are no more vivid memories than those stored in the brains of soldiers who have experienced combat situations. Witness the above account told by a 65-year-old Viet Nam veteran who cannot hear a clap of thunder, see an Asian woman, or touch a bamboo placemat without reexperiencing the sight of his decapitated friend.

Once called combat fatigue, war neurosis, or shell shock, it is now clear that posttraumatic stress disorder (PTSD) results from intense trauma and produces vivid memories that last a lifetime. The memories can be triggered by stimuli associated with the original traumatic event (flashbacks), and in some individuals they are so intrusive that normal functioning is no longer possible.

It is now generally believed that PTSD is due at least in part to a learning process in which formerly neutral stimuli (e.g., a bamboo placemat) are paired with extremely aversive events (e.g., the sight of a head without a body). This is a classic example of Pavlovian fear conditioning, a form of learning that has been studied extensively by psychologists and about which a great deal of basic information has been gained. As witnessed by the quote above, despite the passage of many years and the presence of an environment very different from Viet Nam, the fear persists. Hence, basic studies on the development and reduction of fear and anxiety are proving to have direct clinical relevance by increasing our understanding of these processes and the means by which they may become dysfunctional. Learning to overcome fear: Extinction: Inhibition of acquired fear is studied in the laboratory using a procedurally simple paradigm in which a rat or a human being is conditioned to fear some neutral stimulus, such as a light or tone, by pairing it with some aversive stimulus, such as a mild shock. Following this, the fear stimulus is presented repeatedly in the absence of the shock. This procedure is known as *extinction training* and results in a gradual decline and ultimate disappearance of the fear response as subject learns that the stimulus is no longer predictive of the aversive event (a process known as *extinction*).

Behavioral observations indicate that extinction is a form of learning in its own right, rather than an "unlearning" or forgetting of previous learning. Thus, after extinction training fear memories return over time, when the fear stimulus is presented in a place different from the place where extinction training took place, or an intervening stress. In each of these examples, the reemergence of the fear response indicates that fear was not lost through extinction, but rather that fear was actively suppressed through an additional learning process. Thus, extinction is considered to be a form of acquired inhibition that counteracts or suppresses fear responses that are no longer adaptive.

Much less is known about the neural underpinnings of extinction compared to fear learning. Significantly, however, extinction shares with fear learning a dependence on the NMDA receptor within a brain area called the amygdala. The NMDA receptor is a protein located at the synapse that binds certain neurotransmitters and has been implicated in learning and memory in a variety of situations. We found that intra-amygdala infusions of a compound that interferes with activity of this receptor, an NMDA antagonist, shortly before extinction training dose-dependently blocked extinction. Additional studies using systemic administration of other compounds that block this receptor have confirmed this effect. Blocking NMDA receptors after extinction training was completed also blocks extinction, suggesting that

DOI: 10.1027/0044-3409/a000023

NMDA receptors are important for the consolidation of extinction, a strengthening of extinction over time.

D-cycloserine facilitates extinction: It was known that a compound called D-cycloserine binds to the NMDA receptor and makes it work better. Thus, we predicted that giving D-cycloserine prior to extinction training would enhance extinction. In a series of experiments we administered D-cycloserine either systemically or directly into the amygdala prior to extinction training and then tested retention of extinction the next day without drug administration. D-cycloserine dose-dependently enhanced extinction in rats exposed to lights in the absence of shock but not in control rats that did not receive extinction training. This indicated that its facilitatory effect was specific to extinction and did not result from a general dampening of fear expression. Facilitation of extinction by D-cycloserine has now been replicated numerous times in animal experiments.

D-cycloserine facilitates psychotherapy: Exposure-based psychotherapy for fear and anxiety disorders in human beings resembles extinction in several respects. The clearest example is so-called "simple phobia." People who are afraid of snakes do not look at pictures of snakes, touch a snake, or god-forbid let a snake crawl around their neck. However, if you persuade them to look at snakes and remind them these are just pictures and cannot hurt you, or bring a snake in a closed jar and remind them the snake cannot get them, and then let them touch a snake and remind them most snakes are not poisonous, this is a very effective therapy for getting over snake phobias. People afraid of speaking in public (social phobia) benefit from giving a speech over and over again in front of people. People with panic disorder are taken to the place where they had a panic attack and shown this will not happen again. People with obsessive-compulsive disorder (OCD) with a contamination phobia are forced to touch the bottom of a toilet seat but not allowed to wash their hands learn they do not get sick or die and this treatment has been successful in reducing symptoms of OCD in many patients. All of these examples show that repeated exposure to fearful cues or situations with no aversive consequences (i.e., extinction training) is useful to help people overcome being afraid.

Because D-cycloserine facilitates extinction in rats, we investigated whether D-cycloserine might facilitate the loss of fear in human patients. Consistent with findings from the animal laboratory, patients receiving D-cycloserine benefited more from exposure-based psychotherapy than did placebo-treated controls. In this study subjects who had high levels of fear of heights were exposed on only two sessions to a simulated glass elevator, using virtual reality. This was their only therapy and had been shown to reduce fear of heights substantially after seven or eight sessions. One-two hours prior to these two therapy sessions patients were given oral administration of either placebo or 50 mg D-cycloserine. So, only two pills were given separated by an average of 12 days, one before each therapy session. D-cycloserine had no effect during the first session in the simulated glass elevator: It neither increased nor decreased their anxiety. However, in the second session the patients who received D-cycloserine on the first session perspired less (a physiological measure of anxiety reduction) and 1 week later had a much great reduction in their rated feeling of anxiety in the virtual environment that persisted for at least 3 months, the longest interval tested. They also voluntarily exposed themselves to real height situations, such as driving over high bridges or going up an elevator.

Promise for treatment of PTSD: We will know soon. The ability of D-cycloserine to improve psychotherapy has now been replicated in five independent studies, two in obsessive-compulsive disorder, two in social phobia, and one in panic disorder. At least six studies are currently underway looking at whether D-cycloserine will facilitate psychotherapy in PTSD, including one of ours looking at D-cycloserine in soldiers returned from Iraq exposed to a "virtual Iraq." Soon we will know whether D-cycloserine also facilitates psychotherapy in this devastating disorder.

Michael Davis

Emory University
Yerkes National Primate Center
954 Gatewood Drive
Atlanta, GA 30329
USA
E-mail mdavis4@emory.edu